CAMBRIDGE ECONOMIC HANDBOOKS.—XI
GENERAL EDITOR: C. W. GUILLEBAUD, M.A.

MONOPOLY

MONOPOLY

BY
E. A. G. ROBINSON
M.A.
FELLOW AND LECTURER OF
SIDNEY SUSSEX COLLEGE, CAMBRIDGE

With an Introduction by
C. W. GUILLEBAUD
M.A.
FELLOW OF ST. JOHN'S COLLEGE, CAMBRIDGE

London
NISBET & CO. LTD.
Cambridge
AT THE UNIVERSITY PRESS

First published	.	.	.	.	April	1941
Reprinted	.	.	.	.	September	1943
,,	.	.	.	.	January	1945
,,	.	.	.	.	January	1946
,,	.	.	.	.	October	1946

INTRODUCTION TO THE SERIES
By the General Editor

SHORTLY after the war of 1914–18 there seemed to be
a place for a Series of introductory Economic Handbooks "intended to convey to the ordinary reader and
to the uninitiated student some conception of the
general principles of thought which economists now
apply to economic problems."

This Series was planned by Mr. J. M. Keynes under
the title *Cambridge Economic Handbooks*, and he wrote
for it a general Editorial Introduction of which the
words quoted above formed part. In 1936 Mr.
Keynes handed over the editorship of the Series to
Mr. D. H. Robertson, who held it until he became Professor of Economics in the University of
London.

The judgment of its originators has been justified
by the wide welcome given to the Series. Apart from
its circulation in the British Empire, it has been published from the start in the United States of America
while translations of the principal volumes have
so far appeared in German, Spanish, Italian, Swedish,
Japanese, Polish and Lithuanian.

It is symptomatic of the changes which have been
taking place in recent times in the development of
economic science, changes associated in a high degree
with the work and influence of Mr. Keynes himself,
that within the brief space of fifteen years the text

of part of the Editorial Introduction should have stood in need of revision. In its original version the last paragraph of the Introduction to the Series ran as follows :

"Even on matters of principle there is not yet a complete unanimity of opinion amongst professors. Generally speaking, the writers of these volumes believe themselves to be orthodox members of the Cambridge School of Economics. At any rate, most of their ideas about the subject, and even their prejudices, are traceable to the contact they have enjoyed with the writings and lectures of the two economists who have chiefly influenced Cambridge thought for the past fifty years, Dr. Marshall and Professor Pigou."

When the Editorship of the Series was transferred to Mr. D. H. Robertson, Mr. Keynes consented to the retention of his general Introduction, but subsequently re-wrote the concluding paragraph in the following form :

"Even on matters of principle there is not yet a complete unanimity of opinion amongst professional students of the subject. Immediately after the war daily economic events were of such a startling character as to divert attention from theoretical complexities. But to-day, economic science has recovered its wind. Traditional treatments and traditional solutions are being questioned, improved, and revised. In the end this activity of research should clear up controversy. But for the moment controversy and doubt are increased. The writers of this series must apologise to the general reader and to the beginner if many parts of their subject have not yet reached to a degree of certainty and lucidity which would make them easy and straight-forward reading."

Still more recent events have produced a world so far removed from that which existed when the fore-going words were written, that it has fallen to the lot of the present Editor to provide a new Introduction.

This is perhaps a good vantage point from which to survey very briefly some of the principal trends in the evolution of economic thought in this country during the past thirty years. Prior to 1914 economic theory here was largely dominated by Alfred Marshall; and economists, following him, thought in terms of the long period tendencies of the different sections of the economic system towards positions of equilibrium, even though ever-present dynamic factors were per-petually modifying the existing structure and pre-senting new and equally distant, if equally unattain-able, goals as stimuli to change and adaptation. More-over, in the Marshallian system, those tendencies resulted from the working of persistent underlying forces which were conceived of as largely competitive in character. The increasing trend towards monopoly was certainly affecting thought, but not so much in the realm of the theory of value, as in the emphasis which came to be laid on possible discrepancies between the private interest and the social interest. Under the influence of Professor Pigou a Welfare Economics was developing side by side with, and out of, the Value Economics of the older generation.

After 1918 the long-drawn-out agony of the depressed areas, the weakening of the position of this country in international trade, and the tremendous intensity of the economic crisis of 1930–32 (to mention but a few out of the many contributing causes) combined, on the one hand, to focus attention on problems of the short period and, on the other hand, to throw doubt on the extent to which the self-adjusting, seemingly automatic mechanism, which on the whole had operated so effectively during the nineteenth century, was capable of coping with the deep-seated maladjustments and disharmonies which characterised the post-war world. At the same time value theory itself was profoundly influenced by the emergence of a number of writers who approached value problems from the view-point of monopoly, and emphasised the unrealistic nature of an analysis which was based on the assumptions of perfect competition and a perfect market. Most of all, however, economic thought was dominated by the desire to find a solution for the problem of how to maintain the level of effective demand so as to avoid the recurrence of phases of deep depression and widespread unemployment. There was a growing feeling of impatience with the economics of the long period "in which we are all dead", and a great, perhaps even excessive, concentration on the short period in which we live and move and have our being.

The result was a remarkable ferment of ideas, the challenging of ancient orthodoxies, and " for the moment controversy and doubt [were] increased." This ferment had by no means subsided when the second war with Germany broke out in September 1939, bringing in its train a degree of State interference with the normal peace-time working of the economic system far exceeding that reached even in the last years of the war of 1914–18.

In so far as it is possible to foresee future trends, they would seem to lie in a much greater measure of conscious public control over many aspects of economic activity than has existed in the past. It will no doubt still remain true, to quote Mr. Keynes's Introduction again, that :

" The Theory of Economics does not furnish a body of settled conclusions immediately applicable to policy. It is a method rather than a doctrine, an apparatus of the mind, a technique of thinking, which helps its possessor to draw correct conclusions."

Nevertheless, economists may well find themselves to a greater degree than hitherto called upon to express their views on matters of economic policy, and—for a time at least—the writers of future volumes of the Cambridge Economic Handbooks may be concerned rather with specific problems than with the more general aspects of economic theory.

C. W. G.

Cambridge,
April, 1941.

AUTHOR'S NOTE

MAY I make it clear that the manuscript of this book was completed before I accepted a temporary post in the Civil Service ? To the delays inevitable in war-time production has been added the complete destruction of the type when it was completed and waiting to go to the machine.

E. A. G. R.

CONTENTS

CHAPTER I

MONOPOLY PRICE

CHAPTER II

QUASI-MONOPOLY

CHAPTER III

TYPES OF MONOPOLY

CHAPTER IV

DEVICES FOR ESTABLISHING OR PROLONGING MONOPOLIES

CHAPTER V

THE FORMS OF MONOPOLY ORGANIZATION

CHAPTER VI

MONOPOLY AND INDUSTRIAL EFFICIENCY

CHAPTER VII

MONOPOLIES AND INDUSTRIAL STABILITY

CHAPTER VIII

THE CONTROL OF MONOPOLY

CHAPTER IX

THE LAW AND MONOPOLY IN THE UNITED STATES OF AMERICA

CHAPTER X

THE LAW AND MONOPOLY IN GERMANY

CHAPTER XI

THE LAW AND MONOPOLY IN GREAT BRITAIN

CHAPTER XII

FUTURE POLICY

MONOPOLY

CHAPTER I

MONOPOLY PRICE

§ 1. *The Scope of this Volume.* It is well to start by attempting to make clear what is, and is not, the purpose of this book. It does not attempt to describe and assess the operations and the social effects of existing monopolies in Great Britain or in any country. Other books exist which admirably cover this field. The reader is urged to supplement what he may here discover by a study in such books[1] of the working of actual monopolies. The purpose of this volume is rather to consider what we mean by monopoly, the conditions in which monopolies can be created and can continue to exist, the forms that they take, their virtues and vices in certain respects, and the attitude to them of the law and of public opinion in different countries. It is intended to be, as it were, a tin-opener to open the tin of knowledge. But there is nothing in the world so useless as a tin-opener without a tin, unless it be a tin without a tin-opener.

There is one difficulty with regard to the study of monopolies concerning which the reader must im-

[1] He is recommended in particular to refer to P. Fitzgerald, *Industrial Combination in England*, and to A. F. Lucas, *Industrial Reconstruction and the Control of Competition*.

B

mediately be forewarned. What everyone wishes to know is the answer to the question, " Are monopolies a good thing ? " To that question the economist as such has no answer to give. The economist is, or ought to be, an expert in logic as applied to his own particular field. He deals in consequences, in means to a given end, not in the ends themselves. He aims to be the navigator of the ship, rather than the owner. It is not for him to decide to what port the ship is to be sailed, but once its destination is determined, it is for him to show the sandbanks and the shoals, the quarters from which gales may be expected, the deep channels, and the safe anchorages.

The economist, as economist, cannot pronounce judgment on monopolies. For the judgment will depend upon what is the whole end and purpose of our economic, social and political system. That is a question regarding which the economist will inevitably have views, but on which he has no more claim to the final word than have others expert in politics, in ethics, or in religion. But he can usefully produce for consideration the arguments which may be employed to support or to deny the claims of monopolies to improve the efficiency of the economic system regarded, first, as a means of organizing the technical production of material goods, second, as a means of securing that those goods are produced in the amounts that are desirable, third, as a means of distributing to individuals the incomes which it is proper that they should enjoy. If we can reach some tentative conclusions regarding these matters, we shall have at least some of the weights which must be placed on the scales in the balancing of a final judgment.

§ 2. *The Difficulty of Defining Monopoly.* The nineteenth century, we are often told, was an era of competition, the twentieth century is an era of monopoly. With the broad truth of this statement few would disagree. The last quarter of the earlier century, it is true, saw a transition, more marked in some countries, less marked in others, from the old order to the new. The powerful semi-monopolistic concerns familiar to-day began to emerge in the United States and in Germany, and to a somewhat less extent in Great Britain and in other countries. When we speak of monopoly in this way we most of us have a fairly clear idea of what it is that we mean. But if we are to argue closely regarding the actions of monopolists we must attempt a somewhat more precise definition.

What then is a monopoly, and what is a monopolist ? A monopolist, we might say, is one who is in the position of being the sole seller of some commodity. But that definition has only enabled us to escape from our present difficulties by plunging us into other and worse difficulties. What is a commodity ? The unhappy truth is that there is and can be no comfortable, hard and fast, definition of a commodity.[1] There is no simple homogeneous commodity produced by the manufacturers of motor cars, or of wireless sets, or of chocolates, which we can count and calculate, and compute that so many will be bought if the uniform price is so much, or that so many can be produced at an average cost of so much per unit. There is rather an infinite series of closely competing substitutes.

[1] For the difficulties involved in any attempt to define a commodity, see the *Structure of Competitive Industry* (Cambridge Economic Handbooks), pp. 6–13.

Sometimes, as when a fleet of trawlers catch identical
fish in the same waters and land them in the same state
of freshness, the products of one producer are a perfect
substitute for the products of any other, and no one
producer can charge more than the price ruling in the
market without losing all his customers. But more
often the products of one producer are not a perfect
substitute for those of another. There is some quality,
perhaps real, perhaps quite imaginary, which leads
purchasers to take different views, so that there are
certain customers who prefer the products of one
manufacturer to those of his closest competitors, so
that he may charge a fractionally higher price for his
products without losing all his sales. In the case of
the trawlers the elasticity of demand[1] for the products
of our single producer is infinite, and the competition
can be called " perfect " ; in the more usual case it is
less than infinite, and the competition may be called
" imperfect."

---

[1] Since it will frequently be necessary to employ this concept
of the elasticity of demand, an accurate definition is desirable.
If price is lowered, the amount demanded will be increased much or
little.   If a given small percentage reduction of price (let us say
2 per cent) leads to an equal percentage increase of the amount
demanded (in this case also 2 per cent), we say that the elasticity
of demand is 1, or that the demand is of unit elasticity.   Where the
percentage increase of the amount demanded is greater than the
percentage reduction of price, we call the demand elastic, where it
is less, inelastic.   The measure of elasticity may, for practical purposes and where the changes under consideration are small, be
regarded as being the percentage increase of the amount demanded
divided by the percentage reduction of price.   Thus any finite
increase of the amount demanded resulting from an infinitesimal
reduction of price implies an elasticity of infinity.   It will be readily
seen that it follows from the above definition that the total receipts
from selling different amounts of product remain the same where
demand is of unit elasticity ; they increase as more is sold if the
demand is elastic ; they decrease as more is sold if it is inelastic.

Now if we wish to be precise in our definition of monopoly we should say that every manufacturer is in the nature of things a monopolist of his own products. He alone produces those particular products and he alone sells them. The interesting problem is not who is, and who is not, in this sense a monopolist, but rather in what circumstances a monopolist is strong and in what circumstances he is weak. The strength of a monopolist lies in his power to raise his prices without frightening away all his customers. How much he can raise them depends on the elasticity of demand for his particular products. This, in turn, depends on the extent to which substitutes for his products are available. In the widest sense of the word, everything that we buy is a substitute for everything else. Apart from a few physical necessities for existence, such as salt or water, every use of money competes with every other use. There is some increased margin of price which would induce each of us to forsake one method of satisfying our wants and employ an alternative method. The width of this margin depends on the fixity of our habits and on our respect for convention. Some people will clearly be less willing than others to make a change. Some, again, because of their wealth can longer resist it. But sooner or later a point is reached at which any of us will give up one way of spending and take to another.

Obviously there are some products which are more likely to tempt us away from a given form of expenditure than others. There are, that is to say, closer and more distant substitutes. The closest substitutes may be so nearly identical with the original object of expenditure that a comparatively small difference of price is sufficient to persuade me to substitute them. A Morris Eight is a substitute for an Austin Eight, or a Pye radio set for a Murphy in a much nearer sense than are radio sets for cars. The closer the substitutes, and the greater the elasticity therefore of the demand for a given manufacturer's product, the less he can raise his price without frightening away his customers, until in the limiting case of perfect competition, substitutes are so close and so identical that no increase of price is possible at all without the disappearance of all customers.

Now substitutes do not always form a perfect graduation from the closest to the most distant. More often there is at some point a break in this chain of substitutes. Palm Olive soap is a fairly close substitute for Pears Soap. Any very considerable change of price of the one or the other will persuade us to forsake the black cake for the green one, or *vice versa*. But between soaps of all sorts and the next best alternative there is for most of us a wide gap. We would willingly pay far more than we do for our soap before we would copy the Romans and go to our baths with a scraper and a bottle of oil. Thus anyone who could control the price of all soaps might be able to exploit us considerably. It is the double condition, first, of a gap in the chain of substitutes, second, of the possibility of securing control of all the close substitutes, which makes a monopolist strong ; which enables him, in other words, to advance his price considerably and to make large profits out of his consumers.

There are not only difficulties in defining " a commodity," there are difficulties also in defining what we mean by " the sole seller." It would clearly be ridiculous to assume that no seller is a monopolist unless he supplies 100 per cent of the commodity or service, or to say, for example, that the local electricity supply company is not in a monopolistic position, because one or two people have their own generating plants. It would be equally ridiculous to declare that a group of producers do not form a monopoly because from time to time, or in certain markets, they have been known to compete. This difficulty of deciding where to draw the line between what is, and what is not, monopoly is not a difficulty that is unique to this particular problem. It pervades the whole of economics, and indeed, of many other sciences. For the truth is that there is a continuous gradation between competition and monopoly, just as there is between light and darkness, or between health and sickness. But that gradation cannot conceal the fact that there are essential differences between the two. We shall be largely concerned in later chapters with the difficulties that arise from this continuity.

It should now be clear that any simple definition of the terms " monopoly " and " monopolist " is impossible. In some industries where goodwill is important and difficulties of entry are considerable, it may be legitimate to regard any one of a small number of firms engaged in substantially imperfect competition as a monopolist, in the sense that its power of raising price is appreciable. In other industries where substitutes are closer, and goodwill less important, it may serve no useful purpose to regard firms engaged in very slightly imperfect competition as monopolists, and combination of all firms within the limit set by a gap in the chain of substitutes, may be a necessary condition of any effective monopoly.

§ 3. *The Price Policy of the Monopolist.* We have been discussing in what circumstances a monopolist will be able to raise his price. Before we proceed further we must pause to consider how much it will pay him to do so. The more he raises his price the fewer units of his product will he sell, until at some limiting price he ceases to sell any at all. Now it obviously will not pay our monopolist to raise his price to such an extent that he sells almost nothing. He must choose between selling a larger number of units at a lower price and a smaller margin of profit, and a smaller number of units at a higher price and a larger margin of profit. There is some point of compromise between large sales and small sales where the product of the margin of profit and the volume of sales is at a maximum. How does he reach this point of maximum profit ? If he could know precisely the schedule of demand for his product and consequently its elasticity, it would not be difficult. But in practice such exact knowledge is seldom if ever possible, and he does it, if he does it at all, by a process of trial and error, by a process of balancing gains and losses, which enables him to make a rough approximation to the results that he wishes to achieve. For purposes of analysis, however, it is best to proceed as if the monopolist were in a position to secure the accurate knowledge necessary to any precisely suitable decision.

If, by producing and selling more, a monopolist would add more to his receipts than to his costs, he would increase his total profit by producing it. If, by producing and selling more, he would add more to his costs than to his receipts he would diminish his total profit by producing it. It will pay him, then, to go on producing and selling more up to the point where his final unit of product neither adds to nor subtracts from his profits, where it adds, that is, exactly as much to his receipts as to his costs.

We must now go a little more deeply into what exactly we mean by an addition to receipts and an addition to costs. How much do my gross receipts increase if I sell, let us say, another arm-chair, raising my total sales from 100 to 101 ? If I can sell as many chairs as I wish at £5, the answer is simple. For the extra chair I get an extra £5. But if, in order to sell my 101st chair, I must reduce the uniform price for all the chairs from £5 to £4 19s. 6d., I shall get from selling the extra chair only £4 19s. 6d., less the hundred times 6d. by which I have been obliged to reduce the price of the first hundred. My extra receipts, then, are £4 19s. 6d. less £2 10s. 0d., that is, £2 9s. 6d. It is convenient to give a name to this element of extra receipts from selling an extra unit and we will call it the *marginal revenue*. In more general terms it is clear that *marginal revenue = total revenue from (n) units minus total revenue from (n − 1) units.*

The size of the marginal revenue will depend obviously on two things, on the price and on the amount of reduction of price necessary to secure the extra unit of sales. This latter is dependent on the elasticity of demand.[1] If a considerable reduction of price is necessary to secure the extra sale, the marginal revenue

---

[1] $\text{Marginal Revenue} = \text{Price} - \dfrac{\text{Price}}{\text{Elasticity}}.$

may become zero, or less than nothing. If to sell our
101st arm-chair we had been obliged to reduce the
uniform price of all the chairs to £4 19s. od., the
marginal revenue would have been £4 19s. od. less
100 times 1s., that is it would have been *minus* 1s. If
the elasticity of demand is one, the total receipts from
selling all different amounts are the same,[1] and the
marginal revenue from selling an extra unit is obviously
nothing. If demand is inelastic, then, the total receipts
from selling a greater amount will be less than the total
receipts from selling a smaller amount, and the marginal
revenue is therefore negative.

One point immediately emerges from this. No
monopolist will consciously produce and sell an extra
unit if by doing so he actually diminishes his receipts.
If the demand is inelastic he will contract his output
to a point where the demand becomes elastic. Every
demand curve must at some point become elastic, for
otherwise the least possible output would command an
infinite price. We can see at different times actual
monopolists or would-be monopolists restricting the
amount that they sell, because a smaller amount will
sell for more than a larger amount. John Stuart Mill[2]
has described how the old Dutch East India Company
" were obliged, in good seasons, to destroy a portion of
the crop. Had they persisted in selling all that they
produced, they must have forced a market by reducing
the price so low, perhaps, that they would have
received for the larger quantity a less total return than
for the smaller : at least they showed that such was
their opinion by destroying their surplus." We have

[1] See footnote, p 4.
[2] *Principles of Political Economy*, Book III, Chapter *ii*, §5.

seen much the same thing in more recent times in the case of Brazilian coffee and United States hogs.

§ 4. *Average Costs and Marginal Costs.* We must now return to the question of the extra costs which our manufacturer of arm-chairs is going to balance against his extra receipts. His marginal revenue, if he could sell 100 at £5 each, and 101 only at £4 19s. 6d. each, was, we saw, £2 9s. 6d. from the 101st arm-chair. He will add to his profits by producing and selling it, if his extra cost is anything less than £2 9s. 6d. Now what is it that we mean by this extra cost ? It is the addition to total costs caused by producing 101 chairs rather than 100 chairs. Marginal cost, as we call this addition to cost, is *total cost of (n) units minus total cost of (n— 1) units.* It is marginal cost, in this sense, that he balances against marginal revenue.

Marginal cost is related in a perfectly definite way to the more familiar conception of average cost[1] per unit. Average costs do not rise or fall irrationally. They rise or fall because the extra cost of producing an extra unit is either greater or less than the present average cost. This is perhaps most easily seen by a very simple analogy. If my batting average at cricket is, let us say, 20, it will be raised if I play an additional (marginal) innings of more than 20, it will fall if I play an additional (marginal) innings of less than 20. It is not necessary in order that it should fall that my marginal scores should themselves be falling. If, regrettably, my last marginal innings was 0 and my present one is 10, the latter will still reduce my average

Average cost, of course, is $\dfrac{\text{total cost of (n) units.}}{\text{(n)}}$

though the marginal score is itself higher. My average will remain unchanged only if I play a marginal innings exactly equal to my present average. We can now apply this same principle to costs. Average costs will fall only if marginal costs are below average costs, they will rise only if marginal costs are above average costs, they will be constant only in the conditions in which marginal costs are exactly equal to average costs.

The precise meaning of marginal cost will vary according to the period of time that we are considering. If we are considering a short period, in which both the physical equipment of the factory and the organization, with its management and sales staff, can be taken as fixed and to be paid for in any case, the addition to cost through producing another unit of output is no more than the cost of the labour and raw materials and of the wear and tear which would not be incurred were this unit not produced. But if the factory is already working at high pressure, and above its designed capacity, the extra cost of extra units of output is likely to be considerable, for it will probably involve the use of less efficient staff or equipment, the payment of overtime rates of wages, or the operation of plant at exceptional pressure. In a longer period we must regard the extra cost of producing the extra output as including the cost of the additional plant necessary to produce it, of the extra management necessary to organize it, and of the extra sales staff necessary to sell it, and the effect upon costs of producing a larger output will depend upon the relative efficiencies of organizing a larger and a smaller undertaking. Beyond a point it is likely that the short period marginal cost of extracting additional units of output from already overworked equipment will become increasingly greater the more is to be produced, so that it actually exceeds the long period marginal cost of producing similar amounts with more equipment under better conditions, even when allowance is made in the latter case for the additional overhead charges involved. And similarly in the long period, if the scale of output is increased beyond that which gives optimum efficiency, the marginal cost will be higher than the average cost.

§ 5. *The Balance of Cost and Revenue.* We have now reached the point at which we can see how a monopolist may be supposed to balance marginal cost and marginal revenue. By feeling his way all the time, by asking himself at each point whether the extra receipts from a little extra output will exceed the costs of producing and selling that output (and selling it may be a matter of great expense and difficulty), he will by trial and error reach a point where he will make the best profits for himself. But there is one point here which needs a moment's thought. Our manufacturer of arm-chairs would get a marginal revenue of £2 9s. 6d. by selling 101, rather than 100, arm-chairs. If his marginal cost was just equal to this marginal revenue he would be just on the margin of doubt whether to produce and sell this extra chair or not. But at what price will he sell it ? He will sell it obviously at £4 19s. 6d., for it is by charging that price rather than £5 that he sells his extra chair and gets this marginal revenue.

The result of this process may be illustrated by the following Tables. In Table I (*a*) can be seen the effects upon receipts of selling different numbers of chairs at different assumed prices.

TABLE I (a)

Chairs	(1) Selling Price	(2) Total Revenue	(3) Marginal Revenue
99	£5 0s. 6d.	£497 9s. 6d.	£2 11s. 6d.[1]
100	£5 0s. 0d.	£500 0s. 0d.	£2 10s. 6d.
101	£4 19s. 6d.	£502 9s. 6d.	£2 9s. 6d.
102	£4 19s. 0d.	£504 18s. 0d.	£2 8s. 6d.

In Table I (b) certain assumptions are made regarding the alternative total costs of producing different numbers of chairs.

TABLE I (b)

Chairs	(4) Total Cost	(5) Marginal Cost	(6) Profit (= (2) − (4))
99	£402 10s. 0d.	£2 10s. 0d.[2]	£94 19s. 6d.
100	£404 19s. 9d.	£2 9s. 9d.	£95 0s. 3d.
101	£407 9s. 3d.	£2 9s. 6d.	£95 0s. 3d.
102	£409 18s. 6d.	£2 9s. 3d.	£94 19s. 6d.

It is clear that in the conditions of cost and demand that have been assumed the largest profit is made by producing as nearly as possible that output at which marginal cost equals marginal revenue. The 101st chair, which adds equally to both costs and revenue, neither adds nor subtracts therefore from profits, but an output either of 99 chairs or of 102 yields a smaller total profit, the former because an extra unit of output would still add more to revenue than to costs, the latter

---

[1] If the selling price for 98 is £5 1s. 0d.
[2] If the total cost of 98 arm-chairs was £400.

because an extra unit now adds more to costs than to revenue.

§ 6. *The Effects of Monopoly on Price.* It is important to realize that the monopolist is doing exactly what every other member of an economic community normally does. He is balancing his gains, measured in this case in extra receipts, against his outgoings, measured here in extra cost. When the two are equated, he calls a halt to further activity. This is exactly what every producer does in circumstances of pure competition, but in those circumstances, we suppose a producer to assume that the price of his individual output is determined for him by the current market price, and that he can sell additional units of output without driving down the market price. He will assume, therefore, that his extra receipts from selling an extra unit are equal to the market price, and he will enlarge his production until his extra costs from producing an extra unit are equal to market price. Thus marginal costs tend to equal price in conditions of perfect competition. The difference between the action of the competitive producer and that of the monopolist finds its origin, therefore, in the assumption which each makes concerning his relation to the market, and the significance of his decisions of increasing or withholding output in the determination of the current price. The competitive producer assumes that his individual actions have no effect on price, the monopolist that his actions determine the price. We shall consider later the significance of the assumptions actually made, and of the part which these play in influencing the market price, more particularly in the important middle ground which lies between perfect competition and strong monopoly.

The monopolist secures his monopoly revenue, as we have seen, by limiting his output. He may in practice secure the necessary limitation in either of two ways. He may directly limit output, as has been done in the coal industry, by copper producers, by the International Steel Cartel. The fact that the supply is limited serves to raise the price, and if the output is perfectly adjusted, the monopoly profit may be maximized in this way. Alternatively, he may fix the price at such a level that the demand is automatically restricted, and by adjustments of price, the correct compromise between large margins of profit and large quantities of sales may be discovered. The method of price fixation is that adopted by most monopolists where the organization of the monopoly is unified and centralized. We shall have to study later the circumstances in which the one policy or the other is the more convenient to the monopolist. For the moment, we are concerned only with one obvious point. The monopolist cannot both fix price and fix output unless he is willing to regard one or other of his decisions as the more fundamental, and to adjust the other subsidiary decision to fit in with it. If he fixes output, there is one price and one price only corresponding to that output, at which he can sell his whole output. If he fixes price, there is one quantity and one quantity only that he may expect to sell at that price. There are circumstances in which the controllers of monopoly organizations may find it convenient to fix both price and output in order the better to control the market and the individual members of their own organization, but they must regard one decision, often in practice the output decision, as the more fundamental, and adjust the other to it.

The monopolist secures his monopoly profit by a limitation of his output below the output which would be produced by a group of competitive producers if they could be supposed to enjoy the same conditions of supply. The examination of the circumstances which determine how much the output of the monopolist will differ from a theoretical competitive output is beyond the scope of this book. It may briefly be said on what it depends.

The output which a monopolist will find it in his best interest to produce will vary but little in accordance as the demand is more or less elastic, and but little as the supply is subject to increasing or decreasing cost. But the size of the monopoly profit will depend upon these things. If demand for the marginal unit of output is actually inelastic, the monopolist will, as we have seen, produce less, until he again finds himself confronted by an elastic demand. Within the limits of elastic demands, however, the less elastic the demand, the greater the rise in price which will correspond to any given restriction of output. A monopolist who is open to the competition of comparatively near substitutes will restrict output, possibly, to the same extent as any other monopolist, but a given restriction will lead to a smaller rise in the price offered for his goods. The fact that the demand is more elastic will neither lead him to produce more nor to produce less than he would have produced had the demand been less elastic. Again, the fact that increased quantities of the commodity are produced under condition of increasing cost per unit will affect the most profitable output

C

of the monopolist comparatively little, but it will increase considerably the profit which he may hope to secure by limiting output.

§ 7. *Discriminating Monopoly.* So far we have assumed that the monopolist is forced to sell all his output at the same price, but in certain cases it is both possible and profitable for him to discriminate, charging different prices to different customers. Where individuals can move quickly and cheaply from one market to another market, differences of price cannot long persist. But such movement is not always possible. In some cases, movement does not take place because it is unprofitable. It is not worth my while to go to London at a cost of, let us say, 10s. to buy something on which I save only 5s. It is not worth while for a shopkeeper to buy goods from a distant source if the saving is less than the cost of carrying the goods. In some cases, movement does not take place because the customer refuses to move. I shall not go to live in a slum in order to secure a worse address, and so reduce my doctor's charges. Similar articles may be sold at different prices in the East End of London and in the West End, because not everyone in the West End will travel to Whitechapel to secure the bargain. In other cases again, the movement from market to market may be physically impossible. The different railway fares charged for white men and black men in South Africa do not lead the whites to turn black. Transport may be sold at different prices to those who ship motor-car parts and those who ship cotton goods to India without the consigners of motor-car parts attempting to turn those parts into bales of cotton.

The power of a monopolist to discriminate between his customers may vary from the most complete power of making each individual pay what the article is worth to him, down to an ability to group people into a few broad classifications from which they will not tend to break away in pursuit of economy in this particular bargain. The first type of discrimination resembles more nearly the chaffering of the Indian bazaar, where each individual makes his separate bargain, and the shopkeeper, if he is monopolist, usually seems to get the maximum that the customer will pay. Instances of the latter type may be found where a manufacturer sells his goods at different prices at home and in the export market, or again where a shipping company sells transport at different prices to shippers of valuable and of inexpensive goods. With the morality of price discrimination we shall be concerned later ; for the moment we must consider how a monopolist, possessing power of discrimination, will fix his price. We will assume, as we did before, that his one intention is to make the largest possible immediate profit.

For simplicity, let us assume that there are only two markets between which the monopolist possesses the power of discrimination. The aim of the monopolist, as before, is to maximize his profits. He will do this, exactly as we saw in the case of the simple monopolist, if he sells just so much in each market that his marginal revenue from selling an extra unit in that market is equal to his marginal costs of adding another unit to his total output. The marginal cost of adding another unit is supposedly the same (neglecting transport) whether he adds it in the one market or the other. The marginal revenue from selling the extra unit in each market, which he equates to this marginal cost, must therefore be equal in each market. But unless the elasticity of demand is the same in both markets, these marginal revenues will correspond to different prices. The less elastic the demand, the higher will be the price which corresponds to a given level of marginal revenue. The monopolist will therefore charge a higher price in that market which is less elastic, a lower price in that market which is more elastic. A manufacturer who enjoys, for example, a complete monopoly in his home market, but who must face some competition in his export markets, will thus be likely to make his greatest profit by charging a higher price at home and a lower price abroad.

The simple case of two markets can readily be extended to the problems of three or more markets and to problems where parts of the costs are peculiar to the separate markets. In each market the monopolist will sell just so much that another unit will reduce his aggregate profit in that market. In each market, that is, he will try to equate marginal cost of supplying that market with marginal revenue in that market. The different elasticities of demand in the different markets will, however, make his prices in the different markets unequal. He may obtain a higher price in the market in which he sells fewer goods. But since he has already, we are supposing, expanded his sales in that market up to the point where marginal revenue is equal to marginal cost, it will not pay him to transfer sales from the apparently less profitable market to the apparently more profitable market. Wherever the breaking up of the whole market into smaller markets results in the monopolist charging different prices in the different markets, his total monopoly profit will be greater than if he were to charge one uniform price in all the markets.

§ 8. *Conclusion.* In this chapter we have attempted to examine the probable behaviour of a perfectly selfish monopolist who, possessed of all the necessary information, seeks only to secure his own immediate maximum profit. We have left aside for the time being all questions of monopoly policy, of how a monopolist can secure and retain a monopoly. We have found that the monopolist's aim is such a compromise between large profits per unit and large sales that the product of these two is at a maximum. We have seen that he achieves his aim by expanding his output only up to that point where his extra receipts from selling an extra unit are equal to his extra costs in producing that unit. We have seen further that the monopolist may in certain circumstances increase his profits by breaking up his market into various parts and charging in each part of the market that price which will maximize his profits there, and that he secures his maximum profit in each case by offering for sale just so much in each market that his extra receipts are equal to his extra cost.

Just as in the case of a study of pure competition, some of our assumptions have been highly artificial. We have assumed the monopolist to know exactly what the demand for his product would be at other prices than the ruling price ; we have assumed that he is concerned only to make the largest profit. We have assumed that the fact that he is making monopoly profits has no secondary reactions on his sales by inducing customers to cut down their consumption in an attempt to boycott his products. We shall have to consider in later chapters how far these assumptions modify our conclusions. For the time being, it is sufficient that we have established within the limits of these assumptions the possible action of a monopolist.

CHAPTER II

QUASI-MONOPOLY

§ 1. *The Demand for the Output of a Single Producer.*
In the last chapter we saw that in fixing its price
policy every firm acted, so far as circumstances permitted, as a monopolist of its products, balancing
additions to receipts against additions to costs. We
saw also that the additions to receipts from selling
extra units depended on the reduction of price necessary
to secure extra sales, on the elasticity, that is, of
demand. It is important before we go further to
examine rather more closely the meaning of the
schedule of demand and its elasticity, as seen from the
angle of the individual firm.

Suppose a firm reduces its prices in order to attract
more customers, the extent of its success will depend
partly, of course, on the power of price differences to
induce customers to change their habits, or of cheaper
prices to bring in new purchasers, but to an even
greater extent its success will depend upon the way in
which other firms respond to its action. Let us consider for the moment the increased quantity of home-
grown mutton that one particular butcher will sell if
he lowers his price. The increase in the quantity
demanded from him will be different according as we
assume, first, that the price of all meat sold by other

butchers is reduced in the same proportion ; second, that the price of all mutton sold by others is reduced, but that of all other meat remains unchanged ; third, that the price of all home-grown mutton is similarly reduced, but all imported mutton and all other meat remains unchanged ; fourth, that the price of home-grown mutton in all other shops, and of all other meat everywhere, remains unchanged. The elasticity of the demand for our butcher's mutton will vary from comparative inelasticity in the first case to extreme elasticity in the last. This example helps us to see that there is nothing absolute about the schedule of demand that causes the individual firm's decisions. The schedule is a series of hypotheses based upon supposed responses of other firms to the actions of the first. A variation of these supposed responses will alter materially the consequently estimated elasticity of the individual firm's demand, its expected marginal revenue at different prices, and therefore the price that it will decide to fix.

2. *Cat and Mouse Monopoly.* If, therefore, we are to understand monopolistic or semi-monopolistic price policies, we must delve rather deeper into these assumptions that a firm will make regarding its nearest rivals. If the firm is one of a considerable number of close competitors, so that the preferences for one rather than another are not great, and a small price difference will attract a large increment of sales, and if an increase of its sales makes an insignificant inroad into the sales of any one of the remainder, then the responding price changes of other firms are likely to be negligible. In these circumstances we can reasonably

treat the prices of all substitutes as fixed, and the
demand for the products of the individual firm as
highly, perhaps infinitely, elastic. This fixity of other
prices is the assumption that corresponds to the condition of perfect competition.

But if our firm is one of a comparatively small
number of firms in an industry, and if fairly considerable price changes are necessary to break down
the habits and the more purely economic resistance of
customers, then we can no longer assume that the most
probable action of rival producers will be to leave
their prices unchanged. We must draw up a demand
schedule for the products of our individual firm on
the basis of some more likely policy on the part of
these rival undertakings.

There are, of course, various decisions which they
may make, and the hypothetical demand schedule of
the individual firm will vary according as they are
regarded as making one decision or another. They
may decide to proceed with a given manufacturing
programme, and sell the predetermined output at
whatever price in the new circumstances it will fetch.
They may decide to adopt the policy which we have
already considered, that of leaving their prices
unchanged. They may decide to turn out whatever
output will give them the best profits when allowance
is made for the new policy of the firm we are considering. They may decide to make the same proportionate
price-cut as the first firm has made. All these are
possible decisions by rival firms, and a firm which is
considering its own price policy must make what
assumptions it considers most probable. But each
different assumption will yield, it is important to

remember, a different demand curve, a different elasticity and a different marginal revenue.

We cannot follow out in detail the consequences to price and output of all these alternative assumptions. But it will, perhaps, be profitable to examine more closely the results of the last of these assumptions, that other firms cut their prices to a similar extent. This is in many cases a very probable assumption for an individual producer to make. If he can be certain that a given cut on his part will be followed by an equal cut on the part of his rivals, the only outcome of it will be to leave him with the same proportionate share in the total trade at a smaller margin of profit per unit. In these circumstances, he is likely to refrain from cutting price, unless he believes that the expansion of total sales which will follow from that cut of price will recompense him for the reduction in the margin of profit, his share in the total trade remaining unchanged. Now the elasticity of the demand for his goods (and therefore the marginal revenue), which this one producer is assuming, is exactly equal at each price to that elasticity of the total demand which a monopolist combination of all the firms would take into account in determining price.[1] Thus, if a group of producers all assume that a cut of price is likely to result in equal cuts by their rivals, so that no orders can be stolen from them, something not very different from a monopoly price is likely to be established.

We have, so far, been considering only the probable

---

[1] If one producer turns out 100 units daily out of a total production of 500, and if he assumes that a $2\frac{1}{2}$ per cent reduction of price, which would increase the total demand to 525, would enable him to sell 105 units, he assumes in effect that both the total elasticity of demand and his own are approximately 2.

assumptions of a few rival producers as regards cuts of price. Their probable assumptions as regards advances of price will be more likely to depart from those that an individual monopolist would make. For the individual firm is likely to assume, as regards advances of price, that an advance on its part will not necessarily be accompanied by an advance on the part of its rivals, but that they will prefer to steal its markets. This assumption would appear often to be made even in those circumstances where the rival firms could in fact increase their profits more by accepting the advance of price than by stealing their rivals' markets. The reason for the assumption is obvious. A firm which initiates a cut of price is more likely to increase its proportionate share in the total trade than to diminish it ; on the other hand, a firm that initiates an advance of price is more likely to diminish its proportion of the total trade than to maintain it. But the advance of price is only in the interests of the individual firm if it maintains its proportionate share or only slightly diminishes it. Consequently each firm hesitates to be the first to raise prices. It would appear, therefore, that where a number of firms are watching each other closely, a sort of cat and mouse equilibrium may be established. Reductions of price are likely to be made only in those circumstances in which a monopolist would reduce price, but advances of prices may not be made in all those circumstances in which a monopolist would advance price. Profits may, nevertheless, be increased up towards the level of monopoly if improvements of technique increase the margin of profit, and through fear of competitive price cutting no firm reduces the selling price. It may even happen that, from fear that cuts of price once started will be carried too far, a margin of profit per unit too large, and a volume of sales too small to maximize the monopoly profit, will be accepted.

It will be seen that this cat and mouse monopoly depends upon the assumption by each firm that it cannot, by price reductions, increase its share in the total trade. The assumptions of perfect competition are, as we have seen, that by a small price reduction an individual firm can increase its share in the total trade with no limit other than that of the total trade and with no delay, friction or cost. It is evident that the assumption that an individual firm will in fact make is likely to fall somewhere between these two limits, and price will approximate more nearly to monopoly price or to competitive price, according to the assumptions made. These assumptions will be affected not only by estimates of the price cuts or advances which rival producers will make, but also by estimates of the effects of those price cuts or advances upon the long period competitive position of the firm. For a price cut which may be immediately unprofitable may in longer periods be highly profitable, if a larger proportion of the total trade may be expected gradually to accrue to the firm which initiates the price cut.

Moreover the circumstances in which it will be in the interest of one individual firm to cut prices will depend not only upon the assumptions which the firm makes concerning its rivals' price policies, but also upon the effect of an increased or decreased volume of output upon its own costs of production. A firm which can secure a considerable economy of manufacture from the consequent increased output will not reckon on so great a curtailment of its margin of profit through a given cut of price as a firm which expects no such economies. It will, therefore, regard a smaller increase of sales as sufficient justification for a cut in price. Unless, therefore, all the firms in the industry are in approximately the same stage of development and working to approximately the same proportion of their total capacity, they are unlikely to find that an equal price cut will benefit all equally, and one firm may be prepared to cut prices in circumstances in which the other firms would prefer to take no action. In this case, the cat and mouse monopoly is at an end, and a price closer to that which we may call the competitive price is likely to be established. But in many cases a cut in price is only profitable if it is sufficiently large to attract the attention of customers normally attached to a rival firm[1] and since a cut of this magnitude may be unprofitable, an equilibrium which would otherwise be apparently unstable may continue for long periods.

Two very important conclusions follow from the analysis with which we have just been concerned. First, monopoly price is fully as much a consequence of the attitude of a small number of firms to each other, of the assumptions that they make regarding each other, as of formal or informal agreements. We cannot assume that where there is no agreement, even of a tacit nature, competition exists. It all depends upon what one manufacturer thinks another manufacturer is going to do. It follows, therefore, that what we may call the detective story approach to the study of monopoly, the search for mysterious hidden agreements,

[1] I have been told that in one case the minimum significant cut is of the order of 10 per cent.

is really a waste of time. Their existence may prove
something, their non-existence proves nothing. Second,
if we discover a condition of monopoly it is highly
unlikely that we can with any certainty re-establish a
condition of competition merely by breaking up that
monopoly into a few constituent parts. It is very much
more likely that we shall substitute the uncertainties
of a cat and mouse monopoly for the certainties of an
open one.

§ 3. *Price Leadership.*   It is evident in practice
that in a number of industries one predominant
firm initiates almost all price changes, and that other
firms are as a rule content to follow the example of the
predominant firm, fixing their price lists by its price
list.   If the smaller firms are content to accept this
policy, and do not, by underselling or advertisement,
succeed in reducing the share of the predominant firm,
then a price not widely different from the monopoly
price is likely to be reached. But it will take account
not of the costs and receipts of the whole industry, but
only those of the predominant firm, and may, therefore,
differ to some extent from that which would be fixed
by a single monopolist with the costs of production
proper to the whole industry. But if, while accepting
the price fixed by the predominant firm, the smaller
firms expand their sales, the predominant firm must
suffer a contraction unless the total demand at any one
price is at the moment expanding. If it finds its sales
contracting, it may be forced to revise its price-fixing
policy. It may consider that it must reduce price in
order to recover its share of the market for the future ;
it may on the other hand consider that it is better to

attempt to increase its margin of profit and reap immediate gains before its hold upon the market has gone ; it may again decide that no change of price policy in either direction will improve its position, either because the present price yields the greatest profit, or because it regards the inroads of competition as negligible.

It is not possible to lay down the conditions in which one firm can become so predominant in an industry that it usurps the power of price fixing. In an industry with many small firms, it might be possible for a firm with no more than 10 per cent of the total output to possess this power. There is no doubt that it is in fact possessed by firms in various British industries with outputs between 30 per cent and 50 per cent of the whole, but information is lacking which might show the minimum percentage necessary in different industries.

Between the minimum for the initiation of price changes and complete monopoly there is a wide range of ascending power. The predominant firm will in most cases be materially affected by the output and rate of development of rival firms. Its price policy will be directed partly to maximize its own immediate profits, partly to maintain or to increase its ultimate share in the industry. As regards the former objective, the actions of rival firms in expanding output will alter the price at which it can expect the maximum profit ; as regards the latter, their action will influence its strategic price policy. The policy of the predominant firm is thus likely to be a compromise between these two objectives. Few monopolies, as we shall see later, are absolute, and the policy which might immediately yield the highest profits would in most cases be likely also to destroy the monopoly or partial monopoly, and therewith the opportunity of even more moderate profits. The predominant firm is, therefore, in fact likely to fix the price at such a level that rival firms are just unable to encroach on its proportion of the total market, or are able only to encroach at a rate which it regards as negligible or inevitable.[1]

It would appear that in some industries the part of the predominant firm is normally played by foreign producers, and that price changes are ordinarily the consequence of price changes initiated by foreign sources of supply. Wherever the number of home producers is so small that monopoly, whether by formal agreement, by tacit agreement, or by the cat and mouse process, is likely, foreign competition may be the strongest safeguard against it.

§ 4. *Imperfect Competition.* We have seen in the last few pages that while perfect competition and complete monopoly are two possible theoretical limits, in practice the greater part of modern industry is likely to be found in the no man's land between them, sometimes closer to the one, sometimes closer to the other. If we wish to complete our contrast between competition and monopoly there remains a further point to be considered. A monopoly, as we shall see later, must depend upon some difficulty, either natural or artificial, which stands in the way of new firms entering a trade. In conditions of free entry if demand

---

[1] In one or two cases predominant firms have argued that the survival of a few rivals indicates the moderation of their price policy. A moment's reflection will show that it indicates that they have used their monopoly powers to the fullest extent.

increases, so that price exceeds cost, abnormal profits
are made and these abnormal profits will attract new
firms into the industry until profits are again reduced
to the normal level. Monopoly profits can only continue to be made if for some reason they do not succeed
in attracting new capital into the industry. With the
nature of these obstacles we are not here concerned.
But it may well happen that though new firms which
come in cannot at once secure the custom of all purchasers who are paying prices above those at which
they are able to sell similar goods, they can obtain the
custom of some of these. In this case new firms will
enter the industry, so soon as the increase of demand
is sufficient to attract them, and we must make
allowances for this in our calculations.

Let us then consider some group of firms that can
for our purposes be regarded as composing an industry.
This industry will be in equilibrium if at the ruling
price there is a tendency neither for the total of the
industry's output to be expanded nor to be contracted.
But any expansion may be the consequence either of an
increase of output by existing firms, or of an addition
to the number of firms, or of both. The conditions of
equilibrium must therefore be two. First that each
firm shall be in such equilibrium that it shall have no
tendency to expand its output. Second that the firms
shall be making only such profits that the number of
firms in the industry will remain constant. The firm,
we have seen already, is in equilibrium when marginal
revenue is equal to marginal cost. At that point
neither expansion nor contraction can increase its
profits. The industry is in equilibrium when firms are
making such profits that there is no incentive to alter

D

the number of firms, that is when profits are, for this particular industry, normal. A firm's profits are normal when its average cost is equal to price. Thus an industry in which there is free entry is in full equilibrium only when it is true both that marginal revenue equals marginal cost and that price equals average cost.

Now it is obvious that it may well happen that marginal revenue is equal to marginal cost, but that price is greater than average cost. This in fact is the normal condition of the monopolist. How does the industry move from this partial equilibrium to complete equilibrium? New firms, we have seen, will come in, if they are free to do so. The effect of the new firms coming in is to change the amount demanded from each of the old firms at any given price, and probably also the elasticity of demand. This change in the conditions of demand for the individual firms will alter the marginal revenue of the firm, and will destroy the equilibrium between marginal revenue and marginal cost. The firm will proceed to adjust its output to the new conditions as successive new firms enter the trade, so that at each point marginal revenue is equal to marginal cost, but the consequent profits will gradually fall and it will gradually achieve the double condition of equiilbrium.

This double condition of equilibrium helps us to appreciate another point which will be of importance to us when we come to consider the efficiency of monopolies. We have seen that the conditions of equilibrium are, first, that marginal cost equals marginal revenue, second, that average cost equals price. Now where competition is perfect, and the

demand for the products of the individual firm is
therefore infinitely elastic, the additional income from
selling another unit of output is equal to its price, that
is marginal revenue equals price. Marginal cost must
therefore be equal to average cost, if equilibrium is to
be complete. But we saw earlier that average cost
falls when marginal cost is less than average cost,
becomes constant when marginal cost is equal to
average cost, rises when marginal cost exceeds average
cost. The condition of equilibrium in a perfect market
is therefore that average cost is at a miminum, neither
falling nor rising ; that output is produced, that is to
say, by firms of optimum size. But in an imperfect
market firms will not be of optimum size. Where
entry is prohibited by law, or made impossible by the
ingenuities of monopolists, the firm may be either larger
or smaller than the optimum. But where entry is free,
but limited by imperfection of competition, the firm
will always be smaller than the optimum size, and the
efficiency of the industry regarded as a whole will be
less than if it were organized in units of the optimum
size.

§ 5. *The Instability of Imperfect Competition.* In the
last few paragraphs we have seen that in conditions of
imperfect competition, for an industry to be in equilibrium there are two conditions, that the individual
firm should have no inducement to expand, and that
new firms should have no inducement to enter. But
we must be very wary as to what we do or do not, in
these circumstances, call equilibrium. For a third
condition is really necessary, that the degree of competition itself should be stable. It may be unprofitable

for firms to expand, unprofitable for firms to enter,
but still be profitable for firms to combine.   If there are
two neighbouring firms, and if the price that either can
charge is especially limited by the fact that supplies
are, if need be, obtainable from the other, then the
monopoly strength of the two combined will be greater
than that of either independently.   In such circumstances the continued existence of these firms as independent competitors cannot be explained so long as
we assume that each is conducted with the sole end of
maximizing profits. Were that the case these separate
firms would be progressively combined, progressively
increasing the strength of the monopoly, until it
was as nearly as possible complete. Clearly there would
be situations in which the incentive to further combination was great, other situations where various non-
competing areas were already monopolized, and the
incentive to further combination was almost discon-
tinuous.   But so long as any additional limitation on
the price-fixing policy of one group arose from the
existence of another group, their further combination
would be profitable.

Thus the condition of complete monopoly is stable,
the condition of perfect competition by large numbers of
small firms is relatively stable, since the amount of
combination which must precede any gain from it is
very great. But the condition of imperfect competition
is inherently unstable and is ordinarily a situation of
short-period transition, rather than of long-period
equilibrium in any real sense. For we can explain
the continuance of imperfect competition only by invoking motives other than the pursuit of profit. In particular we must look to the motive of the pursuit of

economic power, or to its unwilling surrender, to reluctance to bury the very personal identity of an old firm in the inhuman ramifications of a new combine, to individual fears of supersession and consequent loss of income or influence in the new organization, to a more general distrust of rival manufacturers, or to hope of achieving individual predominance by destroying rivals rather than combining with them.

But these non-pecuniary motives are always limited by the financial environment in which they are to work. In good times they may effectively preclude further combination. In good times, moreover, the thirst for profits of those who are at the head of the larger separate undertakings may be sufficiently slaked, without invoking the greater monopoly powers that further combination might give. Temporary combinations may even appear now as fetters rather than supports, and be repudiated. But in bad times these considerations may become entirely subordinated to the need for combination as an alternative to extinction, and the movement towards complete monopoly will take another series of steps forward.

The onward process itself, however, is likely to create conditions in which new firms will, if there are no great obstacles, again begin to enter, and re-establish an element of competition. This trimorphic series, competition, combination, monopoly, and then again further competition, thus follow each other in kaleidoscopic permutation, reminiscent in many ways of their political counterparts, democracy, oligarchy and tyranny. In both spheres the tide to-day is set towards monocracy. It must not be thought that time and opportunity can be trusted to re-establish competition.

As we shall see, monopoly, once entrenched, may succeed in creating obstacles to the entry of new firms sufficient to make its position almost unassailable except with the co-operation of a system of law designed to protect the consumer and the small firm. In commerce, to a much greater extent than in politics, monopoly is the strongest and in certain forms the least unstable of the three, and at the same time the least harmonious to the interests of the subject. The process of its establishment cannot be analysed if we confine ourselves to a study of the single motive of profit. We shall understand it only if we extend our horizon to include the pursuit of economic power.

CHAPTER III

TYPES OF MONOPOLY

§ 1. *The Sources of Monopoly.* We saw in the last chapter that monopolies possess strength that is sometimes insignificant, sometimes considerable. With the monopolist whose effective powers are strictly limited by close substitutes we shall not in this book be very much concerned. Our interest lies in the behaviour of the strong monopolist, and the terms " monopoly " and " monopolist " may be taken henceforward to apply chiefly to monopolists whose strength is of more than negligible proportions.

This strength, we have seen, lies in two things : in the existence of a gap in the chain of substitution, and in the possibility of securing control of the whole output of the group of close substitutes. The gap itself depends on the inability or the unwillingness of individuals to satisfy some want in a different way. Certain wants, those for food, for housing, for health, in some cases for transport, must be satisfied by some one or other of a comparatively limited range of alternative means. Other wants, those for comfort and amusement in particular, may be satisfied by a wide range of alternatives. There are more reasonably close substitutes, that is, in the latter case and there is no similar gap between the close and the more distant substitutes.

We need then to consider how it may be possible to secure a monopoly of a group of close substitutes. The monopoly must be based, obviously, on the inability of other producers to bring into the market further substitutes during the period of the monopoly. For the monopolist makes his profits by restriction of output, and the raising of price is thereby made possible. If he cannot restrict output, he cannot raise price. He can only restrict output and raise price, if when he does so others do not immediately come into the market and replace his output by their own. This monopoly is based ultimately on the difficulty or impossibility of entry into an industry.

We can distinguish four factors which render entry into an industry difficult. The first is legal prohibition ; the second is the control by the monopolist of the whole supply of some necessary factor of production ; the third is the existence of goodwill which must be broken down before a new firm can sell any of its products ; the fourth is the difficulty or impossibility of entering on a small scale into an industry that requires large scale for efficient production and selling. All these four have played an important part in the establishment of existing monopolies, and we must consider each in turn.

Legal restriction, as we shall see in a later chapter, played an important part in the limitation of competition from about the time of Edward III down to the Bill of Rights in 1689. Under the Tudors and Stuarts in particular patents of monopolies were granted, sometimes for good reason, sometimes as unwarranted favours. The Statute of Monopolies restricted their grant, and the Bill of Rights finally ended it, save by the consent of Parliament. But even to-day certain legal monopolies are ordinarily awarded. They are given first, as patents, for the encouragement of inventions and improvements ;[1] second, to undertakings in those spheres which Professor Robertson has so happily christened the " octopoid " industries,[2] such things as gas, electricity, water, railways, tramways, where the undertaking must be given what is called the right of eminent domain, the right that is of compulsion over private individuals so that telegraph wires or electric cables can (paying suitable compensation if need be) straddle over or burrow under our property. Naturally such powers cannot be lightly given to every applicant, and in practice they are as a rule granted only to one undertaking in each area. More recently also Parliament has given further monopoly or discriminatory powers to further industries—road transport, coal, milk, hops, bacon and others—in the hope that it will thus help to improve their position or increase the stability of the economic system. Finally Parliament in this country, and other Governments in other countries, have reserved to themselves certain monopolies, sometimes on the ground that they can themselves provide a better service, compulsorily unified, sometimes as a source of revenue. In this country, for example, mainly for the former motive, the Government has a monopoly of the transmission of letters and of telephones. In France, mainly for the latter

---

[1] For a discussion of their necessity for this purpose see Professor A. Plant, *The Economic Theory concerning Patents for Inventions, Economica*, February, 1934, pp. 30 *et seq.*

[2] D. H. Robertson, *Control of Industry*, p. 114.

motive, the Government has also a monopoly of tobacco and matches.

The second limitation on the entry of new firms into an industry is set by the control by a monopolist of the whole supply of some necessary factor of production. Such a monopoly may be based upon a control of the labour, the business management, the capital, or the raw materials required for some particular trade. Any of these factors may be monopolized to some extent. A monopoly of skilled labour is sometimes possessed by a firm able to prevent migration to other employers by restrictive covenants based upon the existence of secret, or supposedly secret, processes. A similar monopoly may be possessed by a Trade Union or some other body of similar type, such as a Medical Council or an Inn of Court, which possesses the power to restrict entry. Such powers may not in all cases be employed to limit entry to such an extent as to raise the reward artificially high. On the other hand, the restriction may be produced indirectly by fixing a high rate of fees for services, to which every member of the profession or organization unquestionably adheres, and, by thus limiting the demand, effectively limiting the supply of the service. The monopoly may survive over a long period if the organizations can secure that all recruits to the industry or profession adhere to it. It may on the other hand collapse quickly, at the end of the necessary period of training of new workers, if when rates are fixed at a high level blacklegs in some form or other tend to enter and accept lower rates of pay.

To base a monopoly on a control of the supply of business management which is made available to any one industry is less easy. For management in these days moves comparatively freely from industry to industry. In the days when the trades were mysteries requiring long apprenticeship, a scarcity of masters might perhaps have been artificially maintained. But though the supply of managing ability to one industry may only with difficulty be monopolized, the supply to all industries may in some circumstances, it has been claimed, be monopolized by a limited group who by the accident of birth or education are placed in the fortunate position of being able to acquire the capital necessary to exploit opportunities of profitable enterprise, or of being able to persuade Boards of Directors that they possess hypothetical qualities required for management.

The two most common opportunities of monopolizing factors of production remain : the monopoly power granted by the ownership of all the available capital, and that conferred by the ownership of all possible sources of raw material. The power derived from ownership of all the available capital is essentially short-lived, for universal capital can hardly be monopolized. It arises from the temporary control of all the existing plant required for the manufacture of some commodity. In normal circumstances it must end when new equipment has been constructed and begins to produce. But the short period control may by various devices which we shall study later be continued over longer periods than that required for the construction of the new equipment. Investment may by such means be made so risky or unprofitable to any one individual investor, that all investors may consider it wiser not to attempt to share in the large profits being made.

The power based on the ownership of raw materials may in certain circumstances last over long periods. If all sources in the world, or available to a particular market, are controlled by one user, the monopoly will be an enduring one. But more often the control is limited to all, or a majority, of sources which during the short period can be productive, or to all sources which can produce at low cost immediately. In a longer period, as in the case of capital, other sources of raw material may be expected to become available if high prices are charged, and the monopoly will then collapse.

Of the four original groups of influences making entry into an industry difficult, the third and fourth still remain to be discussed. The third of these was the existence of goodwill which must be broken down before a new firm can sell any of its products. It is the existence of this goodwill more than anything else which makes the market for goods imperfect and creates those habits among customers which require time and great expenditure to break down.[1] Goodwill, built up partly by solid merit, but more often by effective sales talk and the pressure of advertisement, yields in some cases a monopoly power that is far from negligible, and the great expense of competitive advertising can be used by the large concern as a very effective weapon in preventing the growth or expansion of small competitors.

The fourth influence is closely allied to the point that we have just discussed. The difficulty or impossibility of entering an industry on a small scale may make effective the monopoly or the quasi-

[1] See *Structure of Competitive Industry*, pp. 120–21 and 172–3.

monopoly of those in it already. There are many industries to-day in which both goodwill and large-scale are so important that it is virtually impossible (as well as prohibitively risky) for a new entrant to jump immediately to full output at anything approaching an optimum scale of production. Where that is so, the existing firms have a security of monopoly tenure unthreatened by new competition.[1] If these existing firms can be kept from competitive expansion, the monopoly is complete. This question of the effects of large scale in consolidating a monopoly position will become very important at a later stage when we come to consider the devices used to maintain monopolies. For very many of them prove when analysed to be devices for making the minimum scale for effective competition greater than it otherwise would be. The optimum scale of production depends[2] on the facilities that exist for the vertical disintegration of specialist processes, requiring exceptionally large scale for their efficient working, to specialist firms that will undertake them. One of the most effective means of preventing competition may be to make such vertical disintegration impossible to small rivals.

§ 2. *A Classification of Types of Monopoly.* This preliminary survey has suggested a convenient classification of monopolies, which will much help us at a later stage. First, we have seen that some monopolies are able to survive over comparatively long periods, while others may be effective temporarily, but are likely to collapse so soon as new equipment can be constructed,

---

[1] See, e.g.; Wickham Steed, *The Press*, pp. 82-3.
[2] See *Structure of Competitive Industry*, pp. 26-7 and 110-13.

or new workers trained, or whatever may be necessary to increase productive capacity. Thus we must distinguish between the *long-term monopoly* and the *short-term monopoly*.

Second, we have seen that some monopolies enjoy powers which range widely, others enjoy a purely local monopoly, which is effective only so long as it is not made profitable to import goods into the monopolized area from another outside source of supply. It is convenient, perhaps, to call the latter type of circumscribed monopoly *a conditional monopoly*, and monopolies not so circumscribed by possible competition from outside, *an unconditional monopoly*. Since, obviously, a conditional monopoly, for example, may be either of a long-term or of a short-term character, we have here four separate categories that we can distinguish.

§ 3. *Long-term Unconditional Monopolies.* Having constructed these economic hatboxes, let us try to find some examples to put into them, and see for what reasons a monopoly properly goes into each. Let us start with the long-term unconditional monopoly, a monopoly limited in its power neither by the probability that given time, new capacity will come in and destroy its powers, nor by the probability that, if price is raised beyond a certain point outside, possibly foreign, competition is to be feared. Such monopolies can be established only as a rule by Government action, forbidding both home and foreign competition, or by the concentration of all available sources of raw material in one control. For a long-term monopoly based upon control of capital equipment, or upon control of the supplies of management or labour is seldom possible, and for the moment we will exclude those monopolies of a short-term character which are extended in longer periods by various devices that make new entry difficult.

We have already quoted examples of legal monopolies, such as the Post Office, the railways, gas or electricity undertakings, coal-mining, patented articles, in all of which the entry of new firms free to produce what output they may themselves determine, without let or hindrance, and with all necessary facilities, is for some reason or other precluded. Let us proceed then to the other sources of long-term unconditional monopolies. Scarce materials provide the best examples here. But there are in fact not very many materials so scarce as to be easily monopolized, and so necessary or so desired as to yield any considerable monopoly power. And since even comparatively scarce materials are rarely so localized that a monopoly established in a single country will control the material throughout the world, these monopolies are usually in the form of an international cartel, and are for political and other reasons often somewhat unstable.

One example of a monopoly of this sort is afforded by radium. Its history has been curious. First Bohemia, then the United States, now the Belgian Congo has possessed a virtual monopoly of the product. Until 1922 Utah and Colorado were the main sources of supply. In that year the Belgians began to develop a mine at Chinkolobwe, close to their big copper works at Elizabethville, which yielded ore so rich that in two years the American producers were forced to close down. In the following years the Belgians gradually

increased production from about 20 grams to about
60 grams annually. With no competition beyond the
3 to 4 grams each produced annually by Czechoslovakia
and Canada, the Union Minière de Haut Katanga could
determine the price of radium as it wished. It has in
fact substantially reduced it, and the price per milligram was in 1934 only some 40 per cent of the American
price in 1920. Production was restricted during the
subsequent depression, and it was reported that large
unsold stocks had been accumulated.

Published statistics are few, and accurate information regarding costs is lacking. The cost of American
production shortly before the War was put at about
£7 7s. per milligram.[1] A more recent estimate,[2] on
somewhat uncertain authority, would put costs at
about £7 per milligram. With a varying output of
material, and a substantial uncertainty regarding the
extent and the grade of the ore-body, it is quite impossible to calculate costs accurately. Prices for some time
varied between £12 and £10 per milligram, but after
the depression of 1931 were reported to be considerably
below those figures. The market is small and erratic,
and very dependent on the quantity dealt in. It would
probably not be reasonable on any available evidence
to accuse the owners of the mineral of having greatly
abused their monopoly position, but there is no doubt
at all that great monopoly powers at present rest in
their hands to be used or not as they may determine.[3]

[1] See *Report of Radium Sub-Committee, Committee of Civil
Research*, 1929, Cmd. 3303.
[2] See Fortune, Feb. 1934, *The Radium Mystery*, pp. 70–5 and
100–9.
[3] These paragraphs were drafted some years ago. Since then
there have been significant changes. Important new sources of
supply were discovered in Canada in 1930 and developed during the

By far the most romantic example of a long-term monopoly based upon raw materials is provided by the story of de Beers in the diamond market. When diamonds were first discovered in the neighbourhood of Kimberley in 1870 it was imagined that, as in previous instances, the deposit was alluvial and would soon be exhausted. The discovery that they persisted into the yellow and blue ground beneath led to the attempt to work tiny claims (the unit was about thirty by twenty-three feet) down to depths as great as four hundred feet. Difficulties immediately arose, first from the collapse of roadways, later from falls of the encircling shale and the burial of claims. Consolidation of holdings was necessary. It was achieved, after countless difficulties, by the ultimate surrender of Barnato, the protagonist of one group, to Rhodes, the leader of the other. De Beers Consolidated Mines secured command not only in the Kimberley mine, where Barnato had been dominant, and the de Beers mine, which was controlled by Rhodes, but in the Dutoitspan and Bulfontein mines also. Systematic underground mining was introduced and costs substantially lowered. The monopoly was maintained by

following years by the Eldorado Gold Mines Ltd. The Belgian output had reached 60 grams in 1930 ; the Canadian output was little more than 3 grams until 1936. Since then expansion has been rapid, and the Canadian production was estimated at 70 grams in 1938. For a period there was some competition between the rival producers. In 1938 agreement was reached with the Union Minière, whereby the Belgian company would produce 60 per cent and the Canadian 40 per cent of the world's radium requirements. It is said that prices, after falling to around $20, are now $40 per milligram or higher (see *The Mineral Industry* for the years 1930 to 1938). These changes so admirably illustrate the point that I had wished to make as to the changeable character of monopoly that I have thought it best to leave the passage as originally written and to contrast it with the situation as it is only a few years later.

E

purchases from time to time of other mines, and by rights of pre-emption over new discoveries in certain areas.

By the 1890's de Beers Consolidated were producing 95 per cent of the world output of diamonds and possessed complete control over the price. For the whole forty years to 1927 their influence upon the industry was but little diminished. The discovery of diamonds in German South-West Africa had, it is true, reduced de Beers' share by 1913 to about 76 per cent. But the growth of total sales permitted the payment of 40 per cent dividends with almost perfect regularity from 1897 to 1914.

The marketing of diamonds was comparatively early entrusted to a body known as the Diamond Syndicate which handled the whole output and disposed of it in large parcels of assorted stones. The value of the Cape output, which in 1885 had been below 20s. a carat, mounted steadily to over 31s. in 1889, was between 25s. and 30s. to 1898, and thence rose by stages to about 51s. in 1906 and 57s. in 1913. The Syndicate maintained the price of diamonds by holding large stocks, which, if necessary, it increased greatly during a depression. It acted as selling agent from time to time for the majority of outside producers as well as for the South African output.

The dictatorship of the Syndicate had been threatened temporarily after 1903 by the rivalry of the Premier Mine, which at first stood outside, but it was far more seriously disturbed in the years following 1925. In that year, some 90 per cent of South African output came from the mines, the remainder from alluvial output. By 1927 the alluvial output had increased almost ten times as the result of the discovery of the new and exceedingly rich fields of Lichtenburg and Namaqualand. The share of the mines fell to just above half the Union output, and a bare third of the world's. The Syndicate tried to prevent a collapse of the market by frantic buying of alluvial stones. It is reported to have held a stock exceeding £8,000,000 in value at the end of 1927, and amounting to nearly £12,000,000 by the end of 1929.

But the Union Government could not itself afford to see the collapse of the market. It shares to the extent of 60 per cent in the profits of the Premier Mine, and derives large profits—and income-taxes—from the others. A Precious Stones Act was forced through which made possible the control of alluvial diggings. It enabled the Governor-General, amongst other things, to limit the number of diggers' certificates issued, to declare that no more diggings be proclaimed, to prohibit prospecting, to limit the quantity of stones that might be recovered by individuals or by all producers, and to fix minimum prices for stones.

The first action was to prohibit for a period all diamond prospecting, but hard feeling and threats of disorder among the diggers led to its partial relaxation. Meanwhile, however, the Namaqualand discoveries were proving even richer than had been suspected. The fear that the enormous yields would ruin the market, led the Government to proclaim them a State digging, to be operated by direct labour for its own profit. In ten months the Government secured some £6,500,000 worth of stones for an outlay of £105,000, a ratio of proceeds to cost that would bring tears of envy into the eye of a manufacturer of patent medicines.

Even with a substantially reduced output of alluvial
stones in 1929 and subsequent years (it was scarcely
more than a fifth of the 1927 output after 1932) the
task of the Diamond Syndicate had become more than
it could support. At the expiry of the Syndicate's five-
year agreement in 1930, there was created a new body,
the Diamond Corporation, with a capital of £10,000,000
which was to take over from the Syndicate the burden
of holding the surplus stocks. In this de Beers has a
50 per cent interest, and shortly after its creation they
took over the management of all the other large producers. The negotiations were for a long time complicated by the unwillingness of the Union Government
to accept any quota restriction on its own output in
Namaqualand. It was, however, finally induced to
come in on terms exceptionally favourable to it, and
accepted the position of one of the partners to the
monopoly. The agreement assigned quotas not only
to the large producers, but also to the Corporation, so
that its disposal of stocks should be systematically
regulated.

The liquidation of this difficult situation was further
complicated by the onset of depression, which reduced
the annual sales of South African diamonds from over
£12,000,000 to about £1,500,000. The mines were
closed down completely, and stocks slowly diminished.
Finally in 1933 a new agreement negotiated between
the mines, the Union Government and the Administrator of South-West Africa gave added control. The
Diamond Trading Company was to sell all diamonds
for the Corporation and the producing companies, and
all the various interests were to be represented on its
board. These involved proceedings would appear once

more to have re-established a moderately secure
monopoly, with the balance of power not substantially
changed, and the Union Government will henceforward
collaborate with the producers in securing that the
price of diamonds shall be not too closely related to
their cost.[1]

The story of the diamond monopoly serves to make
several things clear regarding long-term monopolies in
general. First, the security of tenure of monopolies
based upon a control of materials is highly uncertain, in
the absence of legal restriction upon competition. For
competition may appear almost at any moment from
any direction. In other words, the monopolist can
seldom be certain that his monopoly is in fact a long-
term one. Good luck and good judgment may post-
pone the moment, as it did for diamonds from 1887
almost to 1927, but there can be no certainty to form
a basis of policy. And price policy, even if designed to
the end of maximizing profits, is by no means simple.
For it is almost impossible to judge whether greater

[1] As in the case of radium, the situation has changed greatly
since this account was written a few years ago. In 1929, of an output of about 7·4 million metric carrats, about 4·3 million came from
the Union of South Africa and South West Africa. The only
substantial outside producers were the Belgian Congo, producing
about 1·9 million carrats and the Gold Coast producing about
·7 million carrats. By 1938 the total output has risen to some
10·3 million carrats, but that of the Union and South West Africa
was no more than 1·4 million ; the output of the Belgian Congo had
increased to 5·9 million carrats, that of the Gold Coast to 1·3 million,
that of Sierra Leone to about ·7 million and that of Angola to about
·7 million. In the early years of the depression of 1930–1934 the
greater part of the restriction of output had been made by the South
African producers ; the Kimberley mines were completely closed
down. In 1933 the Congo and Angola producers accepted certain
restrictions on sales, and while the natural monopoly of the South
African producers has now virtually disappeared, the price of
diamonds remains subject to fairly effective control by the Diamond
Corporation

profits can be won by making hay immediately while
the sun shines, or by following a more moderate policy
in the hope of postponing the appearance of competition. Second, the type of monopoly is likely to
change with the passage of time. It may start,
apparently, as a long-term unlimited monopoly, its
source of long-term monopoly may disappear and it
may enjoy a period of short-term unlimited monopoly,
while the rival sources are being developed, in the
course of its transition to a more permanent position
of ordinary competition, or of predominant firm quasi-
monopoly. Third, the conditions necessary for long-
term unconditional monopoly based on raw materials
can rarely be discovered. For very few minerals are so
scarce that they can with certainty be controlled.
More often, as happened with radium (and as has also
happened with copper), a monopoly stimulates prospecting and calls into existence rival supplies. On the
other hand few agricultural raw materials can be
effectively monopolized on the scale necessary for long-
period unconditional monopoly. There are a few
instances, such as that of Egyptian or Sea Island
cotton, where a particular crop does very much better
in a certain soil and climate than elsewhere. But the
difference is likely to be so slight that the monopoly can
benefit only to the extent of a small margin over other
sources of supply, and given that the scarcity is
sufficient to secure this margin, the interest of the
producers will often be to produce as much as possible.

§ 4. *Long-term Conditional Monopolies.* Let us try
next to find examples of the second type of monopoly
—that in which the monopoly, while not limited in its

duration to the time taken to construct new equipment
and bring new output to market, is yet limited in its
effective powers by the fact that if a certain price is
exceeded, close substitutes will be brought to market
from a more distant source of supply. One well-known
example of such a monopoly is afforded by the coal
industry in Great Britain since the Coal Mines Act of
1930. That Act both permitted and required the
creation of an organization for the limitation of the
output of coal by quotas and the imposition of minimum
prices. Every undertaking producing coal in Great
Britain is subject to the limitations imposed. But coal
may be, and on occasion has been, imported from
Poland or from other rival sources, so that theoretically
the monopoly is not unlimited. But in practice its
powers are evidently considerable. For clearly the
powers of any conditional monopoly will depend upon
the price of the rival product, and upon the cost of
bringing it to market, including both transport costs
and tariffs. In the case of a heavy not very valuable
product like coal, transport costs are large as compared
with total costs, and the monopoly powers of a conditional monopoly are much greater than they would be
for a lighter, more valuable product. Coal affords
another example of such a monopoly in the case of
Germany before the imposition of import restrictions.
The Rhenish-Westphalian Syndicate enjoyed a monopoly conditioned by the possibility of increased imports
from Great Britain into the disputed territories up the
main rivers and along the northern seaboard.[1]

The sources of a long-term conditional monopoly
may ordinarily be three. It may depend, as does the

[1] See pp. 228–32.

British coal monopoly, on legal restriction upon unfettered entry. It may depend, as did that of the
German Potash Syndicate, before membership of the
Syndicate was made compulsory, upon a local control
of all sources of the material, limited by the absence
of control of more distant sources. It may depend
upon exceptional advantages of large scale production
or marketing which make new entry impossible below
a level of price which yields abnormal rates of profit to
the large concern. These advantages may spring from
economies of exceptionally large technical scales of
production, either giving advantages to very large
outputs of a standardized product, or to very large
organizations of productive resources. They may
spring from economies of selling a very large output, or
from the complete impossibility of designing and
financing a satisfactory sales organization on a small
scale.

Thus it was said some years ago of the Imperial
Tobacco Company :[1] " a business of such magnitude,
commanding so extensive an influence on the retailers
and possessing such large reserves, has it in its power,
by forgoing its ordinary profit for a short time, to
cut prices to such an extent as to place all its rivals
out of business and secure the entire, or very nearly
the entire, monopoly of the tobacco trade." Part at
least of the strength of the Dunlop Rubber Company,
of United Dairies, and of the big oil distributing
companies is derived, almost certainly, from the less
efficiency of small scale competition.

Perhaps the best example of monopoly based upon

[1] *Report on the Tobacco Industry* (Cmd. 558), 1920, p. 4; quoted
by Fitzgerald, *Industrial Combination in England*, p. 142.

advantages of large scale and difficulties of new entry
is to be found in the sewing-cotton trade. Messrs.
J. & P. Coats, with various subsidiaries that they own
and control, the Central Agency which acts as a selling
agency, and a number of branch establishments in
foreign countries, dominate the trade. In 1920 they
were reported to be producing some 80 per cent of all
sewing cotton[1] used in Great Britain for domestic
purposes, and a very considerable proportion of that
used for manufacturing and similar purposes. A committee established under the Profiteering Act of 1919
and 1920 presented three separate reports on their
activities. The problems with which that committee
was mainly concerned, the price of the reel and the
question whether the margin of profit was properly
calculated by having regard to the actual price paid for
cotton or to its current replacement in the open cotton
market, though of great interest, and common to many
industries in which stocks are important, do not
concern us here. What does concern us is the answer
to the question why, if, as was held by some members
of the committee, the margin was in fact excessive,
new competitors did not enter the industry. This may
be partly explained by the existence of a special
agreement between the Central Agency and the
Drapers' Chamber of Trade, whereby the drapers were
required, under penalty of closure of accounts, to
charge the same percentage of profit on competitors'
cotton as on Messrs. Coats'. This agreement had
apparently been enforced by the request of the drapers

---

[1] The first report put the figure at 95 per cent. Messrs. Coats
regarded this estimate as much too high, but provided no alternative
figure ; 80 per cent was the estimate of an official of the Drapers'
Chamber of Trade.

to prevent price cutting, but did in fact offer some obstacle to new competition. But far more important was the great advantage that Messrs. Coats possessed in manufacturing costs, an advantage that is the more surprising in that they actually spun only about one-third of the yarn that they employed. The first committee reported that even if the prices were advanced considerably beyond the level of 7¼d. a reel which then prevailed, Messrs. Coats would still be able to command an immense sale of their production. This was mainly due to the fact that their enormous capital resources enabled them to buy their raw materials at the proper moment, to their highly specialized organization, and to the efficiency of their spinning department. The committee was informed by one of Coats' principal competitors "that he could not manufacture six-cord sewing cotton at a price which would show any reasonable margin of profit to himself or the shopkeeper if it were sold at less than 1s. per reel, as against the current price of 7¼d. for Coats' sewing cotton." This was partly, indeed, due to the fact that Coats had run the risk of buying large amounts of cotton ahead, and had been fortunate in possessing cheap raw material on a rising market, but even more to their great economies.

§ 5. *Short-term Unconditional Monopolies.* These monopolies enjoy monopoly powers which cannot survive the construction of new productive capacity in the long period, but, short of the long-period introduction of new competition, have a complete, or sufficiently complete, monopoly. Such a monopoly depends ordinarily on the control of the greater part of the world capacity, represented either by fixed plant or by ready-developed sources of material. Into this category fall many of the large number of international cartels and restriction schemes, such as have been organized in the sugar, rubber, tin and copper agreements, to quote but a few of the better known examples. In none of these instances can the cartel effectively preclude new entry into the industry if it raises prices appreciably above the level that will yield normal profits in the long period. The strength of such monopolies, may, however, be considerable in the short period, and in particular they may be able to exert an important influence upon short-period prices in a depression when profits would otherwise be substantially below the long-period normal level, and can be correspondingly raised before competition is attracted.

The duration of the monopoly will depend upon the time that is necessary to develop new production. In rubber-growing a tree takes six or seven years to grow to the size at which it can be tapped, and a considerably longer period before it reaches its full yield. Thus a short-term monopoly is long enough lived to yield very considerable profits. But, as was shown by the experience of the Stevenson rubber restriction scheme, that was operated from 1922 to 1928,[1] the increase of production that it stimulates will be likely both to destroy the monopoly and to extinguish profits entirely for a period of years. Where productive capacity already exists outside the cartel, the time required to organize and expand it may be less than

---

[1] See both for the rubber scheme, and for other examples of short-term conditional monopolies, J. W. F. Rowe, *Markets and Men*, pp. 122–151 and *passim*.

would be necessary for wholly new production. To the extent that outside producers have unused present resources, competitive output will be immediately forthcoming. To the extent that mineral output is, for example, limited by the state of development of the mine rather than by the sufficiency of surface or winding plant, it can be rapidly expanded. To the extent that a greater plantation output can be temporarily furnished at the expense of future output, that will immediately be done. Thus the life of a short-term unconditional monopoly may in fact prove very brief indeed, and the effects of the additional capacity that it stimulates in reducing prices over the following years may be so great that there may be on balance extremely little gain from the creation of the monopoly, or even an excess of loss over profit.

§ 6. *Short-term Conditional Monopolies.* We have finally to consider the group of monopolies whose powers are limited by the certainty of new entries in the long period if price is raised appreciably above the normal level, and by the threat of outside competition, if price exceeds costs in neighbouring markets by more than the cost of transport, including any such obstacles to transport as customs duties. This is by far the largest category of monopolies. They are at the same time ordinarily the weakest. But where the Government facilitates such monopolies by imposing import duties, their powers of improving the profits of their members may be very considerable during a depression.

This category includes all the many small local rings and gentlemen's agreements among bakers, hotel-keepers, coal merchants, boat-hirers, and so on. It includes many quasi-monopolies in trades, protected by import duties, where the number of competing firms is so small as to create assumptions regarding each other's reactions yielding approximately monopolistic prices, but where new entry cannot be prevented. It includes monopolistic rings or agreements on a national scale, such as have existed in the supply of building materials and fittings,[1] where import from abroad is possible. In Germany, in particular, the number of local cartels of this kind has for many years been exceedingly large.

§ 7. *Difficulties of Classification.* These categories cannot, unfortunately, be regarded as watertight and invariable. It will, in individual cases, often be by no means easy to determine whether certain factors are sufficiently powerful to lift, for instance, a short-term unconditional monopoly into the category of a long-term unconditional monopoly. In particular where the long-period tenure depends upon the difficulty of entry into the industry of new undertakings owing to the disadvantages of small scale production, the degree of disadvantage that is sufficient is not easy to estimate, and the tenure itself depends upon the monopolist exercising his powers in such ways as not to give more than normal profits to a small scale entrant.

The policy of the monopoly itself may affect the category in which it may be convenient to classify it. Thus the experiment of Copper Exporters Incorporated in the years 1926–1932 might perhaps be regarded as an attempt to create a long-term unconditional monopoly, based upon control over all available sources

[1] See *Report of the Committee on Trusts*, pp. 35–7.

of copper, which was in practice so operated as to reduce the monopoly into the category of a short-term conditional monopoly.

Moreover, even in the case of legal monopolies, the powers of the monopolist cannot in many cases be regarded as wholly unconditional and unfettered. Apart from such direct restrictions as will be considered below, insecurity of political support will often dictate such moderation of price policy as will prevent the flagrant outrage of public opinion, and the policy of the monopoly is likely to be directed, not solely to the maximization of immediate profit, but rather to such a compromise as will secure its continued life.

Though these classifications are thus neither definite in all cases, nor wholly permanent, they serve a useful purpose in drawing our attention to the strength and weaknesses of individual monopolies, and they are a necessary preliminary to the study with which we shall be concerned in the next chapter of the various devices by which monopolies attempt to increase their strength and the duration of their tenure.

[1] pp. 180–3.

CHAPTER IV

DEVICES FOR ESTABLISHING OR PROLONGING MONOPOLIES

§ 1. *Introductory.* In the last chapter we examined the various foundations upon which monopolies could be built, and the various types of monopoly corresponding to differences of those foundations. In particular we saw that in some cases a monopoly would be of a long-term type, in others of a short-term type. In this chapter we have to consider a variety of devices by which monopolists, and firms in the later stages of pursuit of monopoly, are able to consolidate their monopolist position and in some measure to modify its character and to prolong it beyond the limits of the short period.

The majority of these devices will be found when analysed to be methods of preventing or impeding the entry of new firms into the industry concerned by making the minimum scale of possible or effective competition larger than it would otherwise have been. The devices with which we shall be concerned are of interest and importance, because in several cases governments which have been anxious to prevent the creation of monopolies within their territories have attempted to achieve that end by forbidding certain of these " unfair " practices. In the course of con-

sidering them it will become apparent how difficult
it is to define " unfair " practices objectively by their
character, as distinct from the monopolistic intention
that underlies them.

§ 2. *Vertical Integration.* In ordinary competitive conditions when one isolated process requires a considerably larger scale of operations for its efficient conduct
than is required by the other processes of manufacture,
it tends to be " disintegrated " from the remaining
processes, to be handed over to larger, specialist firms
who perform the required tasks for the output of a
number of firms in the main industry. If for any
reason such disintegration becomes impossible, a new
firm must be large enough to perform this disintegrated
process efficiently, before its competition will become
a danger to established firms. But quite obviously the
larger the capital required, and the larger the addition
of output in relation to the existing output of the
industry, the less likely is any competitor to think it
profitable to attempt to force his way into the industry
and the more enduring is the existing quasi-monopoly
likely to be.

There are, broadly, two ways of preventing vertical
disintegration by a potential competitor. First, by
vertical integration with the disintegrated firms you
may attach them to yourself and deny their services
to others. Second, by various types of tying clauses,
or by various threats of boycott, you may give the
disintegrated firm the choice between serving you and
serving your competitor. If the advantage of serving
you is sufficiently great, the threat will be effective.

Vertical integration with the disintegrated firm, or

firms, is likely to be most effective if for some reason these possess some sort of natural or artificial monopoly. The quasi-monopolist position of certain iron and steel firms both in Great Britain and in the United States has derived from vertical integration with undertakings owning exceptionally favourable ore deposits. Breweries have enjoyed in several cases a considerable degree of local monopoly through integration with " tied " public houses.   The monopoly is built upon the known unwillingness of licensing magistrates to permit indefinitely new entry into the industry.

But even where the disintegrated firm enjoys no monopoly from natural resources, or from limitation by authority of possible competition, integration may yield considerable monopoly powers if the minimum scale of operation is very large, and the optimum firm is large in size as compared with the total output. Thus the large producers of copper in the United States enjoyed for a time some considerable advantage over producers in other countries from the fact that they were integrated with the main copper refining, and copper using, undertakings.   Again, the competitive position of the larger motor manufacturers in Great Britain is reinforced by the reintegration, during their growth, of such processes as the manufacture of radiators, the forging of crankshafts, the cutting of gears, the making of the larger castings, so that the specialist firms, that might work for comparatively small new entrants, are usually themselves operating on a smaller scale than the big self-sufficient undertakings.

§ 3. *The Prevention of Vertical Disintegration.* The alternative to vertical integration is, we have seen,

F

to prevent a new entrant enjoying the ordinary advantage of vertical disintegration by presenting the disintegrated undertaking with the choice between serving the existing and serving the new firm. Another variation presents the consumer with the alternatives of depending always upon the old or always upon the new firm.

In different trades the precise methods employed will naturally be different. By far the most important need for disintegration, in most instances, is that to disintegrate the later processes of marketing the produce. For to maintain a private sales organization capable of reaching the ultimate consumer, and wide enough to sell the whole of the output, is quite beyond the financial resources of most firms in most industries. Retailing is almost everywhere, in consequence, disintegrated from manufacture and the earlier stages of marketing. Thus the power to prevent the distribution of a product through the ordinary channels of the retail trade is likely to be a most effective limitation to new entry.

It is obvious that, short of vertical integration, an existing manufacturer can do no more than to present a retailer with the alternatives of handling only his products or handling none of his products. The efficacy of this threat depends upon how far it is possible for a shop selling only the new product to survive in competition. This in turn depends on a series of further considerations ; first, upon the size of shops in that particular trade ; second, upon the extent of other products of a similar nature, made by non-monopolistic firms, which can be freely obtained for sale ; third, upon the possibility of sale through shops of an unspecialized character, or of another specialized character ; fourth, upon the buying habits of the public with regard to the commodity in question. The relevance of these considerations is best seen from a few examples.

At the beginning of the present century the practice of making exclusive agreements with agents selling a given product or group of products was common in the United States. It has persisted to this day in certain trades. Thus Ford still insists on dealers selling no other new cars beside his own. The exclusive agreement has certain points to recommend it. The individual agent is more concerned with the sales of a particular line than he would be if he were not in any way limited as to what he might sell. Such exclusive agreements were made by the International Harvester Company during the years before 1905. A dealer was forbidden to sell agricultural machinery made by other manufacturers. In this case the exclusive agreement was remarkably effective in denying to competitors ready access to markets. The reasons are simple. The number of dealers qualified to handle agricultural machinery in a country town is not large. The business is not readily combined with other wholly dissimilar trades. The International Harvester Company, while subject to competition in certain lines, was almost the sole source of supply in others, so that a dealer who did not handle their products would not provide the whole range of farm equipment. The Company, it was alleged, refused to supply certain types of machinery to dealers who did not order certain other types, thus successfully achieving what is known as " full line forcing."

Somewhat similar attempts by the Tobacco Trust in the United States to make exclusive agreements were never so successful as those of the International Harvester Company, though they were not wholly ineffective. For tobacco and cigarettes are far more widely sold. In the smallest town the number of shops offering them is very large as compared with those in most other trades. The sale of branded tobaccos and cigarettes requires no great skill. It is easily combined with any of a great variety of other activities. Sales which represent only 20 per cent of all sales in the town can nevertheless give a good profit to one or two shops. Purchases are made so often that a customer will learn and remember where he can get his own peculiar brand. Thus the choice between handling the products of the Trust and of the small outside manufacturer will not always end in victory for the Trust. Obviously the larger is the outside manufacturer relatively to the Trust, the greater will be his chance of discovering outlets into the retail trade.

On the other hand, the refusal of the railway companies in Great Britain to permit booking agencies selling railway tickets to sell also tickets for air travel by certain routes has placed a most effective limit upon competition with services provided by the railways. The potential air traveller, because he travels but rarely by that route, seldom knows enough about particular operating companies or the whereabouts of the special booking agencies, to overcome the impediments placed in his way. Thus a device that is less efficacious with more regular purchasers, becomes more efficacious with less regular purchasers.

While the impeding of vertical disintegration of selling is the most common device, the impeding of vertical disintegration of processes of manufacture is not unknown. The Eastman Kodak Company, for example, for a period secured a virtual monopoly of photographic papers by making an exclusive contract with the sole manufacturers in France and Germany for importation of their papers into the United States. In other cases exclusive agreements have been made for the purchase of all machinery of certain new types for a period, thus denying their use to possible competitors.

§ 4. *Deferred Rebates.* The device of confronting the consumer or the retailer with the dilemma of permanent choice between the monopolist and the independent concern has been especially developed by the Shipping Conferences. These Conferences are joint committees of owners of shipping in particular trades which meet to fix freight rates and passenger rates in their respective trades, and for such incidental purposes as the classification of ships into certain categories, based upon their speed, comfort, modernity and so on. The different Conferences have sought by different methods to ensure that as much as possible of the traffic should be carried in ships of the Conference's lines, and as little as possible in ships of other lines, or in tramp tonnage. For this purpose they have developed the system of deferred rebates. While the schemes differ somewhat in detail, their main characteristics are similar. If all goods are shipped in Conference ships during a certain period (usually six or twelve months), a certain rebate (usually 10 per cent) is earned. If during a further similar period all goods are again so shipped, the rebate is actually credited or paid. The differences lie chiefly in the definition of loyalty to the Conference. There are three parties whose loyalty it is sought to secure, the exporting merchant, the importing merchant, and the forwarding agent. In some Conferences the loyalty of one, in some of another, is demanded. In the West African Conference it was the exporting merchant whose loyalty was demanded, and no attempt was made to bind the consignee. In the South American trade the principal resident in Europe, in some cases the exporter, in some the importer, was bound ; but in order to claim rebate both the merchant and the forwarding agent must remain loyal. In the South African and Australian trades the consignee was brought within the scope of the system. Rebate was not payable on the goods of a consignee who had received goods by other than Conference ships. But it did not debar a shipper from receiving rebate on other shipments, if a customer compelled him to ship certain goods by opposition ships.

The justification of the whole system of deferred rebates has been widely discussed. It will be seen that in effect the Conference informs the shipper that he must choose between the alternatives of using the Conference ships continuously, receiving a 10 per cent rebate, and using the Conference ships or others at his discretion, receiving no rebate. If on half the occasions a shipper could secure an economy of 20 per cent, paying 10 per cent less than monopoly rates when rebate is allowed, it would be as cheap to retain his freedom to ship as he might wish. The advocates of Conferences have argued that a regular service cannot be provided unless there is some constraint upon shippers to use only the ships of those who provide it ; that the value of regularity of service, like the value of a telephone to a house where there is sickness, cannot be measured entirely by the use that is actually made of it. The very fact of regular sailings, with a relatively stable tariff of freight rates, enables trades to grow up, and industries to be established where uncertainty would prevent them. Stocks can be more certainly, and often more quickly, replenished ; they need therefore not be kept at such a high level, with consequent savings of interest charges and of risks of obsolescence.

The critics of the Conferences have urged that many of the advantages claimed are illusory. That regularity of empty ships is an extravagance for which they have no desire to pay, that the Conferences have had the effect of forcing competition from that of price, into that of speed and luxury of service, until both those qualities have become excessive. That far from certainty of service, the Conference lines have failed to expand services in times of heavy demand, so that valuable shipments have been delayed and have missed their market.

Even if some of the claims of the advocates are admitted, it would appear that the Conferences have in many instances used their monopoly powers, not to give the best or the most desired service, at a reasonable cost, but to make unreasonable charges. During the more recent years of depression in shipping, their justification has been sought rather on the general grounds of diminishing the catastrophe of a depressed industry, than on the old grounds advanced twenty-five years before. The examination of this aspect must be postponed to a later chapter.

The use of the system of deferred rebates is not confined to the Shipping Conferences. It has been employed also, to quote but one instance, by the National Light Castings Association, as a means of securing that customers buy exclusively from members of the association.

§ 5. *Full Line Forcing.* Some reference was made above to the device of full line forcing. The term was applied originally to the policy of salesmanship adopted by the International Harvester Company whose travellers developed " the practice of requiring dealers to order new lines . . . as a condition to retaining the agency for some brand of the company's harvesting machines."[1] But the policy is best known as employed by the United Shoe Machinery Company. This Company, which made it a practice to lease rather than to sell the machinery that it manufactured, was a consolidation of a number of undertakings, each possessing important patent rights with regard to some one or other of the various processes of manufacture. Some of the machines had effective substitutes among the products of other makers, others were no longer subject to patent rights. But certain of the machines made, and in particular the lasting machine, could not be replaced by any competing machinery. In drawing up leases for its machinery

[1] Report of the Commissioner of Corporations on the International Harvester Company, p. 306, quoted by Stevens, *Unfair Competition*, p. 70.

the Company placed obligations on any user of the lasting machine not to employ it in conjunction with machinery for certain other purposes not manufactured by the United Shoe Machinery Company. Thus the Company was able to force on users of its lasting machines the use also of the whole line of its machinery. No competitor could offer at the time a complete line of alternative machinery, and thus effective competition was stifled. When a manufacturer did in fact develop a complete alternative line, he was forced by the cutting off of all sources of credit to sell it out to the Company.[1]

The power to force a full line of goods in this way may be built upon a monopoly of any kind. But a monopoly established by patent rights was at one time its most common basis. The inclusion of such tying clauses in agreements for sale or lease of machinery has been held to be enforceable in Great Britain,[2] but has been condemned as illegal in the United States under the Clayton Act.

§ 6. *Local Price Cutting.* We have seen that by the prevention of vertical disintegration the minimum size of effective competition may be increased, and the difficulty of competition thus enhanced. The second main group of offensive devices is found, when analysed, to secure its end also by limiting competition to undertakings of great size and financial strength. The drastic cutting of prices by monopolists or quasi-monopolists threatened by competition has always been a main

---

[1] For a detailed account see Jones, *The Trust Problem in the United States*, pp. 164- 85.
[2] United Shoe Machinery Co. of Canada *v.* Brunet (1909).

weapon of offence. Where two firms are of approximately equal size and efficiency, and possessed of nearly equal resources, the cutting of price is an inevitable part of the competitive struggle and likely to leave surviving the stronger, and thus usually the more efficient, of the two. But where the two competing firms are of very unequal size and financial strength, the drastic cutting of prices will almost certainly lead to the extinction of the smaller, and not necessarily the potentially less efficient, of the two firms. For the smaller firm is unlikely to be competing with equal intensity throughout the whole area of the market, or throughout the whole range of products of the larger. A drastic cut of price by the larger firm in some small part of its territory will thus greatly injure the smaller competitor, while leaving the larger able to earn monopoly profits elsewhere.

The price cutting by the larger firm may be a local cut of all its prices, or a general cut of the price of one or more products closely competing with the smaller firm's most profitable lines, or again a local cut of these particular products. Examples of all these possible variations are many. The early history of the Standard Oil Company was filled with instances of the destruction of local competition by such means.

But it frequently happens that there are difficulties in the way of such local price cutting. It may be forbidden by law to sell a product at exceptionally low prices in certain markets for the purpose of destroying competition or creating monopoly. There may be, indeed there very often is, prejudice against monopolists who attempt to destroy small producers, and the knowledge of what is happening may rally consumers to the defence of the small producer. There will often be obstacles to local and temporary cuts in the price of nationally advertised goods whose price is well known, and is likely to be restored at a short interval. Where any or all of these difficulties have arisen, various devices have been employed to achieve the end of local price cutting without its ostensible employment.

The most common of these is the " fighting brand." Thus the American Tobacco Company forced its way into the plug-tobacco trade by the use of a fighting brand, happily named " Battle Axe," which it used to undersell the products of its main rivals. The Eastman Kodak Company, again, employed the device of fighting brands of photographic papers, and the National Cash Register Company made use of " knockers," instruments built specially to meet the competition of certain rival lines. A very similar device has been used by the Shipping Conferences, the device of the " fighting ship," which is put to load freight in competition against an outside rival, and to bid down freights to an unremunerative level. The large motor omnibus companies have occasionally used almost the same method, sending sometimes one, sometimes two, of their own buses to shadow a pirate and to collect as much as possible of its traffic. In most cases these fighting brands are produced at a loss and sold only in those markets where competition is encountered. Elaborate instructions have sometimes been given to agents regarding the circumstances in which they should be produced, so that sales of more profitable lines should not be damaged.

An alternative device for achieving the same object, used as a rule where legal objections to discrimination exist, or where public opinion against monopolies is strong, is the device of the " bogus independent." The Standard Oil Company in its earlier struggle for control of the distributive trade in oil would appear to have made some use of this service. The American Tobacco Company is said to have used it extensively.[1] It had to meet prejudices both of consumers against monopoly, and of union workers against an under- taking with a non-union labour policy, and it attempted to do so by controlling and continuing to operate producing firms believed to be outside the trust. We have seen a similar use of the same device in England during the period of struggle for unification of road passenger transport. The larger undertakings in several cases ran bogus " pirates," either continuing buses in " pirate " colours after they had been absorbed, or decorating non-piratical buses in a temporary, piratical garb.

It is at once apparent that these weapons of offence are dangerous only where the competition is between a stronger and larger firm, selling in a wide market, and a weaker and smaller firm, selling in a narrower market. Price competition over the whole field is an ordinary and entirely proper weapon of economic competition. Price competition, even in a part of the field, cannot be avoided where a younger firm chal- lenges an older. On the other hand price competition in which the strong undertaking employs its monopoly profits obtained in one part of the market to destroy competition, and re-establish monopoly, in another part, cannot be justified on the ground that in wholly different circumstances competition gives the

[1] See Stevens, *Unfair Competition*, p. 22 ; Jones; *op. cit.*, p. 151.

consumer the advantage of the most efficient service.

For this reason certain countries have attempted to forbid price discrimination except in so far as differences of local prices can be justified by differences of cost. It may be that such a policy is the best when all considerations are taken into account. But it is important that it should be realized that such a policy does harm as well as good. It may often happen that some measure of price discrimination is a necessary condition before any of some service can be provided. There may be no uniform price per visit which would enable a country doctor to make a living ; there may be no uniform charge per ton-mile at which a railway in an undeveloped territory could be made to pay. Even where a uniform price would give some service, if costs fall considerably with output and the optimum undertaking is greater than the demand of the local market, discrimination may benefit the parties paying the higher as well as those paying the lower price. Thus discrimination in favour of consumers of electricity for purposes of heat and power may well yield lower and not higher rates to consumers of light.

§ 7. *Unfair Practices.* The devices so far considered have been mostly of such a character that their condemnation is at least ambiguous. Vertical integration, local price-cutting, restrictive contracts, special agencies, deferred rebates may all in their places be proper and legitimate forms of business conduct. But besides these there are other devices that have been employed by monopolists for destruction of their rivals which cannot be so charitably described.

Misrepresentation of competing manufactures has been of many degrees, from the exhibition of the rival product labelled " Junk, 5 cents," to deliberate misstatements regarding the honesty of the manufacturer or the quality of his output. The bribery of employees of the rival producer to disclose trade secrets, or the identity of customers, or to give information regarding tenders, or to withdraw their services, has been sometimes a weapon of offence. The bribery of designers to specify products of a particular character, if possible of a particular firm, has probably been even more frequent.

Intimidation of customers, or of employees, or of suppliers of raw materials, or of credit, has been used as a weapon in certain instances. The financial resources of small undertakings have been exhausted by vexatious legal proceedings against them. Some of these methods of competition, defamation of character, for example, are, of course, illegal even apart from special legislation dealing with monopolistic practices. But evidence is in most cases difficult to obtain, and the damage done may be irretrievable by the time that proceedings can be taken.

There is another type of unfair practice which in the United States at least played a large part in facilitating the growth of monopolies,[1] the securing of improperly advantageous rates from public carriers or public utilities, sometimes by bribery or intimidation. In the United States during the 'seventies of the last century there was no open system of special railway rates for undertakings which consigned exceptionally large, or exceptionally regular, shipments. Special

[1] See pp. 199–203.

secret rebates were given to them, and these were in several cases the basis of the great competitive strength of certain undertakings. The importance of the traffic to a particular railway made threats to withdraw it extremely powerful. Even when the practice had been forbidden by law or excluded by agreement, railways were forced to grant terms to big shippers which temporarily did not so much as cover the prime cost of the traffic.

We shall see in later chapters that different countries have taken different steps to prevent the use of unfair practices for the establishment of monopoly. But it is by no means easy to define an unfair practice with that accuracy which is necessary before a court can take action.

All competition is designed to inflict financial injury on a rival, to reduce a competitor's profits to the point where he will transfer his services elsewhere. The fact that certain competitive practices accelerate or increase this injury is not in itself evidence that they should be made unlawful. The dilemma is best illustrated by the technique employed by President Roosevelt to create temporary monopolies in the United States in order to maintain prices during a depression. The system was built upon the framework of the organization designed to prevent the use of unfair practices. Unfairness was merely extended to include destructive price competition of certain kinds. Thus, if we too strictly protect existing firms against the attacks of potential monopolists, we may end in preventing the creation of one monopoly, by ourselves creating another.

To the economist the criterion of whether a practice

is unfair or not, is the test whether it leads to the substitution of a cheaper for a dearer, or of a dearer for a cheaper source of supply. The public has a right to be supplied by the cheapest producer. A practice which detracts from this right, should thus be made illegal. But if that criterion is employed, the same practice may be fair when used by an efficient, unfair when used by an inefficient producer. Moreover, in very many cases the potential monopolist is the more efficient producer, producing at lower costs. It must be a matter of uncertainty whether his lower costs will lead him to sell at lower prices, or his greater monopoly powers will lead him to sell at higher prices. Again, if we think that we can control monopolies and redress the inequalities of wealth that they cause, our test of unfair competition will be different from what it will be if we fear monopolies, or prefer to stabilize an economy of relatively inefficient small firms rather than see concentration in a few giant undertakings.

But even if the economist is content to judge fair or unfairness by these uncertain tests, the lawyer cannot. He must have an objective test; he cannot depend upon the wholly speculative test of intention. He cannot be asked to define at what point a firm's intention to secure sufficient power to influence prices makes it so nearly a monopolist that its methods of competition become unfair. Thus any definition of unfair competition must over a large part of the field be purely arbitrary and reflect in some sense the pragmatic judgments of society as to which practices can safely be permitted and which are in the given circumstances best forbidden.

CHAPTER V

THE FORMS OF MONOPOLY ORGANIZATION

§ 1. *Introductory.* In the last two chapters we have seen that monopolies may be divided into certain categories according to their duration, and according to the sources of their monopoly powers. Corresponding in some measure to these different categories of monopoly are certain forms of organization that monopolies may adopt.

Before starting to study them in detail it is necessary to say something in general terms regarding the forms of organization that any firm must adopt. A firm must be organized in two separate aspects. It must be organized in respect of its technical control and administration. Thus it may, or may not, be divided into a series of plants or departments. These again may, or may not, be separated geographically. The technical co-ordination, both inside the plant, and between one plant and another, will again provide problems of organization.

A firm must also be organized in respect of its financial administration. If it is a single unit, it may be a private firm outside the provision of the limited liability laws ; it may be a private company ; it may be a public company. If it is a multiple-unit undertaking, the financial organization may be separate for each unit, so as to secure for each the advantage of limited liability, or it may be common to all the units. If separate, then financial co-ordination may be informal, though some such device as interlocking directorates, or formal through a superimposed holding company, or by any of a variety of alternative means to the same end.

The forms of monopoly organization are concerned primarily with the financial aspect, but partly also with the technical aspect. The degree of emphasis on each depends largely upon the expected life of the monopoly. An essentially short-term monopoly will be likely to be concerned mainly with the financial problems of increasing and possibly pooling profits. A long-term monopoly will be concerned also with increasing profits by reducing production costs. The choice between the various forms is not, however, always freely made upon purely economic grounds. For legislation in most countries tends to penalize certain forms more than others, or to make certain types of agreement more difficult, or even impossible, to enforce. Thus even if all else were equal, a monopoly might well take different forms in Germany, in the United States and in Great Britain.

The problems of monopoly organization differ ordinarily in one fundamental respect from those of a multiple plant undertaking. Inside a single undertaking, though jealousies may, and often do, exist, it can properly be assumed that the interests of each are identical with the interests of the whole. But in a monopoly organization the contrary is often the case. The interest of one partner in the organization may be in conflict with that of the rest. Regulations and sanctions to prevent internal strife are thus necessary. They are more necessary in those types of monopoly whose sole end is to raise prices and profits ; they are less necessary in those types which in some degree pool profits, and thus make individual earnings independent of the actual output of the component parts of the organization.

§ 2.   *Short-Term Forms of Organization.*   Let us start by considering the most transient, and therefore the least formal, types of organization.[1] They are mostly terminable at short notice, or at some fixed date. They make in most cases no permanent change either in the technical or in the financial organization of the firm, for it is usually assumed that competition will be renewed at a later date. Even if that is not regarded as probable, the power of a firm to withdraw, fully equipped for independent action, is an important factor in the internal politics of the monopoly.

(i) " *Informal undertakings or ' gentlemen's agreements '* between competing producers or merchants as to prices to be charged or areas to be served." Examples of such agreements have been commonest in such local trades as baking, tailoring, boot-repairing, milk-retailing (in the days before the Marketing Board), coal-retailing, the hiring of cars or punts or tennis-courts. But they are to be found

[1] In the following analysis of forms I am following the scheme prepared by the Board of Trade for the Balfour Committee (see *Factors in Industrial and Commercial Efficiency*, p. 71). The explanation of each form is also taken verbatim from that Report, by permission of the Controller of H.M. Stationery Office. Examples of each type have been added, so far as possible, from Fitzgerald's *Industrial Combination in England.* The reader is advised to study their organization further in that book, or in the other references provided.

also in a great variety of trades working on a national scale.
Thus the price of petrol is informally agreed between the
big distributing companies. The prices of various products
of the iron and steel trades have been similarly agreed
between producers, and particular markets have been
assigned to different producing areas. The Cable Makers'
Association[1] has also regulated prices by such informal
agreement. Examples of this most common type of
arrangement can be multiplied almost indefinitely. The
agreement is sometimes conscious, and so nearly formal as
to bring it almost into the next category. It is sometimes
so unconscious that parties to it might honestly deny its
existence. Thus the traditional fees of certain professions,
the traditional charges for certain services, do not constitute monopoly agreements in the minds of the members
of the profession, but are none the less effective. Prices
which no one cuts, because it is in no one's interest to cut
them, may similarly yield a tacit monopoly[2] without any
conscious effort on the part of the monopolists.

(ii) " *Associations for regulating prices.* These involve a
more formal agreement between competing producers or
merchants, who form an association to fix minimum prices
at which they will sell." Examples of this are again very
numerous. They were to be found in certain districts in the
coal trade before the 1930 Act. The Shipping Conferences
have fixed rates of freight between specified ports.[3] The
Sulphuric Acid Association[4] existed to regulate the price
of the product. The Federation of Master Cotton Spinners'
Association in 1923 attempted to fix minimum selling
prices for yarn.[5]

(iii) " *Associations for regulating output.* The simpler
form of organization is for an association of competing
producers to arrange during a period of depression that
only a proportion of the plant of each firm shall be worked,
in order that production may be controlled and prices
increased or maintained. In other cases the actual output

---

[1] Fitzgerald, *op. cit.*, p. 122.   [2] See pp. 21–30.
[3] Fitzgerald, *op. cit.*, p. 170.   [4] *Ibid.*, p. 84.
[5] *Ibid.*, p. 9.

of each producer may be fixed, and he is expected (whether subject to fine or not) not to exceed it."

An example of an arrangement that only a proportion of the plant shall be worked (or that machinery shall only be worked a proportion of full time) is to be found in the short-lived agreement in the cotton industry of 1924–5.[1] A somewhat similar device was employed in the Scottish coal-field in 1928, where a scheme was introduced to raise a levy on each ton of coal, and to employ it to compensate producers for keeping a pit, or a seam in a pit, temporarily closed. Examples of the fixing of the output of producers have always been numerous, and have become exceedingly common in recent years. The Newcastle Coal Vend of 1760–1840 fixed a vend for each mine, depending on its capacity and the demands of the London market. The early German coal cartels and the British Coal Mines Act of 1930 have used similar methods. The output of rubber,[2] sugar, copper, tin, zinc have all at different times been similarly controlled.

(iv) " *Pooling associations.* A common type of pooling association is that in which each member pays a similar fixed sum per unit of output into a pool, which, at regular intervals, is divided up equally among the contributors after the formation of a reserve fund. Under a more elaborate form of arrangement each producer is allotted a percentage of the aggregate output of all the producers in the association, the percentage being fixed on the basis of ascertained experience in the recent past. If a producer exceeds his percentage of the total output, he pays into the pool a sum proportionate to the excess, calculated on an agreed basis ; if a producer falls short of his percentage he receives from the pool a sum, calculated also on an agreed basis (though not necessarily the same basis as is applicable to excess production), proportionate to the deficiency. In some cases pooling associations also fix prices."

---

[1] Fitzgerald, *op. cit.*, p. 9.
[2] Fitzgerald, *op. cit.*, pp. 164–8, and for the others J. W. F. Rowe, *Markets and Men, passim.*

Examples of the equal division of the pool, though they doubtless exist, are not easy to discover.[1] The agreements among the railways to pool the profits of certain traffics in fixed proportions perhaps come nearest. Of the type of pooling agreement under which there are payments made for excess, and received for deficiencies, as compared with some predetermined share in the total trade, the number of examples is very great. The North of Ireland Corn Millers' Association,[2] the National Light Castings Association (dealing in metal fittings for the building trade), the Bedstead Makers' Federation,[3] are a few of the more notable examples. But this type of organization has covered a great variety of industries turning out products as different as tinplates, cut wire nails and clay drain pipes. Similar pooling agreements also find a place in the more elaborate organizations of many of the German cartels and syndicates.

(v) " *Associations for allocating contracts.* Such associations exist in certain industries where work is allotted by tender. The association decides which firm is to receive a particular contract and it is arranged that other firms either do not tender or tender high. In some cases it is arranged that the members of the association shall each be allotted a particular area." An example of the allocation of contracts is afforded by the Cast Iron Pipe Association, which decides what member's turn it is to receive the next order, and instructs him to quote the lowest price. The allocation of markets on a geographical basis is found in the case of a number of international Combines. Thus the British-American Tobacco Co. co-ordinates in the export market the sales of the (British) Imperial Tobacco Company and the firms which before 1911 composed the American Tobacco Trust. The home market is reserved to the national producers. The British-American Tobacco Co., though it owns shares in firms producing for the

---

[1] I can find no example among the industries surveyed under the Profiteering Act in 1919, nor among those discussed by Macrosty or Fitzgerald.

[2] See Macrosty, *op. cit.*, p. 224, and pp. 353–9.

[3] See Fitzgerald, *op. cit.*, pp. 48–51.

British market, confines its productive activities to the
export trade, and produces cigarettes and tobaccos of the
standard brands sold in the home market for that trade.
Other similar agreements define markets, and diminish or
prevent international competition, in the explosives and
cement trades.

Thus far we have been concerned with forms of
monopoly organization which leave almost untouched
the internal organization of each individual firm. They
retain not only their technical and financial independence, but also their sales staffs. In the last category,
where contracts or territories were allocated, the
degree of sales competition was somewhat less. But in
industries which operate by the method of tender,
selling organization is usually less extensive than in
those which sell by other methods, and in the case of
the allocation of territories, selling organization within
those territories remains unaffected. Thus the essential
characteristic of these terminable associations is that
the competitive structure of the industry remains, but
some central organization (where the association is
formal) is superimposed, which restricts competition.
It may do this either by preventing the competition
taking the form of price cutting, thus limiting it to
competition of quality or of advertisement, or by
diminishing the marginal revenue from additional sales
through the medium of some pooling device.

§ 3. *Transitional Forms of Monopoly.* Intermediate
between the short-term terminable associations and
the long-term forms are a group of forms of organization which, though sometimes in fact long-lived, are
essentially transitional in character. The monopoly

remains an association of fundamentally independent firms. The component firms retain their separate financial and technical identities. Inside the monopoly there is a conflict of interest of firm and firm, which expresses itself in an internal politics of the association which may from time to time erupt into actual dis-integration. But the firms have sacrificed certain parts of the competitive structure, usually their independent sales organizations, and the firms act in concert as regards this particular function.

These forms are sometimes in fact transitional; they are forms, that is, that are taken in the intermediate stage between competition and ultimate consolidation. They are sometimes, and especially so in Germany, more stable variations of the short-term forms. For experience has shown[1] that the purely short-lived forms, in which there is no enforceable contract of participation, are extremely unstable. The most profitable position is always to stand outside a restriction scheme, while others observe it. In Germany, where contracts in restraint of trade are not ordinarily unenforceable,[2] the solution has usually been to bind members of the association to sell the whole of their output (or certain defined parts of their output) to a selling agency, acting for the association, for a period of years. In the United States, where restraining contracts have ordinarily been unenforceable, and in more recent years actually illegal,[3] attempts have been made at different times to use some of these transitional forms to surmount the obstacles imposed by law on any association for fixing prices or regulating output. They have been employed merely as apparently legal

[1] See pp. 232–4.   [2] Ibid., p. 225.   [3] Ibid., pp. 205–7.

substitutes for the short-period varieties, and have largely disappeared as their legality has been discredited.

(vi) "*The Selling Agency*. A number of firms making the same article agree to turn over their output to a common selling agency, so as to avoid undercutting. There may be no regulation of output." An example of such an arrangement is afforded by the Central Agency which acts as selling agency in certain markets for the sewing cotton made by J. and P. Coats and by the English Sewing Cotton Co. It is interesting to notice that the history of the Agency is longer than that of the Coats amalgamation, and that before amalgamation took place the Central Thread Agency was acting as selling agent for the group of firms concerned.[1] Thus the form of organization did in this instance undergo transition from less to more complete consolidation.

(vii) "*The participating Cartel with selling syndicate.* This form of organization was adopted in Germany in a number of industries. The essence is that competing producers agree to establish for a definite period a joint selling agency for the exclusive sale of their products, and that each producer is allotted a participation in the total output. Those who exceed their participation pay a fine, those who fall short of it receive an indemnity. The selling agency or syndicate is registered as a company in which the individual producers are shareholders with votes in proportion to their output. The members fix a base price for their products covering cost of production, and sell to the syndicate at an accounting price that is usually somewhat higher. The syndicate sells to the public at the highest price it can get, adjusting its price to circumstances in different parts of the market, though it does not as a rule sell below the accounting price. A feature of some of the German Cartels, notably the Stahlwerksverband, before the War was the subsidizing of the export trade, especially in years of depression." Examples of this form of organization are very numerous

[1] See Macrosty, *op. cit.*, p. 126.

in Germany; the best known example is the Rhenish-Westphalian Coal Cartel which is described in a later chapter.[1] In this country there have been several recent imitations of the German prototypes, notably the scheme established for the coal industry under the Act of 1930, and subsequently amended and modified to include selling agencies. Of other examples, the outstanding one is that in the salt trade, where the manufacturers were combined in the Salt Manufacturers' Association,[2] and in 1906 made an agreement to sell their output at a fixed rate to a selling syndicate (the North-Western Salt Co.), which in turn sold at the best price it could, and distributed profits in agreed proportions.

(viii) " *Variations of the participating cartel with selling syndicate.* In some cases there are variations of structure in the direction of the trust. The syndicate may acquire a considerable degree of independence or it may fall under the control of a particular concern or group." An example of the domination of a cartel by one concern is provided by the history of the great Vereinigte Stahlwerke A.G. in the German iron and steel trades. In 1926 its participation in the pig-iron, raw steel and A-producers syndicates was in each case a little less than 50 per cent. The concern had in 1935 an annual capacity sufficient to produce 36 million tons of coal, and to make 10 million tons of coke, 9.7 million tons of iron, and 9.25 million tons of steel, in addition to finishing plant of considerable variety.[3] Its influence on the policy of the different syndicates concerned with its highly integrated activities was preponderant. In the potash cartel there has been similar domination by one concern, the Wintershall concern, which by absorbing other undertakings has gradually grown until in 1933 it controlled 41 per cent of the total output of the Potash Syndicate. There have at times been signs of counter-organization by other groups to

---

[1] See pp. 228–32.

[2] Fitzgerald, *op. cit.*, p. 73.

[3] See Levy, *Industrial Germany*, p. 55 ; and Liefman, *Cartels, Concerns and Trusts*, pp. 251–4.

oppose its influence in the determination of the policy of
the industry.

(ix) "*Financial Community of Interests (Interessengemeinschaft*). This is established when two or more companies
agree for a period of years (sometimes as many as fifty) to
pool the whole of their profits and divide them up between
the companies in prearranged proportions. The organization remains in theory temporary, and the companies
retain a separate existence, each with its own management ;
but they may work closely together by means of joint
committees. Experience shows that there is a tendency
for this form of organization to give way to a more complete
union." This form is predominantly a German one.
In that country there are numerous examples, of which
the best known is probably that in the chemical trades,
where the I.G. Farben has created a position analogous to
that of Imperial Chemical Industries in Great Britain.
The combination started as a series of *Interessengemein-
schaften* between the different firms by which they undertook to pool profits for a period of fifty years. Gradually
two large groups were built up in this way, which in 1916
reached a further I.G. agreement. But in 1925 this arrangement was superseded by a new trust agreement, under
which one of the companies increased its capital or
exchanged its shares with the other undertakings. But
the old, and now misleading, name of *Interessengemeinschaft Farbenindustrie Aktiengesellschaft* was still retained.[1]
In some instances I.G. agreements go considerably further
than the pooling of profits, and include the pooling of
secret and patented processes, the exchange of information,
and a considerable measure of technical, as well as financial,
collaboration.

§ 4. *The Long-term Forms of Monopoly.* There is no
very definite boundary between the transitional forms
that we have just considered and the long-term forms
to which we come next. In several instances, such as

---

[1] See Levy, *Industrial Germany*, pp. 64-5.

that of the Rhenish-Westphalian Coal Cartel, the transitional form has already a more or less continuous life of over half a century.   The difference lies chiefly in the extent to which the competitive structure of the associated undertakings survives, so that the association is in fact terminable.   But the motive to terminate the association is also relevant.   This is, we have seen, related to the dependence or independence of the interests of a shareholder in one of the associated undertakings on the specific output of that particular undertaking.   There will only be found to be an internal politics of the association and threats of disruption, if the immediate or ultimate gains of one undertaking can change relatively to those of others. By this test the *Interessengemeinschaft*, which for a period destroys the possibility of such relative movements of profits, should be included in the long-period forms.   The reasons for not so including it are, firstly, that though the short-period relation of one undertaking to another is now irrelevant, the long-term relation is not entirely irrelevant ; secondly, that this form is in fact in the majority of cases transitional.

The long-term forms may be divided as follows :

(x) " *The ' voting' trust*.   This form of organization became prevalent at one period in the United States, until it was held by the courts to be illegal.[1]   A number of competing companies agreed to assign the whole of their stock to a group of trustees, receiving in exchange trust certificates representing the valuation of their properties. The trustees were thus able to exercise complete control over all the businesses.   This is in theory a permanent form of organization."   The most familiar example is that of the Standard Oil Company, which adopted this form

' See pp. 206–8.

during the years 1879–92.[1] During those years a considerable number of monopoly organizations in other
American industries also took this form, and trust agreements were concluded among firms concerned in sugar
refining, whisky distilling, the manufacture of lead, of
cordage and of linseed oil. This form was gradually
superseded in the United States by other forms, usually
that of the holding company, after it had been held illegal
by the Supreme Court in 1892 in the case of the Standard
Oil Trust. The " trust " organization was essentially a
lawyer's device, to surmount legal obstacles existing at
a particular moment in the United States. In other
countries, with different legal backgrounds, the " voting
trust " in its pure form has been rare. The Nobel
Dynamite Trust Company, which co-ordinated British and
German makers of dynamite from 1886 to 1914, did, however, take this form. It held the shares of the subsidiary
companies and exchanged for them trust certificates.[2]
Since the scandals of monopoly were most aggravated in
the United States at the moment when the " trust "
predominated, the generic name of " trust " has stuck to
monopolies possessing a certain degree of financial interlocking. Most of the concerns which are now described
as " trusts " belong properly to one of the two categories
to be described below.

(xi) *Exchange of Shares.* Two or more companies may
link their fortunes together by means of an exchange of
shares. The precise effect depends upon the relative sizes
of the companies and the number and proportion of shares
exchanged. Where one company predominates in size
and purchases the whole or a majority of the shares, the
other company becomes virtually a subsidiary though it
may possess a voice in the management of the larger
concern." The exchange of shares is occasionally, but
not very often, employed as a permanent form of organization, for the purpose of pooling profit. It is more often a
technique of transition to one or other of the two main
long-period forms which follow.

---

[1] See p. 206.   [2] See Liefman, *op. cit.*, p. 314.

(xii) " *Holding Companies.* Another method of establishing unity is for each of a group of companies to sell its shares, or a majority of them, to another company, established for the purpose or already existing, the shareholders of the individual companies receiving in exchange shares in the holding company. The individual companies continue to exist, and to enjoy a greater or less degree of autonomy, but their general policy is controlled by the holding company in the interests of the whole group of undertakings." This form of organization is by far the most common of all the long-period varieties. For it retains a certain flexibility and the advantage of the limited liability of the several parts, while making possible their co-ordination in all essentials, and subordinating the interests of each undertaking to that of the whole group. It was widely employed for a time in the United States. The Standard Oil Company of New Jersey was a holding company, controlling the Standard Oil Companies in the several States. In more recent years the pyramids of holding companies erected by the ingenuities of such financiers as Samuel Insull and the van Schweringens have been notorious. In Great Britain the holding company has also been widely employed. Thus Amalgamated Anthracite Collieries, Ltd., has been a holding company in the coal trade producing two-thirds of the anthracite output. Imperial Chemical Industries, covering a wide variety of products, United Steel Companies, Guest Keen and Baldwins, David Colville, Vickers in various areas and departments of the steel industry, Hawker-Siddeley in the aircraft trade, Electric and Musical industries in the manufacture of gramophones and radio, Tilling and British Automobile Traction in the road passenger transport business, are but a few of the better known examples of this type of organization.

(xiii) " *Consolidations or mergers.* These denote the consolidation or merging of two or more businesses into a single undertaking. The businesses taken over completely lose their separate existence." Of this there are also numerous examples, though few of them are so large as to dominate their respective industries. The Imperial Tobacco Company, Stewart and Lloyds, in the manufacture of tubes, Tate and Lyle in sugar refining, Radiation in the manufacture of gas-stoves, the Distiller Co. in whisky distilling, the Renold and Coventry Chain Co. in the manufacture of cycle and similar chains, the London Transport Board, are primarily examples of merger and consolidation. But in practice firms seldom adopt consistently one single form. They not only change from time to time, but at one and the same time they are apt to have different relations to different parts of their combined organization. " Few of the British trusts," wrote the author of the memorandum that we have been quoting,[1] " are purely of the types described ; few consist merely of companies bound together by exchange of shares ; few are merely holding companies ; and few are entirely unified undertakings. Many are holding companies to some extent and consolidations to some extent ; while they may also have allied themselves with other companies by means of exchange of shares or interlocking directorates."

§ 5. *Reasons for the Adoption of Particular Forms.*
Having completed our survey of the various forms of monopoly organization, can we say anything in general terms as to the circumstances in which any particular form is likely to be adopted ? If we attempt such generalization, it must be made with the greatest caution. For the grounds of adoption of some form are very often predominantly legal rather than economic. The fear, or the actuality, of the persecution of some forms of organization and the relative exemption of others has played, as we shall see in later chapters, a large part in causing the predominance of certain forms in certain countries. The enforceability

[1] Balfour Committee on Industry and Trade ; *Factors in Industrial and Commercial Efficiency*, p. 76.

or non-enforceability of certain types of contract is
similarly important. And even where legal considerations are not of great moment, other non-economic
factors may come in. Some individuals who have
played important parts in bringing about combination
have shown a quite idiosyncratic preference for mergers
and fusions, others again for holding companies. The
very presence or absence of a predominant personality
may explain the choice between a trust or large concern
on the one hand and a cartel on the other.

But if we proceed with due caution, we can trace
certain broad relations of types of monopoly and of
particular characteristics of monopolies to corresponding forms of monopoly organization. Thus for the
terminable association there must be reasons, first,
why firms should be prepared to join the association,
second, and for the moment most important, why
they should desire in certain hypothetical circumstances to free themselves from the association. The
conditions in which producers, and in particular low-
cost producers in an industry, will prefer to submit
themselves to the controls of a restriction scheme rather
than preserve their freedom are usually those of
depression superimposed upon excess capacity.[1] They
will desire to adopt a terminable form of association if
new competition from other low-cost producers is
likely to be forthcoming; that is if entry into the
industry is difficult or impossible to prevent, and if new
entry is more likely to have low costs than to have high
costs.

A low-cost producer will also wish to retain the

---

[1] For an admirable discussion of this problem see J. W. F. Rowe,
Markets and Men, Chapter VIII and *passim*.

possibility of freedom, if the difference of the cost of production of high- and low-cost producers in the industry concerned is considerable. As long as prices are low it may be to his advantage to accept restrictions and husband his resources. But when demand increases there will be an inevitable conflict of interest between the high- and low-cost producer. Consider, for example, the problem of a low-cost member of a copper-restriction scheme. A producer whose prime costs are £20 will prefer a price of £40 with a quota of 100 to a price of £50 with a quota of 60. A producer whose prime costs are £25 will be indifferent. A producer whose prime costs are £36 will make more than twice the profit at £50 that he does at £40. The power to withdraw, and the consequential power to use the threat of withdrawal as a weapon for the increase of basic tonnage, is the inducement which alone can attract a low-cost producer temporarily into the association.

The power to terminate one's membership of an association may also be desired where the association covers a number of producers of not entirely homogeneous products, or of products not sold in one and the same market. For in such a case a restriction of output, or a fixing of price that is dictated by the circumstances of one part of the market, may prove wholly unsuited to the circumstances of the other part, and freedom from control may be desired. Such problems arise frequently where certain undertakings are primarily concerned with the home market and others with the export market. They have been extremely acute in some of the German cartels.

It will be seen that the terminable association is in general to be identified with the short-term varieties of

H

monopoly. The less stable is the basis of the monopoly, the shorter its prospective life, the more probable is it that some terminable form of association will be adopted. On the other hand as the prospective life of the monopoly increases, as its stability increases through less divergence of interest between high- and low-cost producers, or between producers of slightly differing products, or between producers for slightly different markets, so it becomes more probable that firms will consent to adhere to one or other of the transitional forms of organization. These transitional forms have sometimes arisen as a means of escape from concealed competition of one kind or another. It not infrequently happens that where an association is formed to fix prices, competition continues in the form of rivalry in quality of products or in special facilities provided, or in quickness of service, or in grants of allowances for advertisement, or a number of other similar ways. Thus rate-fixing agreements between railways at one time led to substantial competition in facilities ; the same has been true of the competition of shipping lines. The escape has sometimes been that of a short-term profit-pooling agreement, sometimes that of an agreement of the " community of interest " type.

That has been in part the explanation of the growth of the transitional forms, but they have had a second and often more important stimulus. As we have seen, the most profitable position is always that of a firm standing outside a restriction agreement, accepting the improved prices without submitting to the necessary restriction. The more rigid types of association have been fostered by the need to prevent each firm in turn attempting this manœuvre. As we shall see in a later chapter, it was this need which led primarily to their development in Germany, the land of their origin. and the land where alone at first the law assisted their enforcement. But this use of more rigid forms of association to deal with situations which have essentially called for terminable associations, has made these transitional forms highly unstable. As we shall see below, the effect has in many cases been, by preventing withdrawal of unwilling members from time to time, to concentrate an industrial crisis at the moment of renewal. The threat of disruption has invoked political intervention, until in Germany, as in England, these transitional forms have depended mainly upon the big stick of Government.

There remain the four long-term forms of organization. Of these two are important, two unimportant. The " voting trust " was, as we have seen, a lawyer's device which soon outlived its legality and consequent utility. The exchange of shares is but rarely a form of organization. It is more usually, as we have seen, a means of transition to one or other of the two main long-period forms, the holding company and the merger.

The adoption of one or other of these long-term forms is, as we have seen, likely where an important motive for combination is the possibility of securing technical economies which can be achieved only by a wholesale reorganization of all the various undertakings included. A preference for the holding company or for the merger may be explained by a variety of considerations. The holding company may perform any, or all, of three quite distinct functions. It may be a

device for the central office management of a number of
separate plants, it may be a central marketing organization controlling and selling the output of separate
plants ; or it may be a financial device to facilitate the
extension of limited liability to units smaller than the
whole combined undertaking. The first two functions
can, however, be performed if necessary by special
offices or departments within a merger, and the third
consideration must be partially relevant in order that
a holding company may be preferred. But it must also
be remembered that the holding company is usually the
line of least resistance. Less complicated problems of
valuation and adjustment are likely to be encountered.
The existing companies remain as legal entities and
their various financial and legal obligations need not
be affected, mineral leases need not be transferred,
and so on. Thus unless the purpose of the merger is to
secure a complete overhaul of technical production,
and possibly its concentration into a new plant in a
new locality, the holding company is the simpler form
to employ.

The holding company has a further advantage in
those industries in which goodwill applies rather to the
care and methods of manufacture, as it does, for
instance, with motor cars, or gramophones, than to the
selection of raw materials, as it does, for example,
with cigarettes or cement. This may perhaps help
to explain why Rootes and Electric and Musical
Industries, Ltd., in the first two industries are holding
companies, while the Imperial Tobacco Company and
the Associated Portland Cement Manufacturers, Ltd.,
have taken the form of a merger. For the holding-
company method can leave intact where necessary the

individual plants with their special reputations, and even give them (as has been done in the case of the constituent undertakings of E.M.I., the Gramophone and Columbia Companies) added freedom and privacy by restoring them to the status of private companies.

The holding company as a device of central management is most likely to be discovered in industries in which the optimum management unit is larger than that of technical production, or in which, since transport costs are high, production must take place in a number of plants near the market, even though they be of less than optimum size. As a device for central marketing it is most likely to be found in any industry where the optimum scale of marketing is markedly larger than that of manufacture. As a device for the subdivision of limited liability it is most likely to be employed where the anticipated fortunes of different parts of the combined undertaking are most widely different. This will be the case where a combination is lateral as well as horizontal, extending not only into similar but also into dissimilar branches of activity. It will be the case where a horizontal combination contains technical units of markedly different natural efficiency, such as is common in mining. It will be the case where technique is in transition and each unit is something of an experiment, or where fashion can affect earnings in a way not easily retrievable. This may serve to explain the common practice of many shipping companies in making small numbers of ships into separate companies. It will be the case also where different units sell in different geographical markets, so that one may encounter difficulties without all others suffering equally.

The complete merger, on the other hand, is most likely where combination has been strictly horizontal, where the market for all the separate plants is uniform and identical, where the ultimate aim of technical policy is concentration into one single plant. To some small extent there is movement from the slightly less permanent form of the holding company to the more permanent form of the complete merger. But the greater flexibility, the greater security, and often also the greater simplicity, of the method of the holding company and subsidiaries has made it the predominating form of modern industry. To the financial schemer, it has the supreme and convincing advantage that, by dexterous pyramiding, a minute holding of certain key shares can be made to control millions. It has also the advantage that it forms on occasion a convenient compromise between the maintenance of the individuality of the separate constituent units that is found in the short-term forms of monopoly and the complete suppression of such individuality which is a feature of the merger. Recalcitrant members of the combination can be left, for the moment at least, as apparent autocrats at the head of individual subsidiary companies, and be tamed by degrees as the holding company's effective control progressively increases

CHAPTER VI

MONOPOLY AND INDUSTRIAL EFFICIENCY

§ 1. *Some Inductive Inquiries.* If we are to consider the desirability of monopoly as a form of industrial organization, it is necessary to ask how it compares with alternative forms in the efficiency which it achieves in production. We may attempt to answer this question in either of two ways. Firstly, we may consider existing monopolies and inquire how far they have succeeded in reducing costs of production to a greater extent than might have been expected apart from the existence of monopoly. Secondly, we may attempt to decide by deductive argument whether monopolies have incentives to achieve efficiency or opportunities of reducing costs which are not shared equally by competitive forms of organization.

The most fruitful inductive studies of the efficiency and success of monopolies have been made in the United States.[1] The National Industrial Conference Board obtained for some sixteen industries a measurement of the relation of output per worker employed in consolidations and in independent firms for the years 1920 to 1926. The investigation was necessarily con-

[1] See especially National Industrial Conference Board, *Mergers in Industry*, and Livermore, *Quarterly Journal of Economics*, Nov. 1935.

fined to processes which were sufficiently standardized for the unit of product to be comparable in different firms. Thus in the steel industry it was confined to actual steel making, and the output was measured in tons of steel ingots. In eleven of the sixteen industries the consolidations show for the year 1926 superior efficiency. In six of the industries the superiority was very marked, in five it was not great. Thus of the sixteen industries analysed, six showed a substantial gain to the consolidation, five a small gain, five an advantage to the independent. The advantage to the consolidation was greatest in industries concerned with metal refining and with mineral manufacture. In the group of industries concerned with metal manufactures the independents were superior, and in one of the industries grouped among miscellaneous manufactures. The explanation in both these cases is believed to be that, while the consolidation took the form of a central control of a number of scattered plants serving local markets, which did not afford advantages of concentration because of high transport costs, the independent producers had larger plants serving, apparently, more concentrated local markets. In these circumstances we should not expect a measurement of purely physical output per head of technical workers to show an advantage.

The data thus collected also made it possible to measure the changes in output per head in consolidations and independents respectively for eighteen industries over a series of years. These must, of course, be used with caution, for such factors as the relation of output to capacity, the differing intensity of effort of employees according to labour scarcity, the concentration of the completion of work with a long production period into certain years, all affect the figures. Moreover, reconstruction of plant will often cause disorganization during the year or two preceding its completion, and in such conditions the statistical separation of productive from constructional employment is seldom easy. The results show that in nine industries technical advance was greater in the case of the consolidations, in four it was greater in the case of the independents, in five there was no significant difference. The figures would appear to support the conclusion " that industrial consolidations have not impeded technical progress. On the other hand they have been among the foremost leaders in experimenting with and introducing time-saving methods of production."

The success of industrial mergers can be tested secondly by their financial achievements. Once more great caution must be used, for profits measure only the level of costs as related to the level of prices. Given the level of prices, high profits, of course, indicate low costs and a high level of industrial efficiency. But where a monopoly is in question, prices are to some extent within its control, and high profits may indicate not a high level of efficiency but a high degree of exploitation of consumers. The author of the best and most recent study of the success of these mergers[1] denies that, in any save a small minority of the cases that he has examined, the success has been due primarily to the possession of patent rights or to the use of vexatious monopoly practices. Nevertheless, where differences of earnings are small, to define the degree

[1] Professor S. Livermore, *Quarterly Journal of Economics*, Nov. 1935, pp. 68–96.

of monopoly and the extent to which it has maintained very slightly higher prices is almost impossible. Moreover, to the extent that the capital of a merger has been " watered " in the process of its formation, the rate of return on capitalization may give very misleading results. Here again the author argues that water was either unimportant or has now been removed, so that assets are often undervalued.

This investigation has shown that, contrary to earlier beliefs that on the whole the industrial combinations of the period 1888 to 1905 had achieved sadly disappointing results, the success of these combinations has been on average greater than that of the general run of firms. Some 328 mergers of that period were examined. They were divided into two groups, the first possessing some degree of monopoly or of dominance in their several industries, the second possessing no such powers and being little different in scale or importance from other undertakings. These two groups were separately analysed into successes, failures and a "limping group" whose history showed a mixture both of success and disaster. The failures accounted for about 40 per cent in the first group and 45 per cent in the second; the successes for about 49 per cent in the first and 48 per cent in the second; while the "limping groups " contained about 11 per cent and 6 per cent. Among the 76 successful mergers in the first group, 10 were outstanding successes, and 10 achieved success only after a process of rejuvenation. The earnings of a large number of these mergers were further compared with a general index[1] of industrial profits

[1] That compiled by R. C. Epstein; see *Industrial Profits in the United States.*

in the United States. For the period 1919 to 1922 results of the mergers were on the average inferior to those in industry in general. For subsequent years to 1932 they were consistently superior, save only in the freak year, 1929.

These two studies would appear to indicate that in efficiency and earning power, industrial consolidations do not differ very widely from the average of all undertakings. But both investigations involve so many assumptions regarding the measurement of output, degrees of monopoly exploitation, or the relative capitalization of mergers and independents, that some hesitation must be felt in placing any considerable reliance upon them.

§ 2. *A Deductive Approach to the Problem.* Since the results of the inductive studies appear so uncertain let us turn now to deductive argument. How far is it likely that incentive or opportunity exists to make monopolies more efficient than competitively organized industries ? We can say at once that we should expect monopoly to be the most efficient form of production wherever a single optimum firm more than suffices to supply the whole market. Where this is the case there will be greater technical economies or economies of management, of buying and selling, of finance, or of better adjustment to fluctuations available to the larger unit, represented by the monopoly, than would be enjoyed by any smaller unit. The larger, then, is the optimum firm in any given industry, the more likely is monopoly to be a necessary condition of the most efficient scale of production.

Now the optimum scale of technical production

depends partly upon opportunities for the division of labour, partly upon the possibilities afforded by a very large output for running at its full capacity certain plant whose minimum size is large, or which is for some reason substantially more efficient in large units than in small units. An extreme instance of such economy is found in the case of public utilities. Apart from the nuisance which would be created by constant disturbance of roads and pavements, and apart also from the unwillingness of local authorities to grant the rights of eminent domain required for this purpose, there would be a wholly unnecessary and extravagant duplication of capital if water companies, let us say, competed for our custom. Of such " octopoid " monopolies gas, electricity, the telephone and telegraph are, in addition to water, the most familiar examples. Tramways might reasonably be included, and in some cases railways.

But the optimum firm may be larger than will supply a given market in more simple cases than these, just because a large firm enjoys certain technical or other economies. The probability of monopoly in such cases will depend mainly upon the size of the market. But it will depend also upon the exact reasons why the optimum firm is large. If we assume that the unit of management and of financial control is the same as that of technical production, so that each plant is also a separate firm, then the size of the market that can be served by one firm will depend upon the area through which the products can be profitably transported from one place of production. The higher are transport costs relatively to production costs, the less will be the area served from each point of production, and the greater the strength of the monopoly at the centre of the area served by it.

If, however, economies depend upon the scale of management or of financial control, or of buying or selling, rather than on that of technical production, it may not be a necessary condition of maximum efficiency that the firm should possess a monopoly, even though its optimum scale of production is substantially larger than the total market in any one of the individual areas which it serves. For it can achieve its optimum technical scale locally without monopoly, and it can achieve its optimum managerial or other scale by multiplication of these local units. Monopoly is almost certainly not a condition of maximum efficiency, for example, in a chain of retail stores, though the total sales of the whole chain may be substantially larger than the consumption of most towns.

If it were true in any particular industry, or in industry in general, as some writers have suggested, that the optimum scale of production was infinitely large, so that an increase of scale always brought further economies, then one unit of production would always be more efficient than two smaller ones, and thus monopoly would always be more efficient in like conditions than any competitive system. But we must ask ourselves what precisely we mean by efficiency. In a given state of technique, with a given organization and with a staff of a given age and enterprise, an existing undertaking may be more efficient than any two smaller undertakings could be. But efficiency is not a static quality. It includes also the power of continuous adaptation to changing situations. The large, ossified undertaking may be incapable of self-modification. And taking a more dynamic view of the situation, greater average efficiency over a long period of time may be achieved, if the industry is always composed of one older and one younger firm, constantly warring for supremacy, rather than by having one firm, at its prime highly efficient, but falling later to a low level of efficiency, before internal revolution or the threat of competition brings about a drastic overhaul of its management. Some of the largest industrial concerns have, nevertheless, shown a surprising vitality and have used their position not to stereotype old-fashioned methods but to develop new processes and improved locations of plants in their particular trades. No useful generalization can either uphold them as models of progressive management or condemn them wholesale for a tendency to stagnation.

So far we have been concerned only with those economies which a monopoly shares with any large industrial organization. The economies considered were those which any firm of similar size would enjoy ; and they were to be regarded as economies associated with monopoly only because monopoly was a condition of achieving the scale of production or of distribution necessary to secure them. If the market expanded sufficiently, the economies would remain even apart from the continuance of the monopoly. We must now proceed to consider how far there are actual economies of monopoly, economies, that is, which apart from monopoly would not accrue to even the largest of firms.

§ 3.   *The Technical Economies of Monopoly.*   It is convenient for purposes of analysis to divide these possible economies into technical economies, economies of management, economies of a financial character, and economies of buying raw materials and marketing the finished product. These will all be considered in turn, though it is well to remember that the line of division between them is blurred, particularly so as regards the distinction between general problems of management and of technical production. The economies of monopoly in relation to risk will not be separately discussed in this chapter. The broader question whether the existence of monopoly can in certain senses stabilize a particular industry, or industry in general, is reserved to a later chapter. But the effects of diminished risk upon the economies of monopoly make themselves apparent through reactions upon technical organization, or management, or the cost of borrowing, or through marketing costs. They have therefore been considered at each step, rather than in isolation.

Let us start, then, by considering the technical economies of monopoly. The first question which we need to answer is whether monopoly secures more nearly than does competition the concentration of production in units of the optimum size. Before that question can be answered we must ask two further questions. What sort of monopoly have we in mind? What sort of competition have we in mind? If we take first the ordinary forms of short-term monopolies, based upon quotas and restriction of output in some one or other of its many forms, we can say at once that monopoly is likely to be technically less efficient than production by competing firms. For if output were to be transferred from higher cost producers to lower

cost producers, or if certain plants were closed down
and the remainder run at full capacity, costs would in
almost every case be reduced. This is true whatever
the degree of perfection of competition, provided only
that the quota restrictions cause some output to be
transferred from low-cost to high-cost producers, or to
be produced by plants working below full capacity.[1]
Monopoly will in this case be superior to competition
only if for some reason it makes it possible to introduce
new equipment where it would not be available otherwise. The question whether that is likely to be the
case must be deferred for the moment.

Where the type of monopoly to be considered is one
of the more long-period forms, the question is less easy
of answer. The simplest way to approach the problem
is to compare the organization which might be expected under perfect competition with that which
might be expected under a monopoly of this type.
Under perfect competition we should expect every
plant and every firm to be of such size that it would, if
the market were large enough, exhaust all the internal
economies of large scale. Each plant or firm would
secure all the economies which could be obtained from
specialization upon one particular type of product.
If economies are to be secured by the vertical disintegration of certain process, under perfect competition we should expect such disintegration to take
place. But unless competition is perfect firms are
likely to be of less than optimum size, and specialization
is not likely to take place in all circumstances where

[1] Considered diagrammatically restriction schemes secure equilibrium by raising the supply curve until the amount supplied will
equal the amount demanded at some predetermined price.

costs, other than selling and transport costs, will be reduced by it.

A monopoly of the completely fused and co-ordinated type may be expected to reproduce almost exactly the conditions of perfect competition. For, whatever price it may be receiving, it will pay the monopoly to reduce its costs of production to a minimum. If one plant can produce more cheaply than another, the low-cost plant is likely to be instructed to fill orders for a particular product up to its best capacity.

If there are economies to be secured by specialization, the monopoly may be expected to secure them. The extent of this concentration and specialization will be the same for monopoly and for perfect competition whether the period we consider is the long period, in which capital equipment may be conceived as requiring replacement, or the short period in which the greatest economy of prime costs is alone relevant, or such a period, lying between these limits, that plants will be closed down if operating at a loss.

So far we have been concerned only with the scale of technical organization. We must now inquire whether a monopoly may be expected to adopt improvements of technique as rapidly as will competing firms. Once again we must limit ourselves to a discussion of whether opportunity and incentive exist, remembering always that to prove these by no means proves effective action. Let us start by considering in what conditions a firm is ordinarily prepared to substitute new equipment for old. It pays it to do so only when total cost of the required output with the new equipment, including a sufficient return on the capital invested, is less than prime cost with the old equipment. The old equip-

I

ment is there in any case, whether it earns any return or none. If prime cost with the old equipment is less than total cost with the new, the additional profits earned through putting in the new equipment will be less than sufficient to pay the interest on the extra capital invested in it. In saying this we have evidently to be very careful what we mean by prime cost of the old equipment, and by the cost of the new. Firstly, in the prime cost we must include the cost of any necessary overhaul and repair to keep the old equipment running. In practice the demise of old ships, old motor lorries, old locomotives is nearly always occasioned by the increasing urgency of major repairs if the ship is to pass survey, or the lorry or locomotive be made fit for another period of service. The longer equipment lives, the more expensive these overhauls become, and the higher is prime cost, until it must finally equal total cost with identical equipment. Secondly, from the cost of the new equipment must be deducted the scrap value of the old equipment, so that what we measure is the immediate addition to the amount of the capital invested.

So far as they are concerned with these considerations, the actions of plants owned by monopolies and by competing firms may be expected to be identical. There is, however, one further point here that needs to be considered. The profitable introduction of the new machinery may be conditional on an expansion of the output and sales of the firm installing it. In such circumstances the more easily sales can be increased, the sooner will the new plant be introduced. The more perfect is the market and the less the importance of goodwill, of advertisement, of selling and transport

costs generally, the easier will this expansion be.
Thus the more nearly does monopoly reproduce the
conditions of perfect competition the earlier will one
of its plants install the new equipment. A quota-
system monopoly will almost certainly be slower in
introducing such improvements than will competing
firms. A well co-ordinated monopoly will probably
find that it pays it to do so more rapidly. Moreover, a
well co-ordinated monopoly can usually give greater
security than there is in any condition short of perfect
competition, that certain plant will be used continuously. It may, or may not, be true that a larger
technical unit is more efficient than a smaller, so that
in a long-period sense, and when each is working to full
capacity, there are diminishing costs with an increase
of scale. But whatever the size of the technical unit,
it is likely to be true that up to its designed capacity
it will show falling average costs if fixed financial and
technical charges are included and averaged over
increasing outputs. Thus there are always substantial
economies of running full rather than running empty.
The economy in respect of fixed charges may in some
industries be reinforced by technical economies where,
as in steel making, a balance of processes is necessary
to full economy, and intermittent working is difficult.
But in an imperfectly competitive industry continuous
full capacity working is seldom possible, for swings of
taste or fortune are likely to favour one firm at this
moment, another at the next. Each will seize the
opportunity to expand its productive capacity in
order to make the greatest use of its opportunities.
Moreover, if customers won are likely to be retained,
and customers lost to be lost for ever, firms will wish

to have a margin of productive capacity to meet unexpected rushes of orders, and to make it easier to grow relatively to other undertakings if opportunity allows.

In aggregate this reserve capital may be quite large relatively to that which would be necessary to produce the output of the industry by continuous working. Its size will very probably be increased by the unnecessary duplication of equipment used only irregularly due to the insufficient specialization of competing firms in an imperfect market. Thus, after the foundation of the United States Steel Corporation, Judge Gary stated that the combined firms required 50 per cent less capital than they had needed as independents. That was probably an extreme case, and few monopolies have in practice succeeded in giving the opportunity for absolutely continuous running to selected plants. But there is no question that the desire to run full is one of the strongest inducements to join in schemes for pooling and distribution of orders, or that very substantial economies can often be secured if the uncertainty of relative changes of output be removed, and the individual undertakings or plants be assigned a fixed proportion of the more stable output of a cartel or a definite task in a more closely merged monopoly. Where relative fluctuations of output can be thus reduced and comparatively continuous operations guaranteed, equipment that is particularly liable to obsolescence can sometimes be profitably installed by a monopolist where any one competing producer would rightly hesitate to do so.

There is one other technical advantage to the

monopoly that deserves mention. A long-period monopoly that has eliminated the internal rivalries and jealousies of the original component firms is, or should be, able to make available to all plants the experience and knowledge of each. Thus it ought to be true that the technical knowledge and experience available to each individual plant was greater under monopoly than under competition. This may not in fact be the case for a variety of reasons. Firstly, the security of tenure of individuals and the continued working of a plant under the monopoly may depend upon the showing of better results than those achieved by other managers or plants, and the sharing of full knowledge may this be discouraged. Secondly, in a period of rapidly advancing technique it may be found even apart from the existence of monopoly that a pooling of knowledge or of patents may be profitable. Thus American industrialists are in general far more willing than are their European counterparts to publish facts and statistics about their organization, technique, and costs, confident that they can learn as much from others as others from them, and that in the march of progress it matters little if others know what you are doing to-day provided that you alone know what you will be doing to-morrow.

In general terms we may say, therefore, that we should expect a monopoly of the fused and co-ordinated type to be superior in technical efficiency to competing firms, unless the competition is exceptionally perfect and all economies of large scale and of specialization have been exhausted. In practice competition seldom, if ever, reaches this level of achievement. But we should expect monopolies of the prices- and quota-fixing variety to be inferior in technical efficiency to ordinary competition. Those forms of monopoly which are intermediate, we should expect to secure some, but not all of the economies of scale and specialization, and to compare well or ill in so far as they secure them.

§ 4. *The Introduction of New Designs.* In considering the adoption of technical improvements in the last section, it was assumed that the new equipment would turn out products indistinguishable from those of the old equipment, so that the firm was merely concerned to lower its costs of production. We must now consider the allied problem of the probable actions of a monopolist where the product itself might be altered, but where the change would involve a change of the productive equipment. It is often reported that monopolists buy up patents to suppress them, and refuse the public improvements which might readily be made. It is important, therefore, to consider whether it is ordinarily in their interest to do so.

Let us examine first the general conditions in which a firm, which has secured the patent for some substitute for a commodity already on the market, will find it profitable to introduce this substitute. It will take account of the effects of its introduction on its receipts and on its costs. From the side of receipts it may benefit in either or both of two respects. It may benefit because, for a time at least, the receipts from the new product will be greater per unit sold than from the old product. It may benefit because it now enjoys a greater proportion of the total trade in the commodity than it did previously. From the side of cost it may benefit if the new product is cheaper to produce than the old, or if the greater output enables it to secure economies of production. Thus the firm will introduce the new product if its receipts from it may be expected to exceed its receipts from the old product by an amount more than sufficient to cover the technical costs of turning over to the new product, the interest and depreciation of special new equipment required, the initial marketing costs necessary to put it on the market and the excess[1] of the prime cost of producing the new product (alone or in conjunction with a smaller output of the old) over the prime cost of producing the old product. In the extreme case where a new firm is set up to manufacture the new product, the whole of the estimated receipts will be balanced against the whole of the estimated costs.

A firm will be more likely, that is, to introduce a new product, the less is its present profit, and the greater its expected profit. In a depression, when firms are working below capacity, so that competition is keen and profits small, the prospective gain of new products is usually greatest. Thus during the depression of 1932 both American and British motor car manufacturers introduced far more innovations than in earlier and in more recent years, when the probable profits to be made on existing models were greater. But the expected profits from a new model depend largely upon the action of competing firms. If all in a given price-field introduce new models, the gain of none of them may be so great as was anticipated. On the other hand if none introduce new models the loss

---

[1] This "excess" would, of course, be negative, if the new substitute has a lower prime cost than the old.

for each will be less. Thus in better times, when
current rates of profit are sufficient not to tempt any
one manufacturer to break away, we enjoy the spectacle
of rival manufacturers telling the public ostensibly,
their competitors in reality, that orderly progress is
more in the general interest than annual new models.

The motive to introduce a product is somewhat
weakened if the general validity or the insuper-
ability of the patent is doubtful. For the period
during which the anticipated addition to receipts is
likely to last will be somewhat diminished. In practice
the enforcement of patent monopolies is often so
difficult, and so expensive in legal fees, that competing
manufacturers have in some industries preferred to
pool patents, and to look for a sufficient reward for
technical invention in the year or so more's advantage
of priority that earlier experimentation usually gives,
and in the subsequent goodwill that may arise from it.

Let us now consider how these various factors will be
affected if the new patent is controlled by an undertaking which possesses a monopoly of the old product,
and can prevent this or any alternative patent being
exploited. The monopoly will take into account
precisely the same factors as we considered in the case
of the single firm, but it will attach substantially
different valuations to them. In the first place, on the
side of receipts, it will measure the gain only after
deductions have been made for the diminished receipts
from the old product of all the producing plants, and
not the single one only. Secondly, on the side of costs,
it will take account of the induced diseconomies in all
plants due to the reduced scale of output of the old
commodity. This induced diseconomy may, of course,

be non-existent if the monopoly can merely shut down the least efficient of its plants, or reconstruct it to produce the new product.

Thus it would certainly be true to say that a monopoly will often have inducements to resist an innovation where one of a group of competing firms would introduce it. But before condemning the monopoly for being conservative in these respects we must pause to consider what is here most in the public interest. Every individual naturally desires to be allowed to have the precise variety of every product which most perfectly satisfies his own needs and taste. But any reasonable efficiency of production requires a certain degree of standardization. Individuals must be asked to accept something that only approximates to their ideal. Obviously some deviation from complete standardization is necessary, but how far should it go ? Clearly it is desirable to add a new product only if the additional satisfaction yielded by it exceeds the addition to cost. But it is by no means easy to define or measure these two concepts. As regards the addition to satisfaction yielded, much will depend upon whether we regard the momentary impulse of the buyer as paramount, as reflecting his true long-period satisfaction. It is a criticism often levelled against competition that it forces competing firms to change purely for the sake of change, and that by advertisement they cajole consumers against their true interest to buy these new products. If we regard the consumer as always perfectly rational in his own interest, his action must show that he derives greater satisfaction to the measure at least of his greater expenditure. It is only if we are prepared to say that he is sometimes irrational, and to put aside price offered as an index of satisfaction that we can argue (apart from changes of costs) that competition is wasteful in this direction. Some of us, perhaps, would be prepared rather hesitantly to make this plunge, and to say that when a monopoly increases its efficiency by enforcing some measure of standardization on consumers, it may not always diminish satisfaction by so much as the criterion of relative demand prices for competitively advertised goods would suggest.

There remains a second point that also requires consideration. It was desirable, we argued, that a new commodity should be introduced only if the additional satisfaction exceeded the additional cost. In a world of competitive prices it is virtually impossible, where costs fall with increased output, to arrange things so that a marginal consumer pays only the additional cost involved in producing his additional unit of output. He pays as a rule something that approximates to its average cost. Thus the financial inducement to a marginal consumer to accept the standard product is frequently less than it ideally should be. The monopolist's calculations in introducing a new product will often approach substantially nearer to the calculations that from the national point of view are desirable, than will the calculations of one individual firm in a situation in which competition is less than perfect.

Thus far the monopolist has been shown to be more conservative than a group of competing firms in introducing new products. If, however, it finds that it pays to introduce a new product at all, a monopoly will very probably do so more rapidly than would competing firms. For the patent will be common to all the plants of the monopoly. The extension of output will be less limited by considerations of manufacturing capacity, and its progress will be less resisted by competitive advertisement to prevent inroads into the markets for the older product.

It has been assumed throughout the foregoing discussion that the invention, whatever form it might take, was already in existence. But the probability of the invention being made is also relevant. Inventions have sometimes been divided into two groups, spontaneous and induced inventions. The former, like Marconi's invention of wireless, come, so to speak, from the blue. The latter are the consequences of dozens of minds tackling some problem that has arisen in industry as the result of changes of scale or of general technical progress. Monopoly will have no predictable effect upon the former type of invention. Upon the latter its effects are twofold and opposite. The large-scale operation of monopolies will raise, and in all probability yield solutions to, various problems of production and organization. Moreover, large-scale research by first-rate experts will be more likely to yield certain types of results than small-scale research unsupported by sufficient resources. On the other hand there is little doubt that active small-scale experimentation proceeds far more vigorously where the manager or owner of a small firm is free to try new ideas and new processes without the restraining hand of a board of directors, and inspired by the motive that the bulk of the profits will go to his own pocket. This is probably one important reason for the relative predominance of small undertakings in industries which are in the stage of rapid technical development, such as was the radio industry a few years ago, or the motor trade a couple of decades back.

§ 5. *Problems of Management.* In relation to the management of monopolies two main issues require consideration : first, the question whether monopolies necessarily throw upon those whose duty it is to manage them, responsibilities that are too vast for effective control ; second, the question whether the existence of monopoly in itself simplifies or complicates the task.

The problems of management are, of course, manifold. But they may be divided for our immediate purpose into three broad categories, the problems of technical control, the problems of financial control, and the problems that, for want of a better name, we may call the problems of entrepreneuring—that is the group of decisions that are concerned with changes in the scale of operations, and more particularly with possible extensions of the scale.

The creation of a monopoly need cause no change in the scale of technical control. As we saw in an earlier section of this chapter, monopoly of the merger form may facilitate the concentration of output into larger units and thus create new problems of technical management. The limit to such concentration will be set, partly indeed by considerations of the geographical distribution of markets, but partly also by considerations of the size of unit that can be most effectively co-ordinated into a smoothly running whole. This size will depend in its turn upon the regularity of running and the extent to which a central organization

can remove for certain plants in the unified undertaking
the problems created by irregularity.

The unit that can be technically controlled and co-
ordinated is not, it is generally agreed, infinite ; nor is
the number of separate units that can be effectively
co-ordinated by a central organization infinite. For
effective co-ordination presupposes intimate knowledge
and understanding of the units, and beyond a point that
becomes impossible. But the nearer technical control,
through decentralization, approaches to a state of no
control, the larger the number that can be co-ordinated.
Thus by forfeiting certain technical or managerial
economies of larger scale, the managerial diseconomies
may sometimes be avoided. But though decentralization of technical control is possible, decentralization of
financial control and of entrepreneuring is not, or is
not completely, possible. For these involve decisions
which must be uniform for the monopoly undertaking
as a whole. The decisions regarding price and output
policy and regarding the extension or contraction of
activity or its concentration in certain units must be
made for the whole combination. And where a
monopoly is of a unified form (a holding company or
a merger), the policy with regard to the division of
earnings between the alternative uses of satisfying
shareholders and strengthening of the undertaking's
resources, must also be determined centrally, though
not necessarily uniformly for all the subsidiaries.
Such decisions, made for an undertaking whose
resources run into millions and employees into tens of
thousands, involving, as they must, an intimate
knowledge of the conditions of many plants and many
markets, may well tax the abilities of even the ablest.

But far more difficult and responsible in the case of those monopolies whose tenure is insecure, is the task of guiding the strategy of manœuvre by which the monopoly is itself maintained, and handling its relations with the Government, with its employees, and with foreign rivals in a struggle for the division of neutral markets. The qualities required to achieve these purposes, be they desirable or undesirable, are given to few.

It would be foolish to suggest that individuals, or groups of individuals, cannot be found capable of making these great and far-reaching decisions. The history of American Trusts in particular, of English and German monopolies to a somewhat less extent, has shown the ability of individuals not only to create but also to control giant organizations. But such men are not easy to find, and are particularly difficult to replace from the subordinate ranks of an already monopolized industry. The great names that we associate with the trusts were their creators as well as their administrators. They entered these industries and gained their experience when the industry was still unmonopolized, and could attract by its wide opportunities men of vitality and initiative. But once the monopoly is formed and its administration has become more a matter of routine, it will rarely succeed in drawing to itself such men. They will prefer freer fields where the rewards of enterprise are still unlimited.

It may, of course, be true that when an industry has passed through that first period of fundamental reorganization and readjustment that has marked the transition to monopoly, the qualities required in its leaders are those of the Civil Servant rather than of the adventurer.

If that is indeed the case, the monopoly may for a time survive with undiminished vigour and efficiency. But in the history even of routine institutions there comes usually a time when a new invention challenges them, as the railways have been challenged by road transport, and a new fount of leadership is needed to revivify the old organization.

As regards these wider problems, the tasks of management of a great nation-wide monopoly are far more complex than those which ordinarily confront a single firm. But as regards the more ordinary functions of control, the existence of monopoly may simplify rather than complicate them. For the task of management is essentially concerned with problems of uncertainty and change. In a world in which change was rare and foreseeable the problems of management would be far simpler than they are in a world in which change is frequent and unforeseen, and anything which reduces the frequency of change or the uncertainty of it, will simplify the problems of management.

If we consider an industry composed of a large number of firms the uncertainty which confronts each one of them is proportionately greater than that which confronts the industry as a whole. It may be possible to estimate within comparatively narrow limits what will be the total consumption of wireless sets next year. But it is extremely difficult to estimate what part of that total each individual manufacturer will provide. The monopolist is concerned only with the former problem, the competing manufacturer with the latter. The larger is this uncertainty, the more difficult do all the problems of management become. The purchase of expensive machinery or new buildings with a long life may be a most risky proceeding if the favouring breeze of public taste may fade away and leave the firm next year hopelessly becalmed. It may on the one hand pay the firm not to expand excessively under the temporary stimulus ; on the other hand by rapid expansion and cheap selling it may make its goods known and build the foundation of future prosperity. The uncertainty of its future share in the whole trade of the industry complicates its decisions at every turn. This uncertainty is enhanced by a further uncertainty regarding the trend of invention and change. We have seen that a monopolist is sometimes in a position to control and dictate the rate of change. He can seldom be certain that no outside invention can affect the demand for his product and render obsolete his equipment, but he can at least be more confident than a single producer. Thus the management of a single plant under a monopoly should involve less difficult decisions than that of a firm under competition. The task may be further facilitated by such interchange of knowledge and experience as we have already considered.

The tasks of management may in such ways be simplified by a monopoly that is complete and permanent, so that a central office distributes orders to plants, each of which attempts to secure the greatest economies of comparatively regular working. But many monopolies are, as we have seen, not of this type. They are temporary cohesions of firms which preserve an individual identity, and look forward to periods of competition as well as of collaboration. Where this type of monopoly is found, the problems of management are likely to be at least as difficult as those which would exist under competition. For the economic struggles of competition are largely replaced by the internal political struggles of the monopoly. The low-cost producer seeks to secure for himself the share of total output that he claims by virtue of the fact that he could earn profits apart from restriction and would prefer in certain circumstances to see a period of competition. The high-cost producer requires high prices to cover his higher costs, but is unwilling to concede the full demands of the low-cost producer. Where voting is on a tonnage basis and the majority of producers have high costs, the political manœuvres of the low-cost producers, the decision when to threaten to withdraw, when to concede a point, when to prefer immediate profits to growth, when to regard expansion as the condition of full influence in the councils of the monopoly, require a wisdom and statesmanship which are hardly paralleled in more competitive conditions.

In some respects, then, the problems of managing a monopoly may be simpler, in others more difficult than those that arise under competitive conditions. But even if they are simpler, that does not prove that they will on the average be better performed. For the comparatively greater ease with which profits may be earned may lull a management into the torpor of routine, or provide an insufficient spur to the achievement of the highest efficiency. There is little doubt that a loss, or the prospect of a loss, will call out reserves of organizing ability which have lain dormant during a period of greater prosperity. Not a few monopolies would appear to reap their monopoly gains not in the form of exceptional profits, but in a laxity of organization and a conservatism of technique. The very

K

ruthlessness of competition may secure a higher average achievement even of a much more difficult task.

§ 6. *The Financial Economies of Monopoly.* We have next to consider the question whether the monopoly possesses any advantages from the point of view of finance and capital raising which are not shared by any equally large firm apart from monopoly. It is not merely a question of raising funds, but also of spending money out of profits on improvements and maintenance. It is sometimes argued that a temporary or even permanent monopoly may be justified by the fact that it enables firms, which under competitive conditions would be unable to raise funds, to secure an amount of profits sufficient to re-equip themselves and ultimately to reduce their costs and prices. This argument requires examination.

If the net effect of the extra capital is to be a reduction of costs, and if at the same time there is to be an inducement to the firm to invest the capital in new equipment or other internal developments rather than in increasing its holding of external assets, it must clearly be true that the reduction of costs due to the extra capital exceeds the ordinary rate of interest on such capital. But if this is the case, we should expect it to be possible for the firm concerned to borrow money in the ordinary way, thus making unnecessary resort to so complicated a method of capital raising. It will be impossible for it to obtain capital by more ordinary means, but possible to obtain it by this means, only if for some reason the investing public requires a higher rate of return to persuade it to invest than do the directors of the firm to reinvest profits. This may,

of course, happen, and it will occur usually for one or
other of two reasons. Firstly, the public may be
unreasonably unwilling to invest in an industry that
is at the moment making losses. It is profitable and
desirable that an investment shall be made if the
extra yield due to the *extra* capital exceeds the *extra*
interest on that *extra* capital. But the general investing
public is more often persuaded to invest by the *average*
return being paid on existing capital in the industry.
If a higher present return is being paid the shares of
firms are likely to be bid up until new investments in
the industry find willing purchasers. In practice it is
almost universally true that investment is likely to be
carried too far in industries at present making profits,
not far enough in industries which are making losses.
Thus a temporary profit may help an industry to
secure funds which are desirable but otherwise
unobtainable.

The second reason for which a monopoly may
facilitate further investment, is that funds are
frequently reinvested in the firm which made them for
a lower probable return than would secure funds from
outside. This may be due to the greater knowledge
of the risks and prospects involved which the directors
themselves possess. It may be due to a greater willingness to throw good money after bad in the hope of
retrieving the fortunes of a firm and earning a return
not only on the present capital but also on that already
invested. It may be due to the general principle that
any investor, considering a particular scheme, must
assess two elements of risk : first, that inherent in
the scheme itself ; second, that arising from the possible
incompetence or misconduct of the intending borrowers.

A firm reinvesting its own profits is likely to put a lower valuation on the latter element than will any outside investor.

These considerations may indicate that firms will sometimes secure additional capital by the formation of a monopoly in circumstances in which additional capital is desirable. But they are far from showing that it is in the interest of the consumer to be exploited in order that, indirectly, he may provide the capital. If the directors of the firms concerned demand any prospective return on the additional capital with which they have been presented before they invest it in new equipment rather than gilt-edged investments, it will always be more economical for the unfortunate consumers to subscribe directly to new capital issues than to provide others with funds which they can invest, and from which they can draw the proceeds. In any case the perfecting of the machinery of investment will offer a better solution to the problem, and failing all else the same result, so far as the consumer is concerned, will be achieved if the firm goes into liquidation and its equipment is bought up by new owners who are prepared to modernize it.

Another, and somewhat similar, problem arises in connection with the question of the survival of firms in the face of an industrial depression. It is sometimes argued that the encouragement of a temporary or permanent monopoly organization is justified by the fact that, apart from such monopoly, a number of firms would be eliminated by the depression which in the ensuing period of good trade would again be required to provide a sufficient supply of the product concerned. Once again the problem is to explain why the investor is unwilling to provide a service that is in the public interest, and which might be expected to be also in his own.

Let us suppose that a firm, working during a depression at a loss, is trying to determine whether it shall close down temporarily, or permanently, or attempt to carry on at that scale of output which reduces its operating losses to a minimum. If circumstances prevent it taking into account those more sentimental and humanitarian considerations which usually count for so much, it will compare its operating losses in a given period with its maintenance costs closed down. If the operating loss is less than the maintenance costs, it will try to carry on. Before deciding to close down temporarily it must take account also of the capital costs involved in reopening, including both the technical costs involved, for example, in shutting down and necessarily re-lining a blast furnace, and the operational costs involved in re-creating the harmonious team-work of the firm and re-entering a lost market. In comparing these two possibilities with the third possibility, that of closing down permanently, the question to be decided is whether the existing equipment, suitably maintained, will have a value when demand recovers which exceeds the accumulated maintenance costs (including interest) during the interval. If it has such a value that its maintenance is profitable, we should expect it to be maintained by the action of existing owners or possible speculative purchasers. If its maintenance is not profitable, there is no purpose in exploiting consumers in order to maintain it. The problem thus once again resolves itself into the issue whether funds will be available to maintain a concern during a depression in all circumstances when it would be profitable to do so.

It is obvious, of course, that existing owners may reach the end of their own resources and thus be compelled to abandon or to sell plants or properties which they believe could profitably be maintained. This will happen only if these owners are unable to borrow. But banks or other credit institutions may for various reasons be unwilling to lend to them in circumstances which would appear to justify the loans. They may be ill-informed of the prospects of the industry and under-estimate future demand. They may recognize that it is desirable that some firms should receive assistance, but unless the lenders are all perfectly co-ordinated the risks of any one lender lending to any one firm may be too great to justify the loan.

But the problem is likely to solve itself in one or other of two ways. Firstly, existing producers may be forced into capital reorganization or into bankruptcy and new owners may acquire the property freed from all present financial charges and be able to carry on. Secondly, as properties are progressively abandoned, the prospects of the remainder, both immediately and ultimately, improve and their chance of securing loans increases. From the point of view of the consumer it is desirable to keep in existence not the present company, the financial organization, but rather the present machinery and equipment. It is possible to conceive of conditions where the break-up of existing organizations may result in a very great decline of capacity in the industry, and where new capital would be difficult to attract, but these circumstances must be rare, and would in any case offer a substantial return to those who could hold on.   As in the previous case the situation could be better met by the improvement of loan facilities than by the immediate exploitation of the consumer for his own hypothetical good.

There is a further consideration of the side of finance that requires examination.   The fact that a monopoly can, if it desires, reduce the fluctuations of net receipts as between good and bad times, and remove so far as it is profitable the relative changes of output of different plants, will mean not only that it will tend to use less capital than competing firms, but also that that capital will be exposed to a smaller risk of total or partial loss, and to smaller variations of income.   In these circumstances the rate of reward which a lender will require is likely to be correspondingly diminished.   In a competitive industry the risk involved in making a loan is double.   There is the risk that this particular industry will prove to be unjustified by public demand, or that investment in it has in general been carried too far.   There is the further risk that from a number of firms enjoying various degrees of success and failure, the firm to which the loan is made may prove one of the least successful.   If the industry is monopolized, the second type of risk is eliminated.   This is indeed occasionally used as an argument for the grant of monopoly by a government where large amounts of capital have to be invested in a somewhat uncertain piece of development.

In the ordinary way these considerations can affect only the rate of interest paid upon debentures or bank charges or other similar borrowings of a monopoly. For the return on the ordinary shares will include in addition to the normal reward of supplying capital not only this possibly diminished reward of risk bearing, but also some share of the monopoly revenue. But it is not entirely impossible that this reduction of risk should result in a reduction of the price of goods produced under semi-monopolistic conditions. For if in some industry entry in times of good trade could not be prevented, but in times of depression the extreme variations of prices and earnings were mitigated by a cartel, the average level of earnings could not in any case greatly exceed normal, and a lower level of prospective rewards might attract sufficient capital in the less risky conditions.

§ 7. *Economies of Buying.* When it comes to purchase materials or equipment, a monopoly enjoys ordinarily the economy which accrues in this respect to any exceptionally large undertaking. It is able, that is, to give orders so large that the undertakings providing the materials can obtain economies in their production, and to secure that a large part of the benefit is passed on to itself. But apart from these gains which would be shared equally by any other undertaking of corresponding size, there are certain advantages on the side of buying which belong exclusively to a monopolist. For the monopolist is very likely to be the sole purchaser of some of the materials that he employs, and possibly also of some grades of labour, to which the same considerations will apply.

A sole purchaser (we may call him a monopsonist in distinction from a monopolist—a sole seller) will order his purchases similarly to, but sometimes with different results from, any other purchaser. Ordinarily when we buy things at a fixed price we take no account of the effect of the size of our order upon the price. But in those rare cases, such as the purchase of our own note-paper, when we find ourselves temporarily monopsonists, we do in fact ask whether the extra units are worth the extra outlay. The monopolist, in so far as he is also a monopsonist, will employ this principle to his own advantage. For if something that he must buy rises in price the more he demands, by modifying his demands he will be able to reduce the price. By buying less of those factors of production which rise much, and more of those which rise little, in response to his own demands, he will be likely to reduce his total expenditure on them.

But even apart from this important consideration, the fact that a monopolist is also the sole buyer will greatly increase his bargaining power. If we have something to sell, the fact that we can if need be take it elsewhere, strengthens our hand in bargaining. If we know that a failure to sell to the one buyer means a failure to sell at all, we are far less likely to be able to extort from him a fair price for what we sell. The advantage in respect of buying to the monopsonist is not merely great. It is in many cases almost certainly too great. For a monopolist can do damage to the public welfare not only by diverting to himself some part of the income of consumers, but also by diverting to himself part of the income of poor and unorganized producers of primary products or materials. What Marshall wrote almost half a century ago has still much truth to-day :

" The cruellest of all combinations in England are, probably, in the trades that buy up small things, such as fish, and dairy and garden produce in detail, and sell them

in retail ; both producers and consumers being, from a
business point of view, weak relatively to the intermediate
dealers."

If we remember that the earliest complaints against
monopolies in the United States were largely those of
producers against groups that were attempting (as
did the Standard Oil Company) to control their access
to markets and to force them to sell their products
to a monopoly, and if we remember the long-continued
complaints in this country against rings, more particularly in agricultural markets, it is strange to find that
this aspect of monopoly has been until lately almost
neglected by theorists, and remains almost unin-
vestigated by official or unofficial inquiry.   The urgency
of its further examination is increased by the growing
disparity in some trades of the scale of production
and of retail marketing, which has given rise to complaints that these large organizations drive unduly
hard bargains with small producers.   Where a large
store provides a small producer with exceptional opportunities for long runs of work upon standardized
products, it will induce savings of cost which must
properly be divided on some fair basis between the
two.   But where a small producer has come to be
entirely dependent upon a large buyer, it is by no means
clear that a fair price will always be obtained.

§ 8.   *Monopoly and Marketing Costs.*   Let us consider
next the effects of monopoly upon marketing costs.
The combination of a group of firms will almost always
bring some economies of marketing.   For the optimum
scale of marketing is very large in most trades, and
particularly in those trades in which competitive

selling on a basis of quality is necessary.   The greater
the volume of goods to be sold, the more efficiently can
the territory be covered, and yet the more cheaply
in terms of cost per unit of sales.   Moreover as the scale
of distribution increases, it becomes more likely that
the producer will find it profitable to market his goods
directly.   This will not necessarily bring any substantial economy of man-power, though that is often
possible.   But it will certainly save an intermediate
stage of persuasion, in which wholesalers must first
be induced by travellers and advertisement to buy,
and then in their turn induce retailers to buy.   The
change is indeed sometimes marked by a transition of
the independent wholesaler first into a semi-independent
agent and finally into a representative of the producer.
It is likely to result not only in cheaper selling, but also
in more efficient selling, since the goods will now be
pressed upon the retailer by salesmen who have no
alternative lines to offer, and everything to gain by
selling this product.   Moreover, the closer touch
between manufacturer and retailer leads often to the
development of a co-operative sales policy, in which the
retailer with window-space assists the manufacturer,
and the manufacturer by window-dressing experts and
local advertisement helps the retailer.

Thus far, as in other cases, we have been concerned
only with advantages which would have been secured
apart from monopoly by a firm of equal size.   If we
turn now to the special effects of monopoly on marketing costs we find two opposing forces at work.   In the
first place the fact of monopoly is likely to reduce
the necessary expenditure on competitive selling.
Advertising and selling costs are much like military

armaments, your expenditure must depend on the expenditure of your opponents, and its efficacy is not absolute but relative. Some expenditure on advertising is necessary to inform the consuming public of prices and qualities available and of changes in goods, and to keep information regarding sources of supply readily available. But there is no reason to think that, in conditions of imperfect competition, advertising or selling will be limited to the amount that is strictly desirable. The substitution of monopoly for such competition may eliminate the difficulty of selling one product against another variety of the same product and so reduce very greatly these costs.

But though this may be true in many cases it will not necessarily be true in all. Many monopolies, as we have seen, rest upon the difficulty of the entry of new firms into the industry. The maintenance of the monopoly itself may be conditional on the maintenance of such a level of advertising or selling costs that competition on a small scale cannot profitably be attempted, or if attempted will make no headway and rapidly be exterminated. Where this is the case the expenditure on marketing of the monopoly may actually be greater not only during the period of creation of the monopoly, but also during its subsequent career, than the previous expenditure of competing firms. For the monopolist will measure the profitability of his selling expenses by the additional monopoly profits that they enable him to reap.

§ 9. *Some Conclusions.* In the course of this chapter we have studied the comparative incentives or opportunities to reduce cost which confront respectively a monopolist and the manager of a firm in an industry working under competition. Broadly speaking our conclusion has been that so far as concerns these incentives, a long-term monopoly of the completely co-ordinated type, in which the individual constituent plants preserve no separate identity or separate conflicting interests, may be expected to reproduce for any given output almost exactly the conditions of perfect competition. As compared with such a state, the completely co-ordinated monopoly may possibly enjoy certain economies in the purchase of materials and in the elimination of risks and uncertainties, and thus find itself able to employ expensive plant where the probable return to a competing firm would not justify it. As compared with the more normal state of imperfect competition, the completely co-ordinated monopoly is likely to enjoy advantage not only in these respects, but also by approaching more nearly to the optimum scale and utilization of plant than do the competing concerns and by achieving economies of marketing expenses. Against these economies must be balanced any losses due to growth beyond the scale at which management can exercise the most efficient control, or due to the rigidities and inflexibilities which creep into large organizations and prevent continuous and successful adaptation to changing circumstances.

Where the monopoly is of the restrictive types, maintaining separate identities of individual constituent undertakings, and not allocating output within the monopoly on the basis of lowest cost, but rather with some intention to equalize outputs to a greater degree than competition would do, the efficiency of the monopoly will almost certainly be less than that of competition, whatever the form of the latter. Apart from the special economies of monopoly, it would in all cases be less efficient. The real problem then is what sort of competition and what sort of monopoly we are considering. If a perfectly co-ordinated monopoly is to succeed a markedly imperfect condition of competition, the monopoly is likely to be the more efficient. If a restrictive monopoly is to succeed an almost perfect condition of competition, the monopoly is likely to be less efficient. Unless we can know in some detail both the form of monopoly and the degree of competition we can say nothing definite *a priori* regarding their relative efficiencies.

CHAPTER VII

MONOPOLIES AND INDUSTRIAL STABILITY

§ 1. *Introductory.* The deliberate creation of monopolies, or their encouragement rather than suppression, is frequently advocated on the ground that in some way, often unspecified, they assist in promoting the stability of industry. The extent to which, firstly, they have the power to do this should they wish, and to which, secondly, it is likely to be in their interest to do so, requires therefore to be considered. But it is necessary at the outset to make clearer the precise scope of the inquiry. We may inquire, firstly, whether a monopoly in one industry can or will stabilize that particular industry, at a cost, it may be, of de-stabilizing others. We may inquire, secondly, whether a monopoly in one industry can or will stabilize all industries. We may inquire, thirdly, whether a system of monopolies can or will stabilize all industries. Each of these three questions must in turn be divided into two separate problems. We may ask, first, whether a monopoly operating throughout the whole period under consideration will, in some sense to be defined, stabilize industry as compared with competition similarly operating throughout the whole period. We may ask, alternatively, whether a monopoly substituted for competition in the middle of the period will stabilize industry as compared with a continuance of competition. These are distinct questions, and the answers may well be divergent. Finally, we must make it plain what meaning we attach to stabilization. Sometimes the word is used as meaning stabilization of price, sometimes of physical output, sometimes as meaning stabilization of gross earnings, and sometimes again of net earnings. For the moment we shall be concerned chiefly with the stabilization of physical output and of employment.

§ 2. *Effects of Monopoly in one Industry on the Stability of that Industry.* Let us begin then with our first problem : what are the powers of a monopoly to stabilize one industry. We will suppose the latter to be sufficiently small in relation to all industry to allow us properly to neglect the repercussions of its level of activity upon its own level of demand. A moment's consideration will show us that if in this industry demand fluctuates, so that at one moment the whole demand curve is raised, at another moment lowered, a monopoly which attempts to keep *price* fixed will have a larger output in good times and a smaller output in bad times than would be produced by competing firms with a rising supply curve. This is obviously true in all cases in which the amount that the demand curves fluctuate is quite independent of the price that may be charged at any time. But if the range of fluctuation is itself diminished by fixing price it may or may not be true. We shall have to consider this point in detail a little later. Conversely we can see also that if a monopoly fixes *output*, and the fluctuation of demand is independent of the price charged, the price will be higher in good times and may be lower in bad times than it would be under competition. Thus, granted the same fluctuation of the demand curves, any attempt to stabilize price will produce greater fluctuations of output, and any attempt to stabilize output greater fluctuations of price than would otherwise occur. This does not, of course, mean that a monopolist cannot stabilize an industry, in some sense, should he desire to do so, but rather that either of the two policies discussed de-stabilizes in one respect as much as it stabilizes in another.

A monopoly that aims at stabilizing either the gross receipts or the net receipts of an industry is likely to do so partially, if not completely. If, indeed, the monopoly exercises its monopoly powers to a greater extent in depression than in boom it will very probably have some effect in stabilizing gross or net receipts even if that is not its conscious intention. But it will ordinarily do so only at the cost of diminishing the stability of output.

Let us begin, then, by asking what are the inducements under a competitive system to equalize production through time. The predominant effect upon costs will be an economy of overhead costs. The equipment available in an industry which works irregularly must be sufficient to produce, even if it be only under great pressure, the maximum output required. If it were worked continuously its output would clearly be greater than it is in practice, or if a given output were produced at a more constant rate less equipment would suffice to produce it. How far, then, will variations of price induce consumers to assist in achieving this economy ? Let us begin by supposing that some

L

constant output is produced by an industry composed
of a number of competing firms—an output which
can be sold at a price which will cover marginal cost
in bad times as well as in good times—so that the
equipment of the industry will be run always at full
capacity. In these circumstances the price of the
commodity concerned will vary substantially, for the
demand for this fixed output will be greater in the busy
than in the less busy periods. The profits and the
contribution to long-period overhead costs will thus
be much greater at one moment than at another. It
may even happen that almost the whole of the necessary
long-period overhead costs are met out of the profits of
the good times, and almost none from those of the bad
times, and that during the bad times the firms make
losses almost equal to their current expenditure on
overhead costs.

What are the conditions, then, in which one or more
of these firms will think it worth while to expand its
productive capacity so as to increase output in a busy
period even at the cost of having idle plant during a
large part of the less busy periods ? Obviously the
prospective addition to income from the extra plant
during the period that it is likely to be running must
be sufficient to give an adequate return to the capital
over the whole period of good times and bad. Thus
the prospective price of extra output in the good times
must be at least sufficient to pay the whole of the extra
costs involved in its production. It might perhaps be
supposed that this conclusion would be invalidated if
an industry were composed of such a number of firms
that each imagined that it could sell any output that
it could produce at the market price, whether in periods

of general activity or inactivity, and that, whatever might happen to others, it at least would run continuously at full capacity. But if an increase of output by some firms to meet peak demands resulted in the more intermittent running of others, their receipts for the whole period of boom and depression would be diminished, and the average return on their capital reduced. As equipment wore out some of it would not be replaced, and output would be contracted to the point where for the industry as a whole the boom output of the busy times paid at least the full extra cost of its production.

There is a further consequence of the added productive capacity which is relevant. If equipment is increased to meet demand in times of prosperity much of it will be available also during the periods of depression. Thus added equipment will mean that the output that will be produced in the subsequent depression in response to any given price will be greater,[1] and the price determined by any given schedule of demand lower. Thus if average receipts over a period are to be as great as before, the returns during the periods of prosperity must be greater to compensate for the lower receipts during the periods of depression.

The argument thus far would show that, under competitive conditions, if demand is greater at one moment of time than at another, price will tend to rise at the moment of higher demand sufficiently to cause the total costs of the extra output then required to be borne by those who are buying goods at this time. If any purchaser who is free to buy at the

[1] Diagrammatically this means that the short-period supply curve for the industry as a whole will be lowered.

moment of lower demand delays or anticipates his purchase and transfers it to a moment of higher demand, he must pay a higher price; this higher price is sufficient to cover the immediate addition to the costs of the manufacturer caused by the transfer of demand. Conversely, any purchaser who buys at a time of lower demand, can buy at a lower price; the lower price represents the reduced cost to the manufacturer of meeting this demand at a moment when his equipment is not fully utilized. But there are important costs to society other than those borne by manufacturers which must also be taken into account. In the first place there are a number of commodities and services for which for practical purposes it is impossible to alter price to correspond at every moment with marginal cost. Thus even if it were true that all road transport over a period of years paid the full cost of providing the necessary roads, it would still be likely that the extra cost of providing widened roads for additional traffic in periods of congestion would in some cases be greater than the extra receipts from the extra traffic concerned. The same is not improbably true in similar circumstances of railway traffic, of telephone facilities, and of other public utilities. Thus the inducement to equalize traffic between busy and less busy periods may not in practice be sufficient.

But far more important than this is the cost which society bears through unemployment. A certain volume of output produced irregularly will need not only more equipment, but as a rule also more workers than the same volume produced at a uniform rate. Any transfer of demand from bad times to good will increase both the hardships of unemployed labour and the cost to the State of maintaining it. Only a very small part of these costs will be borne by the employer, and only rarely will they show themselves in an increased margin between price in good and bad times.

There is another point that requires consideration, if demand can be regarded as transferable between a period of boom and a period of depression. Added demand at a time of low employment will give rise to further income and expenditure at a moment when it is urgently required, at the expense of reducing secondary employment during a period of activity, when it may be not only less desirable, but even positively undesirable. The gain, therefore, to society as a whole from a transfer of demand from a busy to an inactive period may thus be considerable ; even if the reduction of price during the time of lower demand fully covers the reduction of manufacturers' cost, there is no reason to think that it normally equals the gain to society.

But whether or not the inducement to transfer a unit of demand from times of greater to less activity theoretically equals the whole advantage to society from such a transfer, it remains that in practice the inducement is insufficiently operative. The reasons are several : first, the curtailment of incomes makes inevitable in many cases a curtailment of expenditure ; second, there is in many cases some addition of risk involved in transferring demand, since it involves making at a great distance an anticipation of future trends of demand ; third, there seems to be little doubt that, granted perfect foresight of future prices, the fluctuations of demand would be less than in fact they are, and, as a complement of that, the course of prices could not be what it is, if perfect foresight existed. An inducement to transfer demand, which might be sufficient in a state of perfect knowledge, becomes insufficient through imperfect knowledge of the future course of prices. This raises the question whether a monopoly which offers less financial inducement to transfer units of demand from one time to another, can yet make that inducement more operative by increasing foreknowledge of prices.

§ 3. *The Monopolist's Incentives to Stabilize Output.* We have seen that it is almost certainly in the general interest that output should be stabilized to a greater degree than is achieved under competition. It is important therefore to see how far it is likely that a monopolist will in practice be led to stabilize it. Let us begin by emphasizing one obvious fact. A monopolist secures his monopoly profit by limiting output. If in all circumstances, equally in times of prosperity and depression, he limited his output to a given proportion of the competitive output, the absolute change of output might be less, but the proportionate change would clearly be the same as under competitive conditions. Thus it is only in so far as the monopolist exercises his monopoly powers to a different extent at different times, or in so far as the monopolist's reaction to a given schedule of demand or a given situation on the side of costs is different from that of a group of competing producers, that the proportionate range of fluctuation of output will be different. If monopoly powers are exercised to a greater extent in the depression than in the boom, so that the output in the depression is a smaller proportion of competitive output than the output in the boom, the existence of monopoly will increase the proportionate change of output ; if *vice versa*, the existence of monopoly will diminish that change.

Let us first consider the monopolist's attitude to a given schedule of demand. There is one relevant factor which will encourage him to make output somewhat more stable. Let us imagine that a single competing firm is considering what will happen if it declines a given order at the present moment. The potential buyer has the possibilities of buying immediately the same commodity from someone else, of buying some other commodity now or later, of buying the same commodity later from someone else, or, finally, of buying this commodity later from the firm concerned. Thus to the one firm it is very unlikely that an order declined now will become an order at a later date. But if the firm has a monopoly an order declined now has quite a substantial prospect of becoming an order to the same firm later. As more often happens, a monopolist can afford to offer far less prompt delivery than could a competing firm. Thus a monopolist's response to a given short-period demand schedule may be appreciably different from that of a group of competitive firms, and to treat the two as identical and unalterable is misleading. But though a monopolist sometimes possesses the power to convert demand in the present into demand in the future, it must be remembered that by so doing he will often reduce the price that he receives. He will only transfer demand from the present to the future if the prospective and discounted saving of cost exceeds the prospective and discounted loss of receipts. He will act, that is, on the same principles with regard to markets differing in time, as a discriminating monopolist ordinarily does with regard to markets differing in space.

The monopolist's attitude to costs will also differ in certain respects from those of a single competing firm. We have already seen that one competing firm will take no account of additional costs in which it will involve society by making employment irregular. It is equally true that there are costs of this nature which a monopoly will be able to throw on to others unless it takes conscious steps to avoid it on humanitarian grounds. Some monopolies do in fact use a substantial part of their monopoly advantage to provide better or more stable working conditions for their employees, but there is no security that they will do so. There is, however, one factor on the side of wages which may induce monopolists to make employment more regular than will competing firms. For the individual firm wages are as a rule determined by influences outside its own control, but for the monopolist the level of wages of the particular type of skill that he employs is to some extent the consequence of the level of employment that he creates. During a period of activity a single firm must pay the current rate of wages to attract such labour as it needs, and a reduction of its current activity will make no substantial difference to any increase of wages that boom demands for labour may cause. But the monopolist by limiting somewhat his output in time of activity may prevent a rise of wages, and be able to give better employment and possibly pay higher wages during a subsequent period of depression.

This difference of attitude to an increase of costs will not, of course, be confined to questions of labour cost. If a sudden increase of demand for capital equipment or for raw materials will result in an increase of its price, the monopolist will take this into account, and by limiting his demand avoid an increased payment for all the equipment or material that he may require. His greater knowledge of the current totals of demand and of capacity will also help him to avoid excessive orders at boom prices.

These various considerations may lead a monopolist to be less anxious to expand output in time of activity and help him somewhat to equalize output. But it would be a mistake to exaggerate their probable effect. For we must ask ourselves over what range of time the equalizing effect is likely to work. If we are considering comparatively short periods of fluctuation, such as are due to seasonal causes, the various factors that we have considered might well diminish the amplitude of the fluctuation. But when we come to consider cyclical disturbances, it would appear far less probable that any motives acting upon monopolists can secure a transfer of demand from, let us say, 1929 or 1930 to 1933. The level of uncertainty is usually so great, and the future course of prices, of interest rates and of demand so impenetrable, that no comparatively slight variation of price in a single industry can attract demand on any substantial scale to the empty shipyards or factories at the bottom of a depression.

There is another respect in which the monopolist's calculations may differ from those of competing firms. A single firm in an industry into which entry is free, in deciding whether or no it will pay it to cut a price, has often two alternatives open to it : to make somewhat larger profits in the present at the expense of allowing its competitors gradually to invade its market and destroy the goodwill, or to accept lower prices and profits in the present and continue, perhaps indefinitely, to make a more moderate level of profit. In making its decision the firm must discount future profits into the present. The rate of discount will depend upon the financial position of the firm. If the firm is prosperous it may regard future profits as equivalent in full to present profits. If it will go bankrupt to-morrow, it will discount the future infinitely. Now in a competing industry, the threat of competition to any one firm is normally greatest in a depression. In a boom the firm may well hold that any moderation of price policy on its part will be swamped by immoderate action of its competitors, and if new firms are going to come in, nothing that it alone can do will prevent it. The monopolist, on the other hand, is less fearful of competition in a depression, more fearful in a boom. If large profits are more likely to attract competition than unfilled orders, he may prefer to keep price lower during the boom, and higher during the depression. To the extent that he does so he is likely to increase the range of fluctuation between depression and boom.

§ 4. *The Probable Effects of Stabilizing Prices.*   Let us return at this point to a possibility that was mentioned at an earlier stage. It was suggested that an inducement to transfer demand from one moment to another which might *in a certain state of foreknowledge* be insufficient might in a greater state of foreknowledge become sufficient. Since included in the powers of a monopolist is the power, should it be advantageous, to stabilize prices and advertise their intended stabilization, it is important to see what the effects of such action will be. It has been pointed out that in a given fluctuation of demand such action will de-stabilize output, and the changes of output will be greater than if price is permitted to rise and fall. What we require to know is whether stabilizing price is likely to reduce the amplitude of the fluctuations of demand to such an extent that the fluctuations of output are less and not more than under competition. The classical example of such a policy is afforded by the fixed price of $28 a ton for steel rails maintained by the United States Steel Corporation for over fifteen years between 1901 and 1916.

The effects of stabilizing price may be gathered conveniently into two groups, first, those which arise from anticipation and postponement effects, second, those which are concerned with the total volume of demand. The immediate effects of a cut in price made by a firm are not easy to predict. In the first place a cheapening of goods will obviously bring them within the reach of new sections of the community and stimulate demand in the ordinary long-period sense. Secondly, it may attract demand out of the future into the present, if it leads to a belief that present prices are lower than future prices are likely to be. On the other hand, if it leads to a belief that further reductions of price will take place, an initial reduction may discourage present demand to such an extent that the level of sales is actually reduced. This is the more likely when certain additional factors are remembered. A cut in price is sometimes regarded by consumers as an indication that the commodity is not selling, and as throwing doubt therefore on its quality. Again, a cut in price is sometimes regarded as an indication of financial weakness of the selling firm, a first step into suspension and bankruptcy, and where service and spare parts are important it may reduce purchases. These various considerations all cause short-period repercussions. Their quantitative importance will differ substantially between industry and industry. But in a competitive industry they make the decision when to cut price, and how much to cut it, a difficult one, and not infrequently, where a manufacturer is expected to give credits for stock bought from him before the cut at higher prices, they make any reduction of price a quite substantial investment designed to secure higher profits in the future.

The monopoly may if it wishes escape from this "penumbra of uncertainty." The stronger is the monopoly reputed to be the more likely is it that a policy of stabilizing price will redistribute orders through time up to the limit of the advantage to the consumer in such redistribution.

The second effect of stabilization of price is concerned with the question of the volume of demand. There are a number of circumstances in which a known service, regularly available at a fixed price, may succeed in evoking a greater demand than a service irregularly available at a varying price, even though the average price and the average delay are less. Thus it is frequently argued, and probably with some validity, that shipping conferences, by assisting the provision of regular services at relatively fixed prices, have developed trades which with uncertain services would not have reached the same dimensions. Again, decisions have frequently to be made, for example regarding types of heating or power installation, which involve forecasting the course of prices of rival fuels over a period of years. In many cases a known moderate evil is preferred to uncertainty. Thus a policy of price stabilization may in some cases secure a greater volume of comparatively consistent demand even at a higher average price.

These various considerations may perhaps somewhat mitigate the normal tendency of a policy of price-stabilization to increase the fluctuations of output and employment. It is conceivable that in an extreme case the fluctuations might even be diminished by price-fixing. But much must obviously depend upon the nature of the market considered. A market in which the financial resources and the financial stability of the purchaser are great relatively to the expenditure (as is obviously the case with steel rails) is clearly more capable of such stabilization than one in which changes of income must enforce postponements. A market in which the demand is mainly for foreseeable replacements is, again, more likely to be stabilized than one in which the bulk of demand is for extensions of somewhat uncertain necessity. It must be remembered also that in many cases the terms on which capital may be borrowed, or, indeed, the possibility or impossibility at a particular moment of obtaining capital, may be fully as important in determining the time at which purchases are made as any anticipations of the future course of the prices of the goods con-

cerned. When all these considerations are taken into
account, the number of cases in which a monopoly
will ordinarily achieve any considerable degree of
stability by such methods cannot be expected to be
very many.

§ 5. *Summary of the Preceding Argument.* We have
been concerned thus far with one limited aspect of the
relations of monopoly to industrial stability : the
power of a monopoly in one industry to stabilize that
industry, irrespective of any possible effects upon other
industries. It is important again to emphasize that
the problem was essentially limited by the assumption
with which we started : that the industry we were
considering was of such small size in relation to
industry in general that we could afford to neglect the
repercussions of its individual level of activity upon
activity in general, and thus upon the total level of
demand. We have in effect assumed that the demand
for the products of this industry is given, not only
instantaneously, but also through the course of years,
so that we may ask whether a given aggregate of
production is satisfactorily distributed through time.
The results of such limited inquiry must not be extended to the case of industries which form so large a
part of the whole economy that their scale of activity
affects appreciably the level of activity of industry in
general, still less to the problems of the economy as a
whole. In these somewhat unreal conditions we have
seen that it is desirable that production should be
stabilized to a somewhat greater extent than uncontrolled competition will secure. A monopoly will have
certain inducements to make production less steady,

certain inducements to make it more steady than will competition. To the extent that monopolies are less afraid of creating competition, and therefore exercise their monopoly powers to a greater extent, in the depression than in the boom, they will, with given demand schedules, make output less regular. To the extent also that higher profits in the depression make the attraction of future orders into the present less urgent, they will also make output less regular. But to the extent that they are less afraid that an order declined immediately during a boom will be lost for ever they will make output more regular. They will make it more regular if the maintenance of a policy of stable prices, through effects on postponement of buying, can diminish the fluctuations of demand. They will make it more regular if an increase of their output during the boom will appreciably increase the price of labour, of raw materials, or of equipment. We can say nothing *a priori* as to which of these various factors will predominate.

The foregoing argument has been concerned almost entirely with the comparison of the respective effects of continued monopoly and continued competition. Many of the practical discussions of this problem in recent years have been concerned, however, with the substitution of a newly created monopoly for existing competition. Most of the arguments which would indicate a tendency for a continued monopoly to increase fluctuations of output apply *a fortiori* to the case in which monopoly is substituted for competition in a depression. On the other hand, in few or none of the cases where continued monopoly stabilizes output does the sudden creation of a monopoly reinforce the effects. To substitute monopoly for competition will seldom, therefore, stabilize output over the period covering the two different conditions.

§ 6. *Monopoly and General Industrial Stability.* We have been concerned thus far with the possibilities of a monopoly stabilizing, in some sense, the particular industries in which it prevails. We must turn next to the further question, whether a monopoly in one industry can assist in the stabilization of industry in general. In the case of a single industry, provided that it was assumed to be of small size relatively to the whole economy, it was legitimate to neglect the repercussions of its own level of activity upon the demand for its products. When we come to consider the economy as a whole, it is the continuity of the level of demand that most concerns us. We can no longer discuss the problem of activity in general on the basis of the transfer of demand from one moment of time to another, taking the aggregate output over the whole period as approximately constant. For the maximum output of the whole economy in time of boom is set by limitations of productive resources. The relevant problem is the depth of the subsequent depression, and the ratio of actual activity to maximum possible activity over the whole cycle.

It is frequently argued that if a monopoly is formed by the association, let us say, of the growers of rubber, the incomes of all who are concerned in this industry will be increased, their expenditure on other commodities will be proportionately increased, and the total volume of unemployment diminished. On these grounds a monopoly is held to be desirable. Now this argument, as it has been stated, neglects one most important consideration. The rubber growers, it is true, are richer, but the consumers of rubber are poorer. What income the rubber growers have gained they have gained at the expense of consumers. If both rubber growers and rubber consumers always spend the whole of their incomes, all that will have happened is to transfer purchasing power from one group of people to another. There may in certain circumstances be no evident objection to that on grounds of justice,[1] but the transfer will only affect the volume of employment if for some reason a given amount of money spent by rubber growers gives more employment than the same amount spent by rubber consumers. Now one form of expenditure can create less employment than another only for one of two reasons. Firstly, if part of the expenditure concerned does not pass on down the continuous cycle whereby income creates expenditure and expenditure income, but is saved and held back, the employment given will be greater if it is directed down the stream in which more is spent and less is saved. Secondly, one or other of the forms of consumption may involve the creation of additional incomes and expenditure, because, in order that some present demand (or prospective future demand) may be satisfied, new capital must be constructed and incomes thereby created which are additional to those that arise from the current expenditure on finished goods.

Now it is by no means clear what is most likely to cause an increased expenditure on the construction of new capital goods. If demand is transferred from

[1] See p. 170.

M

industries which already possess superfluous capacity
to those whose capacity is scarcely adequate to supply
existing needs, we should expect further investment
in the latter group of industries. But it is by no means
clear that such a transfer of demand is more likely to
be secured by a transfer of income from rubber consumers to rubber growers than by one in the opposite
direction. We might even expect investment to be
stimulated by changes of demand, in whatever direction
they might occur. Such changes will, however, only
stimulate the construction of new equipment to satisfy
the new demands if they are believed to be comparatively permanent. If a series of transfers take
place, at one moment favouring rubber growers, at
another rubber consumers, and are foreseen by the
producers of the goods consumed by both parties, they
may unanimously hold that the introduction of expensive machinery to meet these intermittent demands is
unwarranted. In these conditions a stabilization of
the income of either party might increase the regularity
of their expenditure and increase, therefore, the investment of those who produced goods for their
consumption.

The volume of employment will alternatively be
increased, we have seen, if income is transferred from
those who are likely to save much of it, to those who
are likely to save little, provided that transfer produces
no effect upon investment. Here again it is difficult
to feel certain of the probable effects of a given transfer.
In the long run it is almost certainly safe to assume that
a transfer from poorer people to richer people will
increase the volume of saving, and that one from richer
to poorer will diminish it. As regards short-period

reactions one can be less confident. A transfer from richer people to poorer people who are heavily indebted may increase saving. Moreover, there is good reason to think that saving is highest wherever there is a sudden windfall increase of income. After a time standards of life are adjusted to the new income, but during a period the rate of saving may even in exceptional cases be greater if income is taken from richer people who will be forced not only to reduce their savings, but also their expenditure, and given to others whose simpler tastes are not quickly altered. This will be the more likely if the richer group save largely through the agency of insurance premiums or on other comparatively rigid principles, so that a reduction of income must be largely met by a reduction of expenditure. But though these possibilities must not be forgotten, it is usually reasonable to assume that saving will be reduced by a transfer of incomes from richer to poorer.

If we think of a more complex industry in which there are producers, merchants and consumers, much will depend upon the extent to which a reduction in the price of the product finds its way into reduced prices to the ultimate consumer. If, for example, a monopoly diminishes during a depression the margin of profit of merchants, and the rate at which they repay overdrafts to the banks, a larger part of the final price may go to create current expenditure, and employment will be increased. On the other hand, if a monopoly simply enables producers to save more and repay their debts while diminishing the other expenditure of consumers, it may reduce employment.

There is, thus, no simple generalization that is

universally true of all monopolies. Each case must be separately analysed by the sort of method that has here been indicated. But one or two things can be said in general terms. A monopoly will add in this sense to stability of demand only in so far as it induces less saving during the depression and more saving during the boom than would otherwise exist. It will achieve its end, that is, only if it transfers income from more thrifty to less thrifty people during the depression, from less thrifty to more thrifty during a boom. If it is true to say that monopoly price is higher relatively to competitive price in a depression (and may in some few cases actually be below competitive price in the boom), then it is only if the monopolist is less thrifty than the average consumer that stability of demand will be increased. Very broadly speaking this will imply that there may be a gain in such cases as monopoly action by comparatively poor agricultural producers to maintain prices of produce. But monopoly action by wealthier groups is less likely to promote stability of demand, and more likely to increase fluctuations.

Statistical evidence would appear to show that the relative shares of manual workers and of others in the British national income as a whole have remained remarkably constant over the last half-century. The total income has, however, been increasing rapidly. Thus postponable expenditure has become a larger proportion of the whole, and the economic system has become to that extent more susceptible to fluctuations. Moreover, it would appear that with increasing concentration of industry and increasing capital per head, the share of the income that goes to capital has only been maintained by an increasing degree of monopoly and this in its turn, as the result of attempts to stabilize net income, has resulted in diminished stability of output.

§ 7. *Certain More Complex Considerations.* There are certain more complex considerations that deserve mention. If there were an increased degree of monopoly in the whole group of industries which mainly supply capital goods, and if the monopoly powers were used to a greater extent in depression than in boom, the effect would be to discourage investment (apart from possible reactions of price-stabilization discussed above) during depression, and thus to increase the incidence at that time of unemployment. Under competitive conditions the decline in demand for capital goods is likely to cause a fall in their price, and this in turn is likely to cause certain manufacturers to seek to replace equipment or build extensions while costs remain low. Their expenditure serves to increase incomes and the general level of activity. Under a regime of monopoly this expansive force is likely to be weakened, and the upward turn of trade thus postponed.

And while it may be convenient for purposes of analysis of a single small industry to discuss the distribution of the demand through time as if its aggregate over a period were given, when demand in total is under discussion, it is impossible, as we have seen, to take its aggregate over a period as given, and to assume that any factor which diminishes it at one moment will increase it *pro tanto* at another. If, because incomes fall off, people in general consume less this year, that does not mean that they will be able to afford to

consume more next year. Similarly, because investment is less this year it does not follow that it will be
greater in a subsequent year. Anything which increases
the cost of investment goods during a time of inactivity
and diminishes the amount of investment, will tend
to have a cumulative effect. For by reducing incomes
earned from manufacture of investment goods and thus
the level of consumption, it will reduce also the inducement to invest, which itself arises principally from the
growth of consumption. In practice it will be found that
it is in the industries which are occupied with the
manufacture of capital goods, and which because of
fluctuations of investment suffer exceptional changes
of demand and of net income, that monopoly is particularly common. Thus, except in so far as price-stabilization may have important effects on the course of
investment, the prevalence of monopoly in such
industries must add to the fluctuations of industrial
output.

§ 8. *General Conclusions.* In this chapter an attempt
has been made to discover, and to give the fullest
possible weight to, all arguments which can support
the claim of monopolies to stabilize either their own
industries or industry in general. When all has been
said that can be said, the evidence that they contribute
to the stability of industrial output remains very slight.
Even if it were true that in exceptional cases the existence
of a monopoly might somewhat stabilize output and
employment in the single industry in which it existed,
it would remain very improbable that the total effect,
not only upon that industry but also upon industry
as a whole, would be in the direction of greater stability.

In many respects, indeed, and in particular in so far
as monopoly powers are used to a greater extent in
depression than in boom, the existence of monopoly
is likely to increase fluctuations of output. The
creation of a monopoly in the course of a depression
is even more likely to increase the fluctuation. No
one can doubt the power of a monopoly to modify the
distribution of income favourably to itself (the problems
that arise from that will be discussed in the next
chapter), and if a monopoly exercises such powers to
a greater extent in depression than in boom it is likely,
as we have seen, to succeed in stabilizing somewhat the
fluctuations of its own income. But if it does so, we
must recognize that it is likely to achieve its ends only
at the cost of increasing the fluctuations both of its
own output and of the incomes and welfare of others.

Such a conclusion forms in itself a most serious
indictment of monopoly. For we must not forget that
it is the main justification of the existence of the
entrepreneur that he carries the main risks of industrial
production. If, through the creation of monopoly, he
seeks to transfer those risks to the shoulders of others,
he will inevitably suffer the universal fate of all redundant members and be replaced by some new organism
better fitted to fulfil this function. Thus those who
seek through monopoly to make the world safe for
capitalism are probably doing more than anyone to
ensure its ultimate destruction.

CHAPTER VIII

THE CONTROL OF MONOPOLY

§ 1. *Monopoly is largely a Problem of the Distribution of Wealth.* We have been concerned hitherto, first with the way in which monopolists will, if they are allowed complete freedom, fix their prices, and second with the efficiency of monopoly as a form of productive organization. We must now consider how far it is necessary that monopolies should be controlled, and what forms that control should take. We have seen that a monopolist differs only in degree from any other producer, for every producer is a monopolist of his own products ; that the strength of the monopoly may be negligible, vanishing completely in the extreme case of perfect competition, or may be very considerable, as in the case of a monopoly of some comparatively necessary product for which there are no readily available substitutes.

It is important, before we proceed further, to analyse a little more closely the damage done by a monopoly. In a previous chapter we examined the relation of the costs of production of a monopoly to those of competing firms. We saw there that in some, though not in all, cases a monopoly might be more efficient than a group of competing firms. If that is the case, for any given output fewer resources will be required. But since the monopoly raises the price of the product, some or all of these resources will be more highly rewarded than they would be under competitive conditions. There will be a transfer of purchasing power from consumers to the producers of the monopolized goods. Thus society as a whole may be better off in the sense that these goods have required fewer resources to bring them into existence ; it may at the same time be worse off to the extent that purchasing power has been transferred from one group to another group. The practical problems of monopoly are thus very largely concerned with the issue of the better or worse distribution of wealth.

If we break up a monopoly that is more efficient, and attempt to re-establish competition, we shall be seeking to redress one evil, that of the worse distribution of wealth, by creating another, that of the less efficient production of goods. We shall be justified only if we can show that the new evil is a lesser one than the existing evil, and that it is the only means of redressing it.

The amount of damage that will be done by the monopoly, with any given volume of output, depends first on the amount of the undesirable monopoly revenue which is secured by the monopolists, and second on the amount of that revenue which can be recovered by taxation or other devices. A country which enjoys a fiscal system which can recover for social expenditure, or to diminish taxes in other directions, a large part of the profits of monopolists will have less motive for attempting to destroy its monopolies than will a country which fails to tax them so heavily, or a country which suffers from the depredations of monopolists of alien domicile who succeed in transferring some substantial part of their monopoly revenue abroad without payment of full taxation.

But not all monopoly revenue is necessarily undesirable. It has long been held, for example, that trade unions which, by monopolizing the supply of labour of a given trade, raise its income above that which would rule in conditions of unmitigated competition, or associations of poor agricultural producers, are as likely to improve as to impair the distribution of wealth. There may therefore be cases where the creation of a monopoly is desirable rather than undesirable from this point of view. The answer in any particular case must depend largely upon the distribution of the monopoly revenue among the various participants in the monopoly.

The monopoly revenue accrues primarily to those who perform in any given industry the functions of entrepreneuring and risk-bearing. They are the residuary legatees of industry, and they enjoy the surpluses. And their share may be increased from another source. A monopolist is not infrequently the sole, or at least the chief, employer of a given grade of labour in the country as a whole or in a particular area. If the monopolist curtails his output in order to raise the price of the commodity he will cause unemployment, and may thus be able to secure the quantity of labour that he requires more cheaply. If this is the case he will, as we saw in the last chapter, take into account the effect of a given volume of output upon his wage and other costs in deciding what output will maximize his profits. Thus a monopolist possesses special powers of exploiting labour and other factors of production, and of securing not only the whole monopoly revenue

for himself, but also some part of what would in
competitive conditions be the reward of these other
factors.

But though monopolists in general possess these
powers, and though it would not be difficult to quote
examples of cases where they would appear to have
made use of them, it would be very far from the truth
to argue in general terms that monopolists pay lower
wages than those that rule in more typically competitive
industries, and that they consistently seize the whole
monopoly revenue for themselves or their shareholders.
Many of the best employers in England owe their
power to pay better wages, and to give better conditions of work, to the possession of some measure of
monopoly. Not a few directors who have surplus
profits available for distribution are as anxious to
reward their workers, whom they know, as their shareholders, whom they do not. In some instances, where
a monopoly rests upon goodwill, a reputation as good
employers may be a valuable asset to a firm. To raise
wages to a level that can only be paid by a large and
efficient organization may, moreover, make the in-
vasions of small men doubly difficult. Self-interest may
thus reinforce the good intentions of the good employer.
But though this may be true of individual industries
which are able to increase the welfare of their employees at the cost of consumers employed in other
industries, it could not be true of all industries simultaneously. If all industries were monopolized, the gain
to entrepreneurs would necessarily be at the expense
of all other sections of the community, including their
workers.

If we look for a moment at the other side of the

picture, it is not difficult to see that in a fiercely competitive industry no employer can give better terms or
pay higher wages than his competitors. If he does, he
will go to the wall. Competition requires that no one
shall be a better employer than he can afford to be ;
that all shall be driven as near as conscience, the law,
or the trade unions permit to the morality of the worst.
Thus in an industry where competition is for some
reason excessively keen, the pressure upon wages and
conditions may become irresistible, and the latter
unfairly bad as compared with those in other similar
industries. Wages or prospects of employment must,
it is true, be such in a contracting industry as to discourage new entry, and to encourage all possible
migration. But there is no reason to think that, where
competition is severe, they will be stabilized at a level
at which the minimum necessary pressure is applied
in both these directions.'

Where excessively fierce competition is pushing
down wages and conditions in this sort of way, there
may be a case for the creation or the permission of a
monopoly. Many who would otherwise hesitate to
support the monopoly powers granted under the Coal
Mines Act of 1930, would, I think, justify it on these
grounds.' A somewhat similar case may be made out
for some of the monopoly powers given to impoverished
farmers both in the United States and in this country.
But whether or not in these specific cases the creation
of a monopoly can be justified, it is nevertheless
evidently possible that monopoly should on occasion
redress an unjust distribution of wealth rather than
create an injustice.

But these cases must in the nature of things be

exceptions. In general the effect of monopoly will be a less desirable transfer of wealth from consumer to producer, and in the main from consumer to the entrepreneur or the ordinary shareholder—a transfer, that is, in most cases from poorer to richer. It may be possible by taxation to recover some part of it, but it will never in practice be possible to recover the whole, and it is difficult to frame an income-tax law so as to recover even a substantial part without further repercussions upon other industries and other forms of earning which do not require similar discouragement. There is thus likely to remain in almost every case a residue of damage created by the monopoly, which may be greater, but which may be less than the gain from more efficient methods of production, and which will enjoy no compensating advantage in those cases where monopoly employs less efficient methods of production.

§ 2. *Monopoly causes a Maldistribution of Productive Resources.* So far we have considered monopoly merely as the cause of a transfer of wealth which may be undesirable, or desirable. But that does not exhaust the effects of monopoly. If it were possible to recover the whole of the monopoly revenue by taxation and to redistribute it, we should not have restored the conditions that would exist under competition. For the monopolist secures his monopoly revenue by limiting his output. If all the effects of maldistribution of wealth could be removed, those of maldistribution of productive resources would still remain.

Let us contrast for a moment the amounts of output that a monopoly will produce and that we should

consider ought in the general interest to be produced.
It is socially desirable that output should be carried
up to the point where the marginal utility of an
additional unit is just equal to the marginal cost to
society of that additional unit. The monopoly is
likely to carry production only up to the point where
the marginal revenue from the additional unit is equal
to the marginal cost to the monopoly of that extra
unit. In almost every possible case the monopoly's
output will be less than the socially desirable output.
Thus in a world in which production was in the case of
some commodities in the hands of monopolists, and in
the case of others in the hands of competing firms, we
should, speaking very generally, expect to find too
little production of those things which were monopolized, too much of those which were unmonopolized,
and we should thus get less satisfaction from a given
income than if production were equally efficient and
no monopoly prices were charged.

But this argument is not completely conclusive.
For it is impossible to discuss with complete certainty
the output that is socially desirable in a world where
people are different and incomes are different. The
amount of utility or disutility measured by a shilling
will be different according as the shilling is spent or
earned by a poor man or a rich man. Something
profitably produced by poor men and consumed by
rich may cause far more disutilities in production than
it creates utilities in consumption. Something produced by richer and consumed by poorer individuals
may yield, even beyond the limit of profitability, an
excess of utility over disutility. A monopoly might,
in the former case, come closer to, and would in the

latter case depart even more widely from, the socially desirable output.

Moreover there is a further complication. The monopoly, when it limits its output, employs fewer workers and less of other factors of production. But these are not all of them likely to remain permanently unemployed. In the long run they may be expected to gravitate towards the highest earnings and to leave earnings in the monopolized industry approximately fair as compared with other industries. But over a shorter period it may sometimes, as we saw in the last section, be the case that they earn substantially less in the monopolized industry, and if the impediments to movement are very great the cost of labour may be so reduced that much of it again finds profitable employment in the monopolized industry, and output during this short period is little if at all below the desirable output, but wages are very greatly diminished. This is the more likely to happen if the efficiency of the monopoly is greater than that of competing firms.

If we may suppose a world in which all industries were monopolized, the distribution of resources would be markedly different from that which we should expect in a perfectly competitive world. This would be partly due to a different attitude to rises of costs on the part of a monopolist and of a single competing producer. It would be chiefly due to their different attitudes to a given schedule of demand. A single producer in a perfectly competitive industry will regard the ruling price as the marginal revenue to be gained by an increase of his own production.[1] The monopolist will be affected by the marginal revenue that corres-

[1] See p. 15.

ponds to the elasticity of demand for the product as a whole. Thus, in a perfectly competitive world, without economies of large-scale, marginal cost will be equal to price. In a world of monopolists, however, each would seek to limit output and employ, for given rewards, fewer factors of production. But, as we have seen, it is not likely that the unemployed factors would continue indefinitely in idleness. They would accept lower rewards for their services. Their reabsorption would depend upn an excess, at these lower rewards, of marginal revenue over marginal cost. The marginal revenue would be greater in those industries in which demand was more elastic,[1] and these would be likely to expand relatively to those industries in which demand was less elastic, until in equilibrium, in each industry marginal cost was equal to marginal revenue. There is no reason to think that the welfare of society as a whole would ordinarily be increased by such a change even if allowance be made for differences of income and of the marginal utility of money.[2]

Though these difficulties of comparison are very real, we can say in very broad terms that monopolies are likely to supply less of the products that they produce than is in the general interest and that their existence results in less satisfaction from a given income, produced with a given efficiency, than we should otherwise enjoy. The practical problem is, then, whether we can secure the advantages of technical efficiency, which monopolies sometimes, but not always, provide, without incurring a countervailing loss in a worse distribution wealth and a worse distribution of our productive resources.

[1] See p. 9.   [2] See p. 174.

§ 3. *Methods of Control : the Suppression of Unfair Competition.* Since, therefore, monopolies are likely in general to do damage in these two ways, it is desirable to exercise a control over their activities, a control that may sometimes be mild, but may on occasions require to be stern. In the three following chapters we shall consider in turn the methods of control that have been employed in the United States, in Germany and in Great Britain, and attempt to derive guidance for future action from the successes or failures of these various devices. But before proceeding to study them in detail it will be useful to consider in general terms the different methods that have been or may be used. We may begin by distinguishing the two alternative policies of preventing monopoly, and of accepting monopoly but regulating it. The former suppresses not only the disadvantages, but also the advantages of monopoly where such exist. The latter seeks to retain the advantages while mitigating the disadvantages.

Let us begin by studying the means of preventing monopolies. In the first place an attempt may be made to prevent the creation of a monopoly by rendering illegal the devices which, as we have seen in an earlier chapter, may be employed to drive competitors out of the market or to keep them out once a monopoly has been established. Thus agreements which make the supply of a firm's goods conditional on an undertaking not to handle the goods of others may be made unenforceable ; discriminating prices aimed at destroying competitors may be forbidden ; misrepresentations of the quality of rival goods may be made illegal, and so on. By such methods monopolies of certain types may, it can readily be seen, be rendered more vulnerable to

N

actual or threatened competition and their monopoly powers curtailed. Moreover, by eliminating only unfair methods of competition, the combination of firms when it is in the public interest by promoting efficiency still, it is argued, remains permissible.

Such outlawry of the more obviously unfair methods of competition is beyond question desirable. But this method of control can seldom alone suffice. There are many and powerful monopolies whose strength depends little, if at all, upon such weapons. Moreover, in practice it is, as we have seen, by no means easy to define an unfair practice with that precision which is necessary if a law is to become a reality. It is easy enough to say that in certain conditions discriminating prices, for example, are capable of being used as a weapon of offence to eliminate a weak but potentially efficient rival. But in other circumstances discriminating prices may be the condition of the provision of a necessary service (in the case of a country doctor, for example), and as desirable as they were elsewhere undesirable. Thus it may become necessary to attempt to define the unfair practice by the intention, and not by the action, with inevitable complexities of proof in the courts.

But even if unfair methods could be eliminated, the contention that combination will only occur where it is justified on grounds of efficiency, will not be valid. For the motive to combine is an increase of profits. If competition is perfect, and combination can do nothing to enable a firm to raise its prices, combination will, it is true, only occur where efficiency is increased by it. But if the market is imperfect and combination makes possible a raising of prices, it may be expected to occur whether or not efficiency is increased, or indeed even

if costs are increased by any amount less than the
addition to monopoly revenue.   Thus if in an industry
there is imperfect competition of such form that the
amalgamation of any two firms will make the market
more imperfect and the monopoly revenue to be earned
greater, there is no position of equilibrium short of
complete monopoly.

§ 4.   *The Break-up of Monopolies.*   A second method
that has been employed in order to escape the consequences of monopoly is the attempted restoration of
competitive conditions by making illegal the forms of
monopolistic combination, the trust or holding company, or whatever shape the monopolist organization
may take.   Here again difficulties arise.   In the first
place, as we shall see, in the struggle of wits between the
company lawyer and the courts, the former is always
one trick ahead, and has apparently always one more
card to play when the present trick is trumped.   This
method has the merit, however, that it can most easily
render illegal those temporary forms of monopoly
which do most to raise prices and least to promote
efficiency, and drives companies into those forms, such
as the complete fusion, which, while least assailable,
do yet make possible the greatest use of technical
improvements.
   But this method of mitigating the effects of
monopoly, applied to any save the most temporary
forms of association, would appear to be founded upon
a fallacy.   It is seldom or never possible to disintegrate
a monopoly into atoms and restore atomistic competition.   What happens is rather that a single monopoly
is broken into a small number of individual units.

But, as we have seen, the competition of a few firms
is something fundamentally different from the competition of a myriad.   The price policy of each will depend
upon how it thinks that others will react to any given
change.   Apart from such assumptions, price cannot be
determined. With certain assumptions it may be almost
identical with monopoly price, and where willing co-
operators have been turned by law into unwilling competitors, such harmony of policy as would produce this
result would be not improbable.   It is thus extremely
uncertain whether the policy of disintegration can in
any case achieve the intended results.

§ 5.   *The Regulation of Monopolies.*   In the third place
it is possible, while accepting the existence of monopolies, to attempt to regulate them and to prevent
any excessive use of monopoly powers.   Such regulation may be achieved, firstly, by publicity.   If all the
facts regarding monopolistic agreements, or regarding
rates of profits being made, are published for all to
know, and the monopoly is confronted with the need to
justify its actions before the court of public opinion,
inexcusable use of monopoly powers will often be
curtailed.   The value of this weapon of publicity
appears to be widely different in different countries.
In some, the force of public opinion is such that a
monopoly hesitates to incur the odium of criticism.   In
others, monopolies have brazenly continued anti-
social practices in the face of an almost universal
outcry.   Where monopoly is based in part or in whole
upon the goodwill of customers, publicity may serve
substantially to diminish it.   Moreover, by making
known excessive margins of profit, potential competi-

tion may be stimulated, or its likelihood be so increased that a less outrageous price policy will be in the interest even of the monopolist.

Secondly, an attempt may be made to regulate prices. This may take the form either of forbidding in general terms excessive prices, and leaving the courts to decide in any given instance whether or not a price is excessive, or it may take the form of imposing a maximum above which for the time being price may not be increased.

Thirdly, an attempt may be made to regulate profits and to impose a limit to the rate of return on capital, either absolutely, or such that any excess over this limit must be conditional upon a reduction of the price to the consumer of the goods or services provided.

The regulation of prices, directly or indirectly, or the regulation of profits are all in a sense variations upon a single theme, and all encounter the same difficulties. Such regulation cannot be effective unless it is possible to say in the first case what is a reasonable price, and in the second case to fix this reasonable price as a maximum. Neither of these things can be done unless it is first possible to decide what is a reasonable return upon the capital invested. But what do we mean by the capital invested ?[1] If we attempt to take the present value of the capital we are arguing in a circle. For the value is determined by capitalizing the present or expected earnings at the current rate of interest. We need, therefore, to take the actual capital invested. But this again is by no means simple and certain. If the owners of a number of

[1] For a full discussion of this problem see A. C. Pigou, *Economics of Welfare*, 4th Edition, pp. 367 *et seq.*

undertakings combined to form a monopoly, they might purchase the existing plants at inflated prices and, though the rate of return on the capital so invested would be normal, the capital on which the return was received would be excessive. Even if the actual expenditure on capital equipment be taken as the index of capital invested, we are not clear of our difficulties. If, as not infrequently happens, prices have changed materially since the date of construction of some of the capital, some not easily calculable allowance must be made. If in certain earlier years earnings have been non-existent or below normal, those years must be treated as a period of investment, and allowance must again be made. These and other difficulties make the determination of a fair price, or of a normal return, extremely uncertain, and if monopoly prices can only be regulated when earnings become so high that they exceed by a significant margin the highest rewards of the most skilful entrepreneurs in competitive industries, the monopolist will suffer little. There are, nevertheless, likely to be cases where, despite these difficulties, regulation is obviously called for, and we must attempt such price-fixing as may be possible.

There is one merit of the method of price regulation that it is well to appreciate. Monopoly has, we have seen, ill-effects upon the distribution of resources between alternative uses as well as upon the distribution of wealth. The method of price fixing has in very many cases a remedial effect upon the output that the monopolist will produce as well as upon his price. The reason is easy to appreciate. The monopolist ordinarily makes his profits by limiting output, since by so doing he raises the price at which his products will sell. If restriction of output will no longer raise the selling price, the motive to restrict disappears, and the monopolist will in most cases maximize his profits by selling the greatest output that can find a sale at the fixed price.

§ 6. *The Problem of Economic Power.* There is another consideration that reinforces the need to exercise some measure of control over monopolies. The steadily growing scale of industry has made the unit of industrial operation—the factory, the steel works or the mine— large in comparison with the unit of social organization, the town or village. To an increasing extent it has become true in certain industries, of which the heavy industries afford the predominant but by no means the only example, that a particular company virtually controls the economic basis of life of a town or even of a whole mining valley or county. The company is faced at intervals with the problem of constructing new plant or of concentrating output into certain works, and closing down old centres completely. To some extent its decisions may be inescapable. Coal or iron may be worked out, or the best location may have been fundamentally changed by the discovery of new mineral resources or a new technique of production. But not infrequently the place of future production is not uniquely determined. Concentration somewhere is necessary, but the place itself may be chosen from a fairly wide field of possibilities.

Where this is the case, considerations other than those which make the concentration of materials and the final transport to market fractionally cheaper in one place than another, ought almost certainly to come into review. From the point of view of the individual, progress is achieved if he himself can reduce costs by unemploying workers, and maintaining his output at a smaller labour cost. But from the point of view of society as a whole, progress is only achieved when the labour thus set free is re-employed and used to increase the flow of goods available for consumption. From the point of view of society it is therefore relevant to ask whether resources are being set free in such places and of such a character that they can be re-employed for other purposes, and whether they are equipped with housing, schools, hospitals, transport facilities and so on, which can continue to serve them when occupied in some other industry. If, at some small cost to the rationalizing industry, usable rather than unusable resources can be released, society will almost certainly benefit. And since the maintenance of unused labour becomes chargeable to society, it has ground for enforcing its preference within reasonable limits.

This general consideration of the relative advantages of locating primary output in different places is greatly reinforced by the effects upon secondary employment. The proportion of all economic activity that is industrially located by considerations of materials and so on, and which serves a national or at least a comparatively widespread market, is probably not more than about 40 per cent of the whole. The remaining 60 per cent represents local services and occupations which meet the requirements of purely local markets and whose fortunes fluctuate almost proportionately with those of the basic industrial activities upon which they are, in a sense, parasitic. The State, in deciding the optimum present distribution of production, would take account of the effects of certain policies upon this local secondary activity, and of the costs of transition and movement involved.

This problem of the great and largely irresponsible political power of big undertakings is not of course confined to monopolies. In mining, for example, it may exist even where the industry is highly competitive. But it is likely to become much more serious in the case of monopoly, firstly, because monopolies increase their earnings by limiting their output, and in some instances, therefore, by shutting down the least profitable parts of the organization ; secondly, because, as we have seen in Chapter VI, the concentration of output and the specialization of work is more easily achieved in monopolies of the merger type.

Where the problem exists, it is by no means easy to deal with it in practice by the usual methods of adjusting the profit motive by tax or subsidy. Such instruments must in general have an intelligible, foreseeable and concrete basis of imposition, and a tax on the closing of works in certain areas would be almost impossible either to assess or to collect. More direct methods of persuasion, such as have been exercised in a few cases with regard to the Special Areas in Great Britain, might be attempted, though they are scarcely efficacious. But whatever means are employed, there will emerge a conflict of interest between the monopoly, pursuing profits, and society, pursuing security and the least painful transition.

Thus not only in the field of price and profit regulation, but also in the field of economic freedom, the monopoly may have to accept or to resist political control. The greater the political power, therefore, of a monopoly, the greater within certain limits will be its freedom to secure profits. This must not be taken to imply that every monopoly is everywhere concerned to inflict the greatest damage that it can upon society. Indeed the existence of monopoly very much reduces the competitive pressure upon individual undertakings to act in the way that will maximize their private profits, and to that extent facilitates the due consideration of these larger issues. But to some extent the interest of the monopoly to restrict production and to concentrate output must come into conflict with the interest of the State to maximize national production and to diffuse output in those places where it is socially most desirable both for the primary output which it will yield, and for the secondary employment that will flow from a given level of incomes earned in primary activity. Where such conflict arises, the political strength of the monopoly is important.

The political power of big business lies partly in its power actually to cause temporary dislocations of the industrial machine, by declining to give continued employment or to increase employment by further investment of resources : partly in its ability to mould public opinion directly, or through influence upon the press, into agreement with its own views. Those views are not, in the majority of cases, deliberately antagonistic to society. Rather they emphasize over-insistently the importance of profit as a mainspring of industry, and the national dangers of a decline of those activities which are motivated by such gains. A Government that is too fearful of the often remote consequences of a temporary decline of profit, and too unwilling to risk the necessity of replacing an organization inspired by profit with some alternative, may with the best of intentions pay undue heed to the claims of the entrepreneuring class.   And all the forces of common social bias and tradition may tend to reinforce its judgment.

The nineteenth and twentieth centuries, which have brought in the democratic countries a progressive extension of the franchise and widening of the basis of political power, have brought simultaneously a narrowing of the distribution of economic power, and a growing concentration of it in the hands of a small and irresponsible industrial oligarchy.   How small and how irresponsible it may be is best illustrated from some facts regarding the control of industry in the United States.[1]   In 1929 the two hundred largest non-banking corporations controlled 49·2 per cent of all non-banking corporate wealth, and received 43·2 per cent of the income of all non-banking corporations.   The latter figure in reality under-estimates their share, for in many cases subsidiaries of the two hundred made separate income-tax returns, and when allowance is made for this the proportion must have been well over 45 per cent.   The rate of growth of the assets of these large corporations over the preceding twenty years had been about half as great again as that of all non-banking corporations.   These two hundred undertakings were managed by some two thousand directors.   In some few cases these are appointed and controlled by owners of a majority of the stock of the corporation. The number of examples of private ownership among

[1] See A. A. Berle and G. C. Means, *The Modern Corporation and Private Property, passim.*   Some of the results of their investigation are briefly summarized in F. L. Allen, *The Lords of Creation*, pp. 239–244.

these large corporations is small. The Ford Motor
Company is not typical in this respect of modern
America. Private ownership accounts for only some
4 per cent of all the capital controlled by these corporations. Control through the ownership of a majority
of closely held stock is even rarer. It apparently
accounts for only 2 per cent of all the capital. Rather
more (about 14 per cent) is probably controlled by
substantial minority holdings, where the remaining
stock is widely distributed. Some 2½ per cent is controlled by the use of some legal device for concentrating
power into certain hands, usually the device of
pyramiding. But considerably more than half of all
the capital resources of these two hundred corporations
(about 58 per cent) is apparently controlled not by the
owners of large blocks of capital, but by a small
group who happen to possess the management of an
undertaking, and who can only be unseated in quite
exceptional circumstances. The stock of many of these
large corporations is very widely held. There were at
one time 182,585 stock holders in the United States
Steel Corporation, including 120,918 holders of common stock. The largest holding was less than three-
quarters of 1 per cent of the whole. The directors, who
included the largest holder, held in total no more than
1·4 per cent of all stock, and 1·9 per cent of the common
stock. That situation is typical of a large part not
only of American, but also of British industry. Yet in
most cases the directors are virtually self-appointed
and self-perpetuating. For their election is in practice
the function of a proxy committee, and the proxy
committee is appointed by the directors. In these
circumstances nothing short of flagrant mismanage-

ment can provoke the revolution which will unseat them. It is only when banks and debenture-holders become nervous that reorganization can proceed.

It does not, of course, follow from the fact that there is a divorce between ownership and control, that control will not be in the interests of the owners. For if the management were composed of persons who were owners of large absolute amounts of capital, even though of a small proportion of the whole, their individual interests as owners might lead them to act generally in the interests of all owners. But the authors of the American study suggest that in a number of respects the interests of those in control may substantially diverge from the interests of all owners. They may be more interested in certain stocks than in others. They may have private interests in subsidiaries, or in firms selling to or buying from the main corporation. They may even be in a position to benefit by its bankruptcy. Where their interest as employees exceeds their interest as shareholders, they may be over-generous in their salary scales. Where they are primarily concerned to enhance their technical reputation as producers, they may be over-lavish with regard to capital equipment, or over-exacting with regard to quality.

But the conflict of the interest and the fiduciary responsibility of the management arises most acutely of all, where the buying and selling of the company's shares by directors is concerned. Within the framework of the company law, the existing managers of a company possess very considerable powers to benefit one class of shareholders at the expense of another. This is possible by a variety of methods, some con-

cerned with the increasing of certain classes of stock as
compared with others, in cases where their relative
participations are laid down, some concerned with the
postponement of dividend payments on prior stocks
and their concentration into certain years, so that
deferred stocks may benefit. Thus there has emerged
a new problem of industry. "*Quis custodiet ipsos
custodes ?*" The old proposition, "Where the risk lies,
there the control lies also," is, even if we define risk to
mean no more than the risking of capital, to-day not
remotely akin to the truth. Moreover, the whole basis
of the distribution of a company's profits has come in
question. Are they a necessary reward for risk-
bearing and waiting, or are they an incentive to
enterprise ? If the former, then they must go to the
shareholder ; if the latter, then the more they are
concentrated in the hands of those who control, the
better. Where profits are at the normal competitive
level, each will presumably get barely sufficient to
induce a supply of these two separate groups of
functions. But where monopoly profits are made,
to which will they accrue ? There is seldom reason to
think that the conflict of these rival interests will
transfer them to the consumer, or even to the consumer in his other character of salaried or wage-
earning producer. Between the other parties it is
largely a question, first, of conscience in a position of
trust, second, of the possible divergence of motive
between management and shareholder. In very many
cases these two factors will unite to promote control in
the interest of the shareholder. But in not a few
instances, the problem of the control of the arbitrary
economic power of an irresponsible minority will

reinforce other arguments for the regulation of monopoly.

§ 7. *The Replacement of Private Monopoly by some Alternative.* It has become plain that there is, in the world as we know it, a fundamental conflict of interest between those who own and control capital on the one hand, and those who work and consume on the other. The additional conflict between those who own and those who control does little if anything to mitigate it, but rather creates additional ground for intervention. We can attempt a solution of the major problem along two alternative paths. We can, as we have seen, try by the familiar weapons of tax and subsidy, or by illegalizing certain practices, to entice the refractory monster into the paths that it should tread. The probable success of such a policy can best be judged from history of such attempts in the following three chapters. We can alternatively seek to resolve the conflict by entrusting the control of production to some organization which, since it combines in itself both the producing and consuming interests, will not be warped by over-emphasis of the former. This organization may be an offshoot of one of the various branches of government, local or central, or it may be an association created for this purpose and independent of the government.

The threat of purchase by a public authority at a price representing approximately the actual current replacement cost of physical assets may in some cases be sufficient to induce a monopolist to moderate both his price and his output policy. For anything which makes it more difficult for a monopolist to raise his price if he produces and sells less, will ordinarily lead him to increase his output. A public authority may also secure the rule of competitive price, and in some cases of competitive output, without itself undertaking the task of operation, by opening the operation of some necessarily monopolistic service to competitive tender, and accepting the tender which provides the service at the lowest price.

But in many cases such methods are insufficient or inapplicable, and the public authority is confronted with the need to provide the service or product itself. A full discussion of the proper field of national and municipal trading lies beyond the scope of this book. Nor indeed can anything valuable be said concerning it in general terms. In recent years there is hardly any branch of industrial activity which has not been undertaken by a national or local government in some country, and most of us would now hesitate to repeat those generalizations regarding the comparative efficiencies of government and private enterprise in different types of industry which were current a decade or more ago. Governments have not shown themselves noticeably less enterprising in their industrial activities than private concerns. We hear proposals, indeed, for the nationalization of electrical distribution on the ground that such operation might result in a quicker extension of facilities and reduction of price. With the steady growth of the scale of large industrial undertakings, their methods have inevitably become more bureaucratic, and the recruitment of the higher staff less nepotic, until the differences of the forms of administration between a publicly controlled and a privately controlled body have become negligible.

This is the more true of those *ad hoc* bodies which have been created in some numbers in this country in recent years for the operation of government-owned undertakings, such as wireless broadcasting or the generation of electricity, or London transport, whose control, though ultimately of course subject to Parliament, has been made as far as possible non-political.

The growth of such bodies is of the greatest interest, for much of the hesitation of those disinterested persons who still question the expediency of governmental ownership and control, springs rather from doubts regarding the wisdom of subjecting industrial undertakings to such fickle and changeable bodies as the House of Commons or local authorities, than from doubts regarding the organizing capacity of those who are likely to be put in immediate charge. A form of administration that can secure at once the continuity of policy that is essential and the consideration of interests broader than those of the shareholder, would commend itself to many who do not so keenly feel the need that others do for the replacement of the motive of profit in industry by the motive of service to the community.

The peculiar merit of the publicly operated monopoly, granted equal efficiency with the private undertaking, is that it permits whatever compromise between the interests of the producer, as represented by a contribution to rates or to national revenue in excess of actual interest charges, and the interests of the consumer, may be held desirable. The output may be made such that total receipts just cover total costs as under competitive conditions they would, or less

o

(the service being subsidized), or more, as may be held to be desirable.

If we are not in general, or in a particular case, anxious to see intervention by the government in industry, an alternative means of escape from the consequences of monopoly is afforded by the consumers' co-operative movement. By combining in itself both the interest of the consumer and that of the producer, manœuvres to promote the interest of one at the expense of the other are rendered irrelevant. Moreover, in theory the type of organization that it represents is exceptionally well-adapted to secure great economies. A very large-scale marketing organization can offer long runs of work on standardized products to specialist producers on a highly competitive basis, and thus secure great economies of manufacture. The fact that the Co-operative Wholesale Society is also a manufacturing organization, capable of extending its operations into any field in which monopolists threaten to raise price, is an effective protection against exploitation even where the weapon of direct competition is not used. It is interesting for these reasons to notice the part played by large co-operative distribution in the Russian economic organization, and the part that it has played in Sweden in the mitigation of monopoly.

In practice the Co-operative Movement would appear to have fallen short of these ideals. Concerned perhaps a little too much to maintain its democratic traditions and the fundamental independence of the branches, it has missed securing some of those advantages of large-scale marketing that have been seized by the large retail chain stores, and has been forced sometimes to depend too much on the loyalty of its members, too little upon solid advantages. There has recently been a welcome desire to think out afresh the functions of co-operation in a changed world, and we may hope that it may once again become the solid safeguard against local monopolistic exploitations that it was in the days of the pioneers.

CHAPTER IX

THE LAW AND MONOPOLY IN THE UNITED STATES OF AMERICA

§ 1. *Reasons for the Strength of Monopolies in the United States.* Monopolies in the United States of America have assumed a more virulent aspect and have provided more difficult problems of control than in almost any other country. The reasons for their greater strength have been several. The great distance which separates large parts of the country from alternative sources of supply outside the United States has substantially diminished the efficacy of foreign competition. The tariff policy has even further reduced it. Moreover, the frontier, pioneering, outlook of earlier days tolerated standards of commercial morality and methods of competition which in other countries and in more stabilized conditions would have been impossible. The sanctions of social ostracism, even if used, were less powerful. Monopolistic prices, again, less quickly attracted competition in a relatively poorer age. Abnormal profits made in one section of industry did not immediately attract supplies of additional capital from outside. Those who could dispose of it had often more immediate outlets of their own which might prove equally advantageous. The double jurisdiction of State and Federal government facilitated sometimes the extravagances of monopolists, since to a single state a monopolist might well bring more of profit than of damage, and thus be regarded as deserving favour rather than repression. Even apart from this he might escape through legitimate doubt concerning the proper sphere of control of the two bodies. The banks, moreover, lent in many cases a helping hand in the process of combination such as circumstances or traditions forbade in other countries. It is again somewhat easier to monopolize the known sources of necessary raw materials in a new country in which they are not yet in long-established ownership than in an old country where land values are higher and owners better appraised of the possible values of their properties.

But more important than any of these considerations is the fact that in the 'seventies or 'eighties the United States was leading the way in the development of the consolidation of businesses into large units. Much of the movement towards monopoly was due to an inevitable supersession of outdated small businesses by modern and more efficient methods. But this natural evolution was reinforced and accelerated by another important force. A general belief in the advantages of combination, even apart from monopoly, led to an excessive increase in the values of combined firms, and enabled the promoters to reap a rich harvest by the sale of watered stock.

§ 2. *An Illustration from the History of the Standard Oil Company.* The problems of the governments of the day will be more readily understandable if we look at them against the background of the history of one of the more spectacular attempts at monopolization. For the methods employed go far to explain the subsequent legislation. Since it was the Standard Oil Company and the person of Mr. J. D. Rockefeller which for public opinion typified the ogre of monopoly, and since it was the revelations concerning that company which more than anything led to legislation, let us very briefly examine its history.

John D. Rockefeller found his first employment as a book-keeper in a firm of produce merchants at Cleveland. In the year 1858, at the age of eighteen, he and a young Englishman named Maurice Clark formed a partnership as wholesale merchants. In the following few years, thanks largely to Rockefeller's energy and ability, and assisted by the demands of the Civil War, they succeeded in building up a substantial business. When oil was first struck at Titusville in 1859, Cleveland, some ninety miles away on the shore of Lake Erie and served by three railways, became one of the chief refining centres. For some years the partners watched the rapidly growing industry and the spectacular fortunes which were being made and lost, without themselves participating. Then, in 1862, they were persuaded by another young man named Samuel Andrews to come to his assistance and provide more capital for the little refinery that he was operating. Andrews, desperately poor, was a mechanical genius, and he and Rockefeller were among the first to appreciate the great advantages of large-scale refining. The undertaking grew rapidly. In 1865 Rockefeller bought out Clark's share in the oil business and sold to him his own share in the produce business. In 1870 Rockefeller and Andrews combined with Rockefeller's younger brother, William, and three others to form the

Standard Oil Company of Ohio. The new company, with its capital of a million dollars, was already the largest refining company in Cleveland, and probably in the United States. But it refined only about 3 per cent of all the oil treated in the country, and was not noticeably stronger than its rivals. Yet by 1879 Standard Oil was refining almost 95 per cent of the total output. It is this decade of breakneck progress that can well illustrate the methods of the monopolies of the period.

Rockefeller neither then nor later attempted on any considerable scale to control the production of crude oil. That was too widespread and too uncertain to be monopolized effectively. It was from the control of the means of transporting and marketing that the Standard's monopoly was derived. The offensive was begun within eighteen months of the incorporation of the new company. The first objective was the control of all the refineries of Cleveland itself, which at the time was treating about one-quarter of the total output, and was faced by fierce competition from refineries in the oil regions themselves, and at New York and Pittsburgh.

The weapon that Rockefeller and Flagler, his chief lieutenant, employed to secure control of their Cleveland rivals was that of unequal railway freight rebates. The rail administrations of the day were accustomed to publish rates which were paid only by the weak and by the foolish. The stronger and the wiser, and the big shippers in particular, were accustomed to demand and to secure such secret rebates as they could extort. This was contrary neither to the law nor to the accepted commercial practice of the day. Railway companies regarded themselves as just as free to do what they wished with their own as any other group of citizens. Rockefeller had already for some years enjoyed certain concessions, but Standard Oil now secured a new variety of rebate for which the precedents, if any, must have been few.

Cleveland was joined to the eastern markets and to the export markets through New York by three railways, the Pennsylvania, the Erie, and the New York Central, as well as by water by way of Lake Erie and the Welland Canal. The lines were in competition, and a skilful man with large shipments at his disposal could play them off one against the other. This for some time had been done. But now Flagler and Rockefeller combined with representatives of the railways to organize a more ambitious scheme. Their object was twofold : " Firstly, to do away, at least in great measure, with the extensive and undue competition now existing between the refining interest, by reason of there being a far greater refining capacity than is called for or justified by the existing petroleum-consuming requirements of the world ; secondly, to avoid the heretofore undue competition between the various railroad companies transporting oil to the seaboard, by fixing a uniform rate of freight, which it is thought can be adhered to by some such arrangement as guaranteeing to each road some such percentages of the profit of the aggregate amount of oil transported, whether the particular line carries it or not." With this object in view they secured control of an old company known by the somewhat inappropriate name of the South Improvement Company, but which had the virtue of a conveniently indefinite charter.

The scheme was this. Freight rates were to be raised

to almost double and enforced without rebate on all other shippers of oil. Standard Oil in Cleveland, suitable other refining interests in the oil regions in Pittsburgh and in one or two other centres were to be given special rebates equal to some 45 per cent of the new rates. The special rebates to the favoured firms would be paid not only on the oil that they shipped themselves but also on all oil shipped by their competitors.

There is reason to think that some at least of the higher officials of the railways imagined that all existing refiners would be given an opportunity for associating themselves freely with the company. In fact it became a weapon to force suitable firms into the combination on Rockefeller's terms. Armed with the proposed rebate, within three months he secured twenty-one of the twenty-six refineries in Cleveland. But an accidental premature disclosure of the intended railway rates led to such outcry in the oil regions that the railways disowned their proposed contracts with the South Improvement Company, and undertook to give in future no such special and secret rebates, and the company itself was deprived of its charter.

But despite this apparent reverse Rockefeller and his associates had in this short time secured control of about one-fifth of the refining capacity of the country. Moreover the railways, within a month of their under-taking to the oil producers, were once more giving Standard Oil special terms. Once more the company began to make efforts to secure control of other refineries. Having failed by secret methods, they turned to open advances. They formed a National Refiners' Association, and secured the adherence of four-fifths of the refineries, but when trade was temporarily depressed many broke away and refused to limit production.

The next step was to secure from the railways an agreement putting all the refining areas, Cleveland, Pittsburgh, the oil regions and New York, on an equality with regard to transport costs to the eastern market, whatever might be their natural advantages. That done, Rockefeller approached the strongest producers in the other centres, and under the cloak of the formation of a Central Association of Refiners, he succeeded in associating them with his own company, giving them stock in Standard Oil in payment, but leaving administration in most instances in the hands of the original owners. Through the Acme Oil Company he quickly acquired control of many of the independent refineries in the oil regions. This time his success was complete and permanent. Inside the group of companies that he now controlled, he was able to determine the output and to negotiate the freight rates.

But the producers and the remaining independent refiners did not surrender without a series of further fights. The most serious of these came from the development of a new type of oil transportation, the pipe-line. These had been used since the early days of the industry, but mostly for the short-distance transport of oil to the railroads for shipping in tank cars. Now long-distance pipe-lines began to be built. The railways, interested in the rival method, naturally did their utmost to oppose them. Since the right of eminent domain had not yet been granted to pipe-lines, at any point where it became necessary to cross a railway track, the railway company could block them ; and this, encouraged by the Standard Oil Company, they proceeded to do. Standard Oil meanwhile proceeded apace with its own construction of pipe-lines, and used its influence with the railways to make the provision of tank cars to its rivals both uncertain and insufficient. Of the pipe-line companies the strongest was the Empire Transportation Company, developed with great ability in connection with the Pennsylvania Railroad. Driven by the pressure of the Standard organization into the refining business it became at once a direct challenge to them. Rockefeller persuaded the rival railways to assist him in defeating the Pennsylvania. Drastic cuts in rates killed the Pennsylvania's profits. A fortuitous strike of its workers brought the railway to its knees. It was forced not only to abandon its protégé, but even to exercise an option to buy it and hand it over to Standard Oil.

Even now the independents were not finally defeated. A company was formed to attempt the hitherto impossible by pumping oil over the Alleghany mountains to the sea. Contrary to all expectations they succeeded, and the monopoly of Standard Oil was again vitally threatened. But quietly the company bought up the independent refineries on the coast which were to have been supplied, and when the Tide Water Pipe Company replied by building its own refineries, Standard Oil succeeded in buying surreptitiously a sufficiency of the stock of the company, and its independence was at an end.

The monopoly once established was maintained by similar manœuvres. The influence of Standard Oil over the railways was used to make shipments of rivals uncertain, irregular and costly. The construction of new pipe-lines was impeded by every artifice. Moreover the monopoly was reinforced by the gradual elimination of wholesale dealers, as Standard Oil pushed further into the market, and began to serve retailers directly itself. These dealers were eliminated, not in many cases by the slow pressure of more efficient competition, but by the more rapid and effective weapon of drastic local price cutting, until almost nine-tenths of the business was in the company's hands. The virtual monopoly, once created, was held with the assistance of a remarkably perfect intelligence system which secured knowledge of every move and every outlet of a rival, by " bogus independents " which competed fiercely with a genuine independent, and by the same drastic price cutting which had first established it.

It is difficult to measure the relative efficiency of Standard Oil and of the independent concerns. Certainly, both in the early days and later, Rockefeller's amazing capacity for organizing every detail of his business afforded substantial economies in refining. The large-scale distribution of oil provided a wide field for further economies, and these the Standard Oil Company unquestionably achieved. But it consistently held the price of oil above that " normal " price at which smaller rivals could produce and market it, apart from those obstacles which were invariably put in their way If its results are to be measured by price, it diverted into the pockets of its shareholders not only the whole benefit of its very considerable economies, but also monopoly profits derived firstly from a price of oil higher than that at which even small refineries could profitably work, and secondly from the strength of its bargaining power as against the comparatively unorganized producers of oil.

Such methods of competition, even if they were not wholly abhorrent to the commercial morality of the time, were condemned by public opinion, not only in those districts which had suffered from Rockefeller's widening powers, but also more widely throughout the country. While Standard Oil was possibly more notorious than other similar organizations, it was in many ways less evil. Where others had profited by the watering of stock, and out of the fictitious profits of the flotation of combinations of uncertain value, Rockefeller and his associates had created a great industry and brought it to a remarkable level of efficiency. Many of the complaints of the time were, judged by the standpoint of to-day, wholly unjustified. For Rockefeller was only in part the great monopolist injuring the consumer. The outcry came loudest from the displaced producers, and here it is important to remember that he, in his own industry, was the incarnation of a great industrial movement. For it was in the 'seventies and 'eighties that the change began in the United States from the small family business to those great and highly organized corporations which to-day we regard as the optimum that we are seeking to secure. Mingled with the legitimate objections to monopoly was the eternal chorus of those who cry to have the clock put back. Rockefeller's sin was impatience. He habitually took a short cut through history by using weapons of doubtful morality to achieve results which time would in most cases more slowly have accomplished.

§ 3. *The Sherman Act.* The legal defence against the inroads of monopolies came first in the individual

States. Before specific legislation was adopted, monopolies were subject to control only under the common law which the United States had derived originally from England. But it had been interpreted there to restrict the right of contract more extensively than in England. Under common law any agreements to restrict output, to divide markets, to pool profits and for similar purposes were almost always held to be void as being in restraint of trade and against public policy. That is to say, such agreements could not be enforced with the assistance of the courts, but they were not in themselves illegal. Thus there was control over the monopoly only so far as it took the form of a loose association of ordinarily competitive producers, and only then so far as the interests of individual producers diverged.

Apart from the restraints of common law, in several States there were constitutional provisions which declared monopolies or combinations in restraint of trade unlawful. In 1889 four States introduced legislation against monopolies, and in 1890 they were followed by two more. This legislation was directed primarily against the formation of Trusts. In 1879, when Rockefeller had secured control over some thirty separate companies, the problem of their co-ordinated administration had arisen. An astute company lawyer had solved the problem by suggesting the formation of a Trust agreement under which nine trustees would hold and manage the property of all the individuals who were associated in the Standard Oil combination. They were to issue Trust certificates in proportion to the value of the properties brought in by each person. Dividends were to be distributed to the holders of certificates at the discretion of the trustees. This method of control, once inaugurated in the oil industry, was quickly copied by associations in other industries, and in the early 'eighties a trust movement swept through the country.

It almost immediately awoke the resentment both of small producers, threatened by the encroachment of the Trust, and of the general consuming public, and in 1890 Congress passed what came to be known as the Sherman Anti-Trust Act for the control of these forms of industrial combination. The Act made illegal what had hitherto been merely unenforceable. First : " Every contract, combination in the form of trust or otherwise, or conspiracy, in restraint of trade or commerce among the several States, or with foreign nations is hereby declared to be illegal." Second : " Every person " (a person was in a later clause defined to include any corporation or association) " who shall monopolize, or attempt to monopolize, or combine or conspire with any other person or persons, to monopolize any part of the trade or commerce among the several States, or with foreign nations, shall be deemed guilty of a misdemeanor. . . ." It provided for penalties for such actions, and authorized the seizure of property in course of transportation belonging to prohibited combinations (the Federal Government had, of course, no jurisdiction except over property being moved in the process of interstate or foreign commerce). The circuit courts were given powers " to prevent and restrain violation of this Act," and the district attorneys the duty of initiating proceedings. Moreover persons (or corporations) injured by actions forbidden by the Act were to be entitled to sue for damages, and to be granted three times the damage sustained.

Almost from the first difficulties of enforcement and interpretation of the Act arose. It was difficult to enforce, partly because several of the early cases brought under the Act failed, partly because several Attorneys-General were either opposed to, or inactive in, its enforcement. The Act applied specifically to " interstate commerce." The first case which came to the United States Supreme Court was one in which the Government was attempting to secure the cancellation of Share-Exchange agreements within the Sugar Trust. The Court held that the agreements were between " manufacturers " of sugar and the Act gave no power to control manufacture. " Commerce succeeds to manufacture and is not a part of it." This result was probably in part at least a consequence of bad pleading, and in more recent cases of a similar nature the prohibitions of the Sherman Act have been held to apply. But the immediate effect was to throw grave doubt upon the efficacy of the Law and to discourage prosecutions under it.

Certainly until the presidency of Theodore Roosevelt in 1901 prosecutions under the Sherman Act had been rare. But under the Roosevelt administration, and as a result of the " muckraking " campaign of those years, which made knowledge of the actions of the trusts far more widespread, government activity was considerably increased. The Sherman Act became under the Taft and subsequent administrations, if not always an effective weapon for the dissolution of existing monopolies, at least an effective deterrent to the creation of new ones.

The companies against which action was taken during these years included the United States Steel Corporation, the United Shoe Machinery Company, the American Sugar Refining Company, the International Harvester Company and the National Cash Register Company. In 1906 an action was commenced against the Standard Oil Company. The original Trust formed in 1879 had been declared illegal by the Supreme Court of Ohio in 1892. Standard Oil was immediately reorganized. Twenty of the eighty-four constituent companies took over the shares of the remaining sixty-four, and the shares of these twenty companies were divided between the holders of the Trust certificates. The original trustees were majority shareholders in the twenty companies and continued as before to control them. Further but unsuccessful attempts were therefore made to enforce the order of the Court. Standard Oil once more changed its form of organization. This time the Standard Oil Company of New Jersey (a State whose legislation was less unfavourable than that of most others to trusts) was made a holding company, and exchanged its stock for that of the twenty companies. This was the form of organization when in 1906 proceedings were instituted under the Sherman Act.

The proceedings were protracted. In 1909 the Circuit Court unanimously decided against the Standard Oil Company both on the issue of restraint of trade and of monopolization. Appeal was made to the Supreme Court, and in May 1911 that Court finally gave its decision. This confirmed the earlier decision of the circuit Court, while slightly amending the time granted and the conditions imposed for dissolution. But the judgment had an importance far wider even than

P

the ramifications of the Standard Oil Trust. For in the course of their interpretation of the Sherman Act a majority of the judges gave it as their opinion that the Act must be interpreted in accordance with " the rule of reason." They argued that the classes of acts made illegal were inevitably broad and ill-defined, and called for the exercise of judgment, and of some standard whereby to determine whether the prohibitions concerned had been violated ; that standard was the standard of reason applied in the common law. Thus they said (to quote the words of the dissenting judge) : " You may now restrain such commerce, provided you are reasonable about it ; only take care that the restraint is not undue."

The Standard Oil Company was thus once more forced to slough a skin. This time it distributed to shareholders *pro rata* shares in all its subsidiaries. Co-ordination was maintained by interlocking of directorates and community of interests. There was no more effective competition than before between the different producing or the different distributing units in the group.

The history of Standard Oil and of other cases will show that the policy of " trust-busting " had been singularly unsuccessful. The skilful company lawyer was always one move ahead. There is scarcely an instance in which effective competition was restored, and in those few cases where a semblance of such competition was created, it was rather of that " oligopolistic " form, which we have earlier seen to be as likely to yield a price near to that of monopoly as of competition. But it was at least clear that the Sherman Act alone was insufficient to meet the situation.

§ 4. *The Clayton Act and the Federal Trade Commission.*
In 1914, therefore, the Wilson administration strengthened the control exercised by the Federal Government
in two respects. First it created the Federal Trade
Commission, second it passed into law the Clayton
Anti-Trust Act. To consider the Act first, its purpose
was specifically " to supplement existing laws against
unlawful restraints and monopolies." It did this,
first, by forbidding certain unfair practices, such as
price discrimination (beyond such differences as might
be properly accounted for by differences of quantities
purchased or of transport costs involved), or tying
clauses, making it a condition of sale that competitors'
goods should not be handled, in all cases where such
practices tended substantially to lessen competition
or to create monopoly. In the second place, companies
were forbidden to acquire the stock of other companies,
where that might lessen competition between the companies concerned. Thirdly, industrial companies with
a capital (including any surplus or undivided profits)
exceeding one million dollars were forbidden to have
common directors, if those companies had previously
been in competition with each other. A similar
restriction, but with a different maximum of capital,
applied also to directors of banks and Trust companies.
Fourthly, any common carrier was debarred from
having dealings with any firm in which its own directors
or officials might have interests, or any other basis
than that of accepting the lowest tender, whether from
that or another firm.

The Federal Trade Commission Act of 1914 was
designed to strengthen the powers of inquiry into the
actions of Trusts. During the period of rapid develop-

ment of combination in the years 1898 to 1902 there had
been created a body known as the Industrial Commission whose function was to investigate industrial
questions, and in particular the growth of large corporations. Its investigations were hampered by lack of
documentary evidence, and its report recommended the
establishment of some official inquiring body, with power
to collect and publish information. Such a body was
created in 1903 in the Bureau of Corporations. It was
given extensive powers to subpœna witnesses and compel
the production of books and papers. Its functions were
both to advise the President with regard to legislation
and to keep the public informed by the issue of reports.

The Federal Trade Commission superseded the
Bureau of Corporations. Its functions included not
only those of its predecessor, but a number in addition.
It was to investigate the organization of any corporation concerned in business other than banking or
transport ; it was given powers to require annual or
special reports ; it was to report on how the decrees
of the Courts under the Anti-Trust Acts were being
carried into effect by the companies concerned ; it
was to investigate alleged violation of the Acts, if so
instructed ; it was to make recommendations for the
readjustment of offending companies ; it was to investigate conditions abroad where combinations might
affect the trade of the United States.

The Commission is composed of five members, not
more than three of whom may belong to one political
party. Its method of conducting business has differed
somewhat from time to time, but in broad outline it is
as follows.[1] If a complaint of an infringement of the

[1] For more detailed information, see Seager and Gulick, *Trust
and Corporation Problems*, Chapter XXIII.

Sherman or Clayton Act is received it is referred to the chief examiner, who decides whether to proceed formally, or informally, or not at all. In many cases the complaint will be set aside either as frivolous, or because the Commission has no jurisdiction. Or again because ordinary action in the courts would give the complainant sufficient opportunity for redress.

If the Commission decides itself to act, it may deal with the case informally, by conference or correspondence, and the firm concerned may agree to abandon the practice of which complaint is made. Alternatively the Commission may decide to take formal action. In that case notice of the complaint is served on the offending firm. The Commission itself, and not the complainant, is in the position of prosecutor. In many cases the defendant firm does not contest the charge and agrees to abandon the practice in question ; if it does contest it, the facts of the case are established before a Trial Examiner, who prepares a statement of facts to which either party may file exceptions. The case is finally argued before the whole Commission, and if it upholds the complaint a " cease and desist " order is issued.

Many of the decisions of the Commission have been concerned with what does, and what does not, constitute an " unfair practice." In working this out in concrete form, and for individual trades, the Commission has made use of the method of trade practice conferences in which the firms in a particular industry meet to discuss doubtful practices, and to help to establish given standards for the industry concerned. These standards are then applied by the Commission, and practices, which the trade itself has condemned as unfair, are forbidden by means of " cease and desist " orders to those who employ them.

Criticisms of the Commission have arisen partly from the inevitable circumstances of such a body, which make it simultaneously prosecutor, judge and jury ; partly from its policy with regard to publicity. One of the intended functions both of the Bureau of Corporations and of the Federal Trade Commission was to keep the public informed with regard to monopolistic actions and practices. In its earlier days the Commission was accustomed to publish information regarding a given complaint at the same time that it served notice on the defendant firm, and before the latter had opportunity of answering the charge. Since hearings were often long delayed, a firm might sometimes have unfounded accusations hanging over it for considerable periods. More recently the Commission has been less prone to publish complaints, and has given no publicity to cases in which firms immediately abandoned an unfair practice. Many observers would now hold that it has gone too far in protecting the interests of those who have employed unscrupulous methods.

The Clayton Act and the Federal Trade Commission have done much to fill the gaps in the original Sherman Act. And more important has been a gradual change of outlook. In 1890 the ideal was the forcible reestablishment of competition. With time there has been a growing acceptance, and even a worship, of the giant corporations. By degrees the efficiency that they could yield has come to be recognized, and policy has shifted insensibly from that of " trust-busting " towards that of acceptance and control. Already by 1914, at the time of the new legislation, this change was beginning to make itself felt. Control has taken the form of outlawing unfair methods of competition, so that the supersession of the small by the large undertaking should be the consequence of greater efficiency and not merely a greater competitive resource. While combination, with monopolistic intent, was prohibited, growth was not and undertakings large enough to give monopoly power, or few enough to cause " oligopolistic " monopoly, are probably no more rare, despite the Sherman Act, than in other countries. American legislation, if it is to be criticized, has been more concerned with monopoly as it affects competitors or would-be competitors, than with monopoly as it affects the consumer. It has relied for the protection of the consumer on a conflict of interest between one producer and another. It has done little or nothing to protect the consumer in those cases where all producers are agreed as to the methods of exploiting him, or where the competition of the small producer is little to be feared.

§ 5. *The Webb-Pomerene and Robinson-Patman Acts.* In the years from 1914 to 1939, while the precedents in the courts, and before the Federal Trade Commission gradually established the precise legal position of monopolies, nothing further was done to strengthen the law, apart from an Act concerned with packers and stockyards and the Amendment described below. On the other hand it was substantially weakened in one important respect. The Webb-Pomerene Act of 1918 set free from the controls of the Sherman Act associations which were concerned exclusively with the export trade, and not only enabled American industries to act, if circumstances permitted, monopolistically at the expense of foreign consumers, but also permitted American firms to enter into international associations, such as shipping conferences, or restriction schemes. But the effects of the Act have almost certainly been wider than the export trade. An association, once permitted, can with difficulty be prevented from discussing the whole range of an industry's problems, and export associations would appear to result not infrequently in surprising harmonies of opinion with regard also to the home market.

More recently, in 1936, the Robinson-Patman Act was passed to reinforce and clarify certain provisions of the Clayton Act. Under the earlier Act price-discrimination had been made illegal, except so far as it could be justified by differences of grade, or of quantity, or of transportation cost. It was a matter of widespread complaint, more particularly of the smaller retailers against the very large chain stores and mail-order houses, that the latter were obtaining terms from manufacturers that were in no way to be explained by the relative sizes of the orders given. The small retailers had pressed the Federal Trade Commission to take action, but with little or no success. The attempts of the latter body to prevent discrimination of a manufacturer between his various customers on the ground that the competition of such customers in the retail markets would be diminished had, indeed, been frustrated for a time by decisions of the courts, which appeared to uphold the view that the only relevant competition was that of the manufacturer with other manufacturers. Though this narrower view was later

overruled, the need for further definition remained.
The Robinson-Patman Amendment forbids any discrimination, so far as inter-state commerce is concerned,
between buyers of commodities of similar grade and
quality " where the effect of such discrimination may
be substantially to lessen competition or to create a
monopoly." Differentials are permitted only so far
as they may be justified by reasonable allowances for
differences of the costs of manufacture, sale or delivery
which result from differences of quantities purchased,
or from differences of the method of sale or delivery.
The simpler methods of evasion by payment of allowances for advertisement, or similar devices are prevented. The efficacy of the Robinson-Patman Act has
yet to be shown, however. It is not likely to be easy
for the Federal Trade Commission to prove to the
satisfaction of a highly critical court, in the face of the
opposition of a defence supported by technical and
financial expert witnesses, and armed with statistical
and technical data, the proposition that in certain
circumstances a differential of a certain magnitude was
not reasonable—the more so if in that industry raw
material costs are highly fluctuating, and the relations
of particular purchases to particular orders are ill-
defined.

§ 6. *The Roosevelt Experiments.* For a short period,
under the administration of Franklin Roosevelt, the
United States appeared to have reversed completely
the policy embodied in these earlier acts, and to have
attached itself to that of the fostering of associations
and restrictions by official action. This *volte face* was
so sudden, its permanence so doubtful, its legality

under the existing constitution so much in question, that no useful purpose would be served by any attempt to analyse it in detail. But something must be said of its broad outlines.[1]

The system which for two years did most to render nugatory the developments of half a century of monopoly control, was built, paradoxically, on the foundation of the control organization itself. Among the functions assigned to the Federal Trade Commission had been that of preventing the use of unfair practices for the establishment of monopoly. In the furtherance of this end it had, we have seen, developed a system of trade practice conferences, which assisted the Commission in defining the fair and unfair practices to be respectively permitted and forbidden for different trades. The National Industrial Recovery Act gave to the President very wide powers to approve codes of fair competition submitted by associations representing their various industries, provided that they did not permit monopolistic practices, and gave effect to the policy, very broadly defined in the Act, of inducing united action under governmental supervision, and promoting the fullest possible utilization of productive capacity. The Act specially provided that during its operation, and for a short period after its lapse, any actions required by a code to be exempt from the provisions of the Anti-Trust laws of the United States.

The administrator almost immediately made it clear that he would not ordinarily approve codes which were frankly fixing minimum prices or quotas. But in several ways the pursuit of fair competition ended in

[1] For a more detailed account see Lyon and others, *The National Recovery Administration*, or A. R. Burns, the *Decline of Competition*, to whose work the subsequent account is specially indebted

devices scarcely distinguishable from the ordinary framework of a cartel. In the first place fair competition was held in the case of certain industries to include a requirement that firms should not use their machinery for more than a limited number of hours a week. In some cases the number was so reduced as to set an effective upper limit to total production and to distribute it between firms in accordance with their capacity.

In many more instances fair competition was held to require that firms should not sell at a price below the cost of production. Inevitable difficulties of definition arose. Cost of production was variously defined in different codes as the cost of the actual firm, of a representative group of firms, of the average of all firms, of the lowest cost firm. Provisions had to be made for defining what amount of overhead costs was to be covered, what percentage of full capacity working was to be assumed in spreading the overheads, what costs of plant were to be taken. It was necessary to demand uniformity of cost accounting, and to attempt to establish uniform systems for each trade. It is hardly surprising that the hastily improvised machinery encountered problems that proved, for the moment at least, insoluble.

But the attempt to prevent sales below cost provoked such an outcry both from consumers generally, and from the advising board which was entrusted with the safeguard of their interests, that the price regulation policy was early modified, and its extension to further codes abandoned, except in certain defined conditions of emergency. But destructive price cutting continued to be outlawed, and the effective control of price once granted to associations was not lightly abandoned by them.

There was a further regulation which facilitated price fixing and impeded price cutting. Many of the codes imposed as an obligation on firms the " open-price " policy which had been voluntarily adopted for many years by some industries. A list of the prices of all goods produced by a firm, and of all discounts and allowances had to be deposited with the code authority. No firm was permitted to charge any other than the published price without informing the authority. To prevent momentary changes for the purpose of securing a particular order, a minimum period of notice and a minimum period of continuance were sometimes required. Special regulations in some instances permitted quicker changes in response to cuts made by others, and special prices for surplus and damaged stock. In this case again there was outcry, partly from consumers, who urged that pressure was brought on those producers who announced an intention of reducing prices not to proceed with their cuts, partly from producers who found that knowledge of their fixed prices made it easier for unscrupulous rivals to secure their trade. In consequence greater flexibility and greater secrecy were gradually introduced into the system.

Having limited price competition, it became necessary also to limit non-price competition. This involved control not only over the whole system of credits and discounts, sales conditions, service facilities, repurchase agreements and exchange allowances, but also over the qualities and standards that might be offered at the various prices.

These were some of the difficulties with which the Administration was struggling when in 1935 the Supreme Court declared the Recovery Act unconstitutional, partly on the ground that it involved an unconstitutional delegation of powers, partly on the ground that the regulation of commerce within the individual States by the Federal Authority was limited to those aspects of commerce which affected inter-state trade directly and in a narrowly defined sense. This decision annulled, of course, the exemption of codes from the operations of Anti-Trust Acts, and made the code authorities subject once more to the Sherman and Clayton Acts and to the Federal Trade Commission. Attempts have been made, in some cases, to salvage codes by withdrawal of any sections which might be held to infringe those acts. The Federal Trade Commission has lent its aid by revising its views of certain practices. One code at least has secured its approval which prohibits sale below cost with intent to injure a competitor, or to lessen competition or to create a monopoly—yet another instance where the " fair " merges so imperceptibly into the " unfair " that the drawing of lines is almost impossibly difficult. Some codes are being continued under these conditions, others have more or less lapsed. But there can be little doubt that it is far harder to destroy associations than to prevent their creation, and the Recovery Act will almost certainly leave a posterity of gentlemen's agreements and of habits of concerted action which are likely to contribute more to the future welfare of the industrialist than of the consumer.

It is early yet to assess this great experiment and to pass a verdict of success or failure. It will never be easy to estimate what part of its achievements were due to the quasi-monopoly powers put into the hands of the code authorities, and what part to other wholly distinct features of the wide range of activities that Franklin Roosevelt set in motion. This we can say. He would be a rash man who would argue from events in the United States that monopolistic restriction is the key to unlock the treasure house of plenty.

§ 7. *More Recent Changes.* Since 1936, largely as a consequence of improved trade conditions, there has been renewed interest in the depredations of monopolies and of their control.   Under earlier Administrations enforcement had varied considerably from time to time. It has been said[1] that

practically, under the Harding, Coolidge and Hoover administrations industry enjoyed, to all intents and purposes, a moratorium from the Sherman Act, and, through the more or less effective trade associations which were developed in most of our industries, competition was, to a very considerable extent, controlled. The Department of Justice acted with great restraint and intelligence, and only enforced the Sherman Act against those industries who violated the laws in a flagrant and unreasonable manner.

The best of legislation requires both zeal and funds to make it effective.   The standards of the 1930's have thus been described :[2]

The routine disposal of cases of " unfair methods of competition " by the Federal Trade Commission without

---

[1] By a leading cost accountant in 1934, quoted by P. T. Homan. *Notes on the Anti-Trust Law Policy, Quarterly Journal of Economics,* November 1939.

[2] Homan, *loc. cit.* ; the whole article deserves attention.

effective follow-up ; the selection of a few cases for prosecution by the Department of Justice under the Sherman Act without effective follow-up ; the stagnant disuse of the investigatory powers of the Federal Trade Commission ; the widespread and sometimes notorious violations of the Sherman Act ; the existence of varied means of evading the Sherman Act in ways difficult to reach under the terms of the law as judicially rendered ; the absence of an effective intelligence service for turning up cases of violation ; the absence of any body charged with the study of market structures for the purpose of recommending means either of adapting them to the purposes of the law or of excepting them from its provisions ; the absence of financial support, and therefore of administrative staff, commensurate with the effective performance of the enforcement duties.

Even if we may suppose that a reforming zeal has contributed something of acid to the writer's pen, it is very clear that the United States was still far from having solved the problems of monopoly control.

Thus, in 1938, Mr. Roosevelt secured the appointment of a committee to consider the improvement of Anti-Trust procedure, and to examine such problems as mergers, consolidations and acquisitions, financial controls, investment trusts, bank-holding companies, trade associations, patent laws, together with possible means of encouraging competitive enterprise by tax correctives. The final report of that committee is not expected before late in 1940. An interim report recommended the modifications of the patent laws and the prohibition of their use for the establishment of trade restrictions, legislation to prohibit a corporation from acquiring the assets as well as the stock of a competitor, and to provide civil as well as criminal remedies for the enforcement of the Anti-Trust laws.

These and other amendments of the existing legislation will, if brought into effect, do something to stop up the breaches in the system of defences. Their necessity after half a century of experience serves to show how difficult it has proved to create an effective network of legislation which will permit what is desirable in industrial reorganization and exclude what is undesirable. This, indeed, is the core of the problem. The complications of the problem have largely sprung from a changing estimate of what is and is not in the public interest, and of the rival merits in particular cases of excluding monopoly and of permitting and controlling it.

CHAPTER X

THE LAW AND MONOPOLY IN GERMANY

§ 1. *Reasons for the Predominance of the Cartel.* The
policy of the Government towards monopoly in
Germany has been fundamentally different from that
in the United States.[1] Whereas in America the earlier
policy at least can broadly be described as one
of maintaining competition wherever possible, in
Germany it has been one of accepting, and even
encouraging, monopolies while controlling their actions.
This wide difference springs mainly from an initial
difference of the law with regard to contracts in
restraint of trade. In America, we have seen, such
contracts were at first unenforceable, later actually
illegal. In Germany similar contracts were both legal
and enforceable, unless they could be shown to be
either *contra bonos mores* or likely to damage the
public interest. The courts had, however, interpreted
these vague phrases to permit agreements even for the
purpose of raising prices. In one case the Imperial
Supreme Court had declared, in pronouncing on a
common selling agency agreement among producers
of wood-pulp.

---

[1] This chapter is mainly concerned with the attitude of the law
and of legislation to monopoly in pre-Nazi Germany, since it is the
experiences of that period which have most relevance to our own
problems.

" If in any branch of industry the prices of products sink too low and if the thriving operation of the industry is thereby made impossible or endangered, then the crisis which occurs is destructive not only for individuals, but also for the social economy in general, and it is therefore in the interest of the whole community that unduly low prices in a branch of industry shall not permanently exist."

In such an atmosphere monopoly associations could multiply freely. Whereas, in Great Britain and in the United States, monopolies tended to be driven into the form of fusions and giant undertakings on the one hand or gentlemen's agreements on the other, in Germany an association of independent undertakings was of a more stable nature than in those countries, and tended to predominate over other forms of monopoly organization. Trusts, fusions, giant undertakings, and in particular vertical combinations have, it is true, been common in Germany, but until recent years their importance has been subordinate to that of the cartel, the association, that is, of independent undertakings.

These cartels take various forms, which have gradually been complicated since the first experiments in the 'seventies. In Germany many associations are known under the name of cartel which serve purposes quite remote from those of monopolization. They may represent attempts at common action to secure economies from joint purchase, or to establish standards regarding such things as discounts, or periods of credit, or methods of packing. Of the more strictly monopolistic forms we may distinguish those to fix prices, to fix outputs, and to fix geographical areas to be served by individual members.

The earliest monopolies were informal, unregistered associations. Any firm could join or withdraw at will, and since, as we have seen in an earlier chapter, the most profitable position is always to be free of restrictions while others are raising price by restriction. these early associations were constantly breaking up because the form of organization was too loose to make them effective.

An example of a loose association of this kind is afforded by the Rhenish-Westphalian coal industry during the 'seventies. Rapid expansion had led to excess capacity, prices were falling and an informal, unregistered association was formed which included at first some 90 per cent of the industry. The association attempted as a beginning to reduce output by 10 per cent, but the attempt soon failed through the withdrawal of members and the collapse of restriction. Further attempts were made to secure the same end by fixing prices. These too failed for similar reasons. The history of these early cartels in the Westphalian industry is thus curiously similar to that of the Five Counties Scheme and other schemes in the British coal-fields in the years 1928 and 1929, and shows the same weaknesses arising from the inability of such associations to bind their members.

These and similar experiences indicated that some more formal organization was necessary if the cartel was to be permanently effective, and various types were by degrees evolved. One form occasionally adopted was that of the registered association. This method gave the association a legal entity ; it could sue and be sued. But it could not at that time prevent withdrawal for reasonable cause, and its life was limited to two years. Most of the more permanent cartels took, therefore, one of two remaining forms : that of the double company, or that of the limited liability company, pure and simple. In the double-decker form there is an unregistered informal association, consisting of all the independent manufacturers concerned, and a separate company, usually with limited liability, of which the shares are held by the members of the association in accordance with some predetermined scheme, and which performs certain functions (more particularly that of selling the combined output) on behalf of the members. In the limited liability company form of organization there is a similar company, owned by the firms in a particular industry, which makes contracts with them to take over their output and sell it on their behalf, and to divide profits on some agreed basis.

§ 2. *An Example from the Rhenish-Westphalian Coal Cartel.* The first successful example of the double company was the Westphalian Coke Syndicate, formed in 1890. Its methods were copied in 1893 by the Rhenish-Westphalian Coal Syndicate. We will take the organization of the Coal Syndicate as an example to illustrate the problems that we have to consider. The whole organization (the cartel) consisted of an unregistered association, and a limited liability company (the syndicate). The association elected a quota commission and an advisory council. In its capacity, moreover, as a meeting of general shareholders of the syndicate, it appointed the board of directors and the supervisory committee of the limited liability company. Output was determined by applying a percentage of production curtailment to the " quotas "[1] of the individual mines. A certain percentage share in the total quota was allotted to each undertaking at the outset. It could be altered only by the quota commission, which was an impartial arbitrating body. The percentage of curtailment, on the other hand, was determined by the advisory council of the association and varied according to sales.

The cartel had for its own purposes three distinct prices for any grade of coal. First the advisory council established at intervals a standard price for the guidance of the syndicate, below which it would not ordinarily sell that grade of coal. Secondly, the directors of the syndicate established an accounting price, usually above the standard price, at which the syndicate paid for coal bought from members of the association. Thirdly, the directors of the syndicate fixed a selling price for each grade of coal at which it would sell to dealers or consumers. The selling price had to be above the standard price, but might on occasion be below the accounting price.

The member firms made a profit by the excess of the accounting price over their individual costs. The syndicate made a profit by the excess of the selling price over the accounting price. Profits made by the syndicate were divided between the members of the association in proportion to their quotas. Losses were made if the selling prices fell below the accounting prices, and these were met by a charge on the members

[1] It is important to understand that " quota " represents in the case of the German scheme the standard tonnages of the British Act of 1930, and that the word " quota " in the British scheme is equivalent to 100 minus percentage of production curtailment, in the German.

of the association in proportion to their quotas. There have been times when the syndicate charges have been quite substantial.

The cartel depended upon contracts made by each individual member of the association with the syndicate, which bound the members to hand over to the syndicate for sale the whole of their outputs (with certain specified exceptions) ; the syndicate, in its turn, contracted to take all the coal (within certain limits) and to divide the profits. The original contract was for a period of ten years.

At the end of its first period of life, in 1903, the cartel was renewed for a further twelve years. On the whole it had worked successfully, but certain weaknesses had appeared, and these were in some measure remedied. In particular the monopolization of such an important raw material had gravely handicapped firms in coal-using industries which did not possess their own mines, and which paid, therefore, the syndicate's monopoly price, in competition with firms owning their own mines, and thus obtaining coal at cost. This had led to a great increase of vertical combination, particularly in the iron and steel industries. These " mixed " mines succeeded at this stage in extorting peculiarly favourable terms for their adherence to the cartel. They were permitted to supply as much coal as they wished to their own works. They were subject to quota restrictions only on that part which they sold through the syndicate, and were charged for the expenses of the syndicate only in proportion to coal sold through it. Apart from this the chief changes were concerned with the organization for the sale of coal, and with the adjustment of quotas in periods of busy trade.

A scheme so favourable to the " mixed " mines could hardly be expected to survive indefinitely. As the date for further renewal in 1915 drew near the strain increased, and it was further enhanced by the withdrawal from the cartel of the Prussian Government which owned large mines in Westphalia. But by 1915 war had made restriction irrelevant, and when the moment came the cartel would not have been continued, had not the Federal Government compelled it. After the war and during the occupation of the Ruhr the cartel was renewed, under pressure from the Government, for comparatively short periods at a time. Apart from such pressure it would on several occasions almost certainly have collapsed. Gradually a compromise was hammered out, whereby the " mixed " mines were prevented from throwing almost the whole burden of restriction on to the " pure " mines. Under this scheme the quota of a mine was divided into two parts, one part for consumption by an associated undertaking (carefully defined) and the other for sale. The " mixed" mines accepted a restriction on their consumption quota equal to 35 per cent of the restriction imposed on the " pure " mines, and, of course, on the sales quota of the " mixed " mines.

A second problem that had troubled the cartel had been concerned with sales in export markets and in " disputed " territories within Germany, areas, that is, where foreign competition, usually British, had to be met. It had been the custom of the syndicate to fix higher prices for the undisputed territories, and to accept such prices as it could secure in the disputed territories. But not all mines were concerned with these markets, and sales to them substantially increased the syndicate charges. It was finally decided to distinguish between output for the home market and output for the purpose of export. The syndicate would act merely as selling agent in the export market, and costs or losses would be distributed between the firms on the basis of their sales in that market.

The history of the Coal Cartel well illustrates several difficulties common to almost all such associations. It shows first how hard it is to reconcile the very divergent interests of different producers in an industry in which non-homogeneous products are being produced for a variety of different markets. Of the undertakings in the German coal industry some are concerned almost exclusively with the production and sale of coal. Others are more interested in by-products. Others again sell scarcely any coal, employ it solely as a raw material of some finished product, and are interested therefore, not in the difference between cost and selling price, but in the absolute level of cost.

The second problem that emerges is that of holding the members of the cartel to a common policy of action. The diversity of interest implies that almost certainly during any period of contract, the accident of events will favour some members of the cartel more than others. It may even damage certain members over the whole period as compared with their probable fortunes had they not been members at all. But it is more likely that there will be moments when the policy of the cartel will produce results particularly favourable to a given group of members and other moments when it will produce results unfavourable to them. It is not reasonable that members should claim the right to restrain others when circumstances are favourable, and the right themselves to escape restraint when circumstances are unfavourable. Yet such claims are frequently made. Nor must a freely entered contract be annulled, apart from any fundamental change of circumstances, merely because events have not precisely fulfilled expectations. The conditions in which withdrawal from the cartel may be permitted have always been a matter of difficulty and dispute, and more will be said regarding them at a later point.

But even apart from withdrawal during the life of a given agreement, very grave difficulties have arisen at each moment of renewal of the contract. Not only in the case of the coal cartel, but also in many other instances, it has been necessary for the Government to apply the forces of law to secure the prolongation of a cartel. The first example of this was provided by the intervention of the State to continue by law the potash syndicate in 1910. More recently the sanctions of law have been employed not only to continue cartels through a period of dispute and negotiation, and to compel a settlement, but also to force recalcitrant producers to join. Thus in 1924 a number of mines were forced against their will to submit to the control of the Rhenish-Westphalian Cartel. Clearly to compel unwilling parties to enter into some contract is something wholly different from holding to their bond parties to a freely entered contract, and the justification of such a policy is far more difficult to discover. For one of the strongest safeguards of consumers has elsewhere been the willingness of low-cost producers to break away from temporary restriction agreements and thus to prevent a restriction of output sufficient to raise price to the level at which high-cost producers can reap undeserved profits. The possible competition of producers outside the combination was, for example, a most important factor in limiting the monopoly powers of the Newcastle Coal Vend in the early years of the nineteenth century, and the possibility of withdrawal always strengthened the position of the low-cost producers in their bargaining within the organization.

But, above all else, a dispassionate study of the history of the Coal Cartel and of other similar bodies cannot fail to arouse doubts regarding the claims that such bodies afford order and stability. Rather is it true that for the struggles of industrial competition are substituted acute issues of cartel politics. In the absence of Government intervention, these associations exhibit ordinarily periods of temporary tranquillity, interspersed between periods of extreme instability. The comparatively gradual changes of competitive prices may be far less upsetting to industrial calculations than the uncertainties and the catastrophic changes, where suddenly for excessive restriction is substituted a form of competition in which firms are manœuvring to secure, by large immediate output, large participations in some future system of quotas. There can be little doubt that weak and unstable associations of the cartel form are more dangerous than either strong associations or none at all. A government is sometimes, therefore, faced with the alternatives of suppressing and of strengthening them.

§ 3. *The Legal Control of Cartels.* Germany has chosen the alternative of making them stronger. The reasons for this choice were probably several. In part it was because at any moment that seemed the lesser evil. In part it was because the Government preferred to have an organized industry with which to deal for purposes of war. In part it was because order and system in industry came sometimes to be regarded as ends in themselves, contributions to an orderly State, and not merely as possible means to a democratic greatest good of the greatest number. But though the cartels have on the whole found favour with the Government and vigorous apologists among the most able of German economists, they have not throughout been equally popular with the consuming public, nor have they been left uncontrolled. There have been two important inquiries into their operations, the first during the years 1902-5, the second in 1928-9. In both cases while the cartels came in for criticism on minor points, their fundamental acceptance as a basis of industrial organization was not weakened.

Before the war of 1914-18 the limitations on the powers of cartels and of monopolies generally were imposed mainly by the ordinary company law of Germany. In the first place the regulations governing the incorporation of a public limited liability company prevent many of those methods of exploitation of the investing public which were common in the United States and not unknown elsewhere. They make it difficult for such a company to be formed except by individuals or institutions of substance, such as the banks, and do much to eliminate the less responsible type of company promoter. They demand the fullest revelation, supported in some cases by outside auditors, of the value of property acquired in exchange for stock, and the organizers of the company are made personally liable in substantial amounts for the truth of certain statements, which must be published, regarding prices paid and the earnings in preceding years of assets so acquired. Moreover every company must have two independently responsible boards, the first a committee of management, the second, a supervisory committee. No person may serve on both, and both must independently satisfy themselves of the truth of all statements.

These supervisory committees afford in practice a means by which the banks and other large shareholders can exercise a general influence upon policy, and it is through such committees that the banks have in Germany frequently been responsible for the creation of monopoly organizations. In this respect it is interesting to contrast the part played by the banks in Germany and in the United States. In the latter country the predatory escapades of many of the earlier promoters of industrial combinations would have been quite impossible without the sympathetic assistance of powerful banking houses. But the banks themselves were influenced mainly by opportunities for grasping exceptional speculative profits. In Germany the banks have also played a large part. But they have on the whole been concerned rather to prevent wasteful competition of a number of firms that they control through these supervisory committees, and to secure their reward from an increased earning capacity and a consequent steady appreciation of their shares, than to secure windfall profits from the temporary manipulation of the stock market.

Apart from the company law of Germany, restraint upon unscrupulous acts of aggression by combinations or the promoters of combinations against other busi-

nesses was exercised at first through the ordinary civil
code which made anyone who wilfully inflicted an
injury upon another in a manner repugnant to good
morals liable for damages. This provision was reinforced in 1896 and in 1909 by special legislation
designed to prevent unfair competition, more especially
by misrepresentation and corruption, and by making
it easier to secure an injunction against the continuance
of an unfair practice.

The more specific legislation for the control of cartels
belongs almost exclusively to the years since the war
of 1914-18. The first steps were taken during the period
of academic socialism that followed the revolution of
1918. During the years 1919 and 1920 Acts were
passed for the reorganization and national control of
electricity supply, and of coal, potash and iron and steel
production. The Coal Industry Act, together with the
regulations made under it, provided for a completely
unified organization for the national control of the
industry. There were to be eleven regional syndicates,
a National Coal Union and a National Coal Council.
The syndicates were to be fashioned closely according
to the Rhenish-Westphalian model. The Coal Union
was to be a body representative of the several syndicates
and of the labour in the industry. Its function was
to distribute the total output between the different
syndicates, to define their markets, and to co-ordinate
their price policies. The Coal Council was to be a
supervisory body. Of its sixty members, half were to
represent employers and employed in the coal industry,
in equal proportions ; half were to represent the coal-
using industries, the dealers, consumers large and small
and the Government. Its functions were to act as

a court of appeal for complaints regarding actions of the syndicates, to regulate imports and exports, and, by a later amendment, to exercise control through its committee over the prices fixed by the Coal Union and the syndicates.

These bodies would appear never to have worked in quite the way that their sponsors had expected. Many of the functions to be performed by the National Coal Union have either not been performed at all, or have been a matter of negotiation between individual syndicates. The functions of the National Coal Council as regards prices have frequently been exercised in practice through the power of veto of the Minister of Economic Affairs. But the legislation was not entirely a dead letter. The Coal Council came to be regarded as an integral part of the system of control of the coal industry, and its continuance, possibly in a somewhat modified form, was generally regarded as desirable. Both the coal industry and the other industries covered by similar legislation, since they are already subject to control, lie outside the ordinary provisions of the subsequent Cartel Decree.

§ 4. *The Cartel Decree.* The more general legislation came in 1923. The hyper-inflation of that year and the consequent problems of prices had, quite illogically, reinforced the very general demand for a revision of the legal position of cartels which had arisen as the result of their rapid growth in numbers and influence during the preceding years. The Decree against the Abuse of Economic Power was signed by Stresemann on November 2nd, 1923, in the exercise of extraordinary powers granted to him some few weeks earlier. Its subsequent acceptance by the Reichstag gave it the permanent force of law.

The Cartel Decree[1] did three things. It laid down certain requirements regarding cartel contracts; it gave certain powers to the Reich Minister of Economic Affairs; it created a Cartel Court and established certain rules to guide its procedure and decisions.

As regards cartel contracts it required that " all contracts and agreements imposing obligations in respect of the conduct of the production or sale of goods, or of the terms of trading, or of the methods of determining prices, or of the prices to be charged (syndicates, cartels, conventions and similar agreements) shall be in writing." Further clauses gave three weeks of grace for existing unwritten agreements to be reduced to written form (failing which they would become void), and prohibited the reinforcement of these written agreements by any private undertaking, or the inclusion of any clause placing difficulties in the way of application to the Cartel Court. Another clause gave power to the Minister of Economic Affairs, if he regarded some contract as likely to endanger the national economy or the public interest, to call for the production of all agreements and papers concerned with that contract. Thus the whole system of private, informal, gentlemen's agreements was brought to the surface, and the conditions of enforcement or non-enforcement came within the scope of legal control.

[1] English translations of the Decree are to be found in Liefman, *Cartels, Concerns and Trusts*, Appendix I, and Gordon, *The Problem of Trust and Monopoly Control*, Appendix A. Neither is entirely to be trusted in detail. An admirable discussion of it will be found in Seager and Gulick, *op. cit.*, Chapter XXV; see also Levy, *Industrial Germany*, Chapter IX, and Kessler, *The Quarterly Journal of Economics*, August, 1936, pp. 680–93.

There was a second important restriction imposed on cartel contracts. A clause forbade the exaction of penalties, the forfeiture of deposits, or the application of boycotts or other sanctions that might be employed by a cartel, except with the prior consent of the President of the Cartel Court. It expressly laid down that permission to employ these sanctions would be refused if they involved possible injury to the public welfare or unreasonable restriction on the economic freedom of the persons affected. Thus the strongest weapons employed by cartels against recalcitrant members were brought also under control.

The Decree gave powers to the Reich Minister of Economic Affairs (or where proper the Reich Minister of Food and Agriculture), in cases in which a given cartel contract appeared likely to endanger the national economy or the public interest, to do any of three things. He might apply to the Cartel Court for the Court to take action. He might publish an order that any party to the contract could terminate it and withdraw without notice. He might order that copies of all agreements should be sent to him and that they be not enforced until such a copy had been sent. The initiative in dealing with misbehaviour of a cartel was ordinarily entrusted to the Reich Minister. But the State Governments were given the power of making submission to the Reich Minister, and if after a period he should not himself have taken action, he was required to transmit their application to the Cartel Court for its decision.

The most important feature of the Decree was, however, the establishment of the Cartel Court. It was laid down that this should be a part of the general commercial judicature of the Reich, but the decision of the Cartel Court was final and binding on all courts of law and all arbitration tribunals, even in so far as concerned its own competence in a particular case. Moreover, if a case in another court should turn upon an issue which was in the competence of the Cartel Court, that other court was to adjourn its proceedings until the Cartel Court should have given its decision.

The Cartel Court was to consist ordinarily of five members, a President and four Assessors. The President of the Court was to be nominated by the President of the German Reich, and was to possess legal qualifications. Of the four assessors, two were to be properly qualified experts in the issues at stake, drawn from a panel provided by the Minister of Economic Affairs ; one was to be a member of the Federal Commercial Court, nominated by the President of that Court ; the fourth was to be an independent economist, also drawn from a panel, whose function was to represent the general interest of the community. The President could sit without his assessors, but, if he did so, appeal might be lodged to the whole Court within three days of the delivery of a decision given by him alone.

When a case has been brought before the Cartel Court and it has decided that in its view the contract is damaging to the public interest, it has two alternatives open to it. It may declare the contract void in whole, or in part. If it does the latter it must define in what respects the enforceable parts of the contract must be modified because of the excision of the unenforceable parts. It may alternatively issue a general permission to injured parties to terminate the contract without notice. This alternative thus permits it to

R

take the action after hearing a case which the Minister might himself have taken without reference to the Court.

So far we have been concerned with the procedure in cases submitted to the Court by the Minister or by the State Government. A most important, and much criticized, clause gives also to an individual member of a cartel the right for urgent reason to terminate a cartel contract without notice. Urgent reason is defined as including unreasonable restriction on the economic freedom of the party concerned, more especially with regard to production, marketing or price-fixing. It was left to some other party to the restriction to apply within a short period to the Court for a decision as to whether the grounds of withdrawal were sufficient. But the onus of proving that the restriction is unreasonable is on the party thus terminating the contract.

This clause has been criticized as impairing seriously the binding force of cartel agreements. Under other sections, it has been argued, an injured party already possesses the right to be released from a cartel contract, if that contract is contrary to the public interest. If the upholding of cartels is a central principle of German industrial policy, " why permit members who enter into cartel agreements voluntarily to withdraw at will without first securing authority from the governmental agencies provided for that purpose ? "[1] The section may be justified in part because that membership is now not in all cases voluntary, in part because it is this section alone which gives an aggrieved member of a cartel the right to secure the intervention of the

[1] See Seager and Gulick, *op. cit.*, pp. 591–4.

Court directly, and not indirectly through setting in motion the political machine.

In practice it is this section which, measured by the number of cases coming before the Cartel Court, has been the most useful. Nor have events entirely justified the gloomy anticipations of its critics. The decisions of the Court have established a series of precedents which enable the parties to a contract to judge fairly accurately the probable line that the Court will take in any case.[1] And generally speaking the Court has tended to uphold cartel contracts, and to refuse permission to withdraw, unless the circumstances have been changed in some material respect by the actions of the cartel itself since the contract was made. Ground for withdrawal is not ordinarily held to exist, if the factors complained of were already in operation when the contract was made, or if, within the cartel's own constitution, machinery for adjustment exists. Nor can a member withdraw merely because of a disagreement with regard to cartel policy, or because of a new grouping of parties within the cartel.

The main grounds that have been regarded as sufficient to justify permission to withdraw have been, first, such a growth of outside competition, or such a decrease of the percentage of output controlled by the cartel that it has become ineffective ; second, mergers within the cartel itself which have substantially altered the balance of power in the cartel and have brought it under the domination of a particular concern or group. This latter ground is not always held to be sufficient, if increased representation has

[1] See Michels, *Cartels, Combines and Trusts*, p. 54, and Warriner *Combines and Rationalization in Germany*, pp. 137–40.

been offered to the minority affected. Other principal grounds for withdrawal that have been accepted are, third, fundamental changes in the policy of the cartel, and, fourth, a failure of the cartel to adapt itself to changed conditions. Finally, if a member's economic existence is really threatened the general rules governing withdrawal may be relaxed.

This clause was, unfortunately, so drafted originally as to make damage to the restricted party the main, and probably the sole criterion, on which withdrawal could be justified. Some interpreters have held that the public interest, considered throughout the Decree, applied here also. But the present view would appear to be[1] that consideration of the public interest is excluded, and serious damage to the complainant contracting firm must be proved. Such a view necessarily emasculates the clause as a protection to the consumer.

It is not easy to estimate the effect of the Cartel Decree. The Government has not employed its powers to the serious detriment of existing monopolies. The Minister has made free use of a permission granted by the Decree to invoke first the voluntary organizations for arbitration. There have been no cases that have caught the public attention as did the early prosecutions under the Sherman Act. It must not, however, be inferred from this that the Decree has been wholly without effect. The threat of action directly by the Minister, or indirectly through the invocation of the Court, has been an active deterrent to certain misuses of economic power. But it is important to remember how limited is the scope of the Decree.

[1] See Kessler, *op. cit.*, pp. 688–9.

Even the comparatively wide definition of a cartel
embodied in it, limits its range of control to associations of independent units.   The degree of dependence
which makes a group of such units a trust rather than
a cartel is an academic issue which has been widely
debated.   Its immediate relevance is not great, for no
trust has reached such dimensions that it embodies
the whole membership of a cartel.   But the German
law in its present form controls trusts and large
vertically integrated concerns scarcely at all.   It has
been argued that this greater restriction on the freedom
of associations of firms has been a stimulus to the
creation of trusts.   This is perhaps only partially
true, since even the trust will almost certainly be a
member of a cartel, and subject to that extent to the
jurisdiction of the Court.   But it cannot be denied that
the growth of large trusts and concerns, stimulated by
the post-War inflation, has proceeded rapidly until
they have come to play a very large and increasingly
important part in German industrial organization.

§ 5.   *The Control over Trusts and Concerns.*   These
trusts are controlled only in so far as the wider control
over the cartels of their industries incidentally provides.   A general raising of prices by the whole cartel
at the instigation of an increasingly dominant concern
may, however, meet resistance from the Minister and
the threat of action under one or other of his various
powers.   In 1925 when it was generally held that the
regulated prices of cartels were excessive in the changed
situation of the time, the Minister threatened proceedings before the Cartel Court, and, if necessary, the
amendment of the Decree.   The powers granted have

been used in one case at least to dissolve a monopolistically inclined cartel.[1] In other cases[2] the Minister
has used the powers requiring production of all
agreements where an unreasonable increase of prices
was suspected. But the threat of action has often
been efficacious without actual proceedings, and the
effective control over prices cannot be measured by the
cases brought to court.

There are certain other provisions of the Decree
which give some added measure of protection against
the threat of monopolization by large integrated
concerns. The section which prohibits the use of the
weapon of boycott and similar sanctions, except with
permission of the President of the Court, naturally
makes impossible their use purely as a weapon of
offence in the struggle of monopolistic competition, and
thus affords a partial parallel to the Clayton Act.
Moreover, the section which gives power to the Cartel
Court on the motion of the Reich Minister to permit
parties to a contract to withdraw from it if the conditions of trading or methods of price-fixing " endanger
the national economy or the public interest " is so
drawn as to include not only the contracts of cartels,
but also the contracts of trusts, interest-groups and
similar combinations with their customers. But the
control does not in general go further than making the
re-creation of competition easy, if anyone is prepared
to compete with the giant concern. Both public and
legal opinion has demanded further action. But it is
doubtful if that can be best be provided by an extension
of the Decree. The failures to control trusts, and the

[1] A Cartel of Berlin Asphalt Factories, see Liefman, *op. cit.*,
p. 170.　　　　　　　　[2] E.g. the Steel Cartel.

facilities for their creation and domination, spring mainly from defects of the Company Law, and it is a reinforcement of that, responsible critics have suggested, that is most urgently required.

§ 6. *Criticism and Extensions of the Cartel Decree.* The Decree as originally drafted was, we have seen, an emergency measure inspired rather by immediate political necessities than by prolonged and careful study. The cartel problem and the Decree itself have since been re-examined both officially, by an extremely thorough and searching Committee of Inquiry, and unofficially by legal and economic associations. The Court has been criticized by lawyers as unnecessary, and it has been suggested that those of its functions which are truly required would be better entrusted to the ordinary courts. That view is, I think, misconceived. It is of the essence of control over monopolies that decisions call, not for the precise interpretation of general rules, but for the exercise of judgment. Critics have pointed to the impossibility of defining the meaning of endangering the " national economy or the public interest."[1] It is precisely because these things cannot be defined that a purely legal court is unsuited to these tasks. Cabinet ministers, parliamentary bodies, local authorities are compelled hourly to make decisions which involved an estimate of public welfare. They do so by exercising judgment and not by interpreting statutes. Since the exercise of judgment is an essential part of the duties of such a court, it is necessary that it should in part be governed by other forms of procedure and other habits of mind

[1] Gesamtwirtschaft oder Gemeinwohl.

than those of the purely legal, though built on the
solid foundation of respect for law and contract. It
would be idle to suggest that the history of the Cartel
Court has shown hitherto that consideration of the
public interest and power to exercise judgment in its
preservation that its critics would demand. But that
is not ground for substituting a system even less likely
to provide it.

Partly in the light of these discussions, but more
immediately as a consequence of the force of circumstances, the Decree has been amended or reinforced
by subsequent legislation in several important respects.
In 1933 additional powers were given to the Minister
of Economic Affairs, almost all directed to increasing
the possible strength of cartels to meet the circumstances of a depression. The Minister could order the
federation of separate enterprises into an existing cartel,
or into one to be created for the purpose. He could
prohibit an increase in the number of competing firms
in an industry or an extension of the capacity of
existing firms.

The power to federate units into a cartel has been
used both for the purpose of bringing in recalcitrant
outsiders, and for the cartellization of such industries
as the cigarette, soap, glass, cement and printing trades.
The power to refuse admission to an industry is more
serious. A Cartel Court decision had refused to permit
the exclusion from a cartel of new entrants prepared
to subject themselves to the ordinary conditions of
membership. Thus the first condition of effective
monopoly, the power to prevent entry into a trade,
was threatened. Apart from other opportunities[1] of

---

[1] Such as have been discussed above, Chapter III.

discouraging new firms, it might therefore be expected that these would increase so long as the prices fixed by the cartel yielded a more than normal return on the capital invested, when that capital was used with the intensity permitted by the quota restrictions. The final result would be a normal return on a volume of capital excessive to the real needs of the industry.[1] Monopoly returns could only be restored by some such action as the German Government was induced to take. The political reasons of action were more complex, and the existence of depression was held to justify action which on long period grounds was less obviously expedient. This power of preventing expansion has been used, to quote but a few examples, in the industries producing textiles, radio, paper, cellulose, and steel tubes.

The powers of cartels have been restricted also during recent years by the system of price control instituted during the financial crisis of 1931, and since continued and extended. In 1933 cartels were forbidden to fix minimum prices for foodstuffs without the approval of the controlling authorities, and in 1934 this was extended gradually to all necessaries, and finally to all goods and services other than those already under the control of other departments. In the early stages an official price-controller was appointed, but from the middle of 1935 his functions were taken over by the relevant departments in the Ministries of economic affairs and agriculture.

" The methods of control have included the laying down of minimum, standard or maximum prices, profits and

---

[1] This was in fact the history of the Newcastle Coal Vend.

discounts, coupled with a strict control of turnover by volume, the cancellation of uneconomic price agreements, and measures to protect the consumer such as compulsory marking of prices, packing regulations and explanatory communications to the press by the control departments."[1]

But these later restrictions, though interesting as an indication of the direction in which experience had shown that modification was necessary, represent rather the transition from liberal to corporative economics than a pure development of the former. To explore the full ramifications of the relation of the cartels to the Corporative State would not be relevant to our present purpose of deriving such lessons as we may from German experience for employment in our own, fundamentally liberal, economy. The control of industry generally, and of the cartels indirectly as contributing to the ordered framework of industry, has become a function of the Estate of Industry and Trade.[2] Industry proper, as distinct from handicrafts, trade, banking and so on, is divided into six main groups, according to a broad classification of type, and these into trade groups, roughly corresponding with a wide definition of an industry, and these trade groups again into more specialized sections and sub-sections. These national groups are subdivided into local groups in the different industrial regions. Every firm must register as a member of its local and functional organization. Every unit in this organization has a leader appointed from above, who represents his unit

---

[1] Department of Overseas Trade, *Economic Conditions in Germany* to March 1936. Report by E. C. Donaldson Rawlins, p. 148.
[2] *Organisation der Gewerblichen Wirtschaft.* See D.O.T. Report; *op. cit.*, pp. 1–5 and 82–97.

in all vital matters. The leader is assisted by an advisory council, and is subject to dismissal by the authority that appointed him if he fails, at an annual meeting of members of the unit, to secure a vote of confidence.

Into this system it is by no means clear how the cartels will ultimately fit.

" Germany, the original home of the cartel idea," wrote a leading German city editor early in 1936,[1] " with its three thousand or so cartels and syndicates, including the oldest and most refined varieties, has entered a fresh phase of development, and is at the moment in a stage of compromise and transition.   We are to-day swaying between the policy of self-administration through cartels and the policy of comprehensive market regulations by Government, between liberalism and socialism in industrial affairs, between partial and total market control, between voluntary agreements and compulsory regulations, between State control of a general type and the establishment of a full dress State market regulation administrative system."

[1] Quoted by D.O.T. Report, *op. cit.*, p. 85.

CHAPTER XI

THE LAW AND MONOPOLY IN GREAT BRITAIN

§ 1. *Restriction on the Grant of Monopoly.* In discussing the relation of the Government and the law to monopolies in Great Britain it is convenient to start by making a distinction between the conditions, on the one hand, in which monopolies may or may not be granted to individuals and the methods of control, on the other, that are exercised over monopolies that have come into existence, or the steps taken to prevent them coming into existence.

Let us consider first the question of the granting of monopolies. It should be emphasised that the original attitude of the English common law was in general anti-monopolistic. Grants of monopolies, where they were made, were exceptions to this general principle, made by the Crown in virtue of its role as " arbiter of commerce." But, in the exercise of that function, the privilege of sole manufacture, or of sole importation, or of sole dealing in some particular commodity, was given to individual private persons at least from the time of Edward III. Such patents were usually granted in order to encourage the development of some new trade, or the introduction into Great Britain of some industry practised abroad. In this sense they were to be compared to the patents of monopoly granted now to inventors and were generally regarded as being in the public interest. This policy was vigorously followed by the Tudors, at first with the original intention of developing new industries ; but later under Elizabeth and James I patents came to be granted to persons who had done nothing to improve technique or to establish new trades. In 1602 the grant of a monopoly in the manufacture, import and sale of playing-cards was challenged before the courts. The grant was held illegal and void on the ground that it was a monopoly and against the common law, and for a time such grants of monopolies ceased. But James I revived the practice by making illegal grants and in 1624 Parliament finally passed the Statute of Monopolies.

This statute declared that all monopolies were contrary to the laws of the realm and so, apart from certain exceptions, chiefly in favour of chartered companies and inventors of new appliances, were void. This Act was evaded, sometimes openly, sometimes by the device of the creation of chartered companies, by the later Stuarts ; but after the passing of the Bill of Rights in 1689 the claims of the Crown to grant monopolies without reference to Parliament were finally renounced, and from that time monopolies have been granted only with parliamentary approval. Certain categories of monopoly, however, of which patents and copyrights form the chief examples, have been recognized as being in the public interest, and have been regularly granted, without reference to parliament in every case, subject to the fulfilment of certain registered conditions,

Parliament has used its power more sparingly. It has granted special monopolies on occasions to such bodies as the Bank of England, in exchange for services or concessions of value. It has created monopolies in the case of such organizations as those for railway transport, or the provision of gas, electricity or water, which need to derive compulsory powers from individual Acts of Parliament or from individual orders under a general Act, by granting as a rule the necessary powers of eminent domain to no more than one supplier within a given area. Until recently such grants as these have almost exhausted the total of monopolies conferred by Parliament. But in recent years a new category has appeared. The first example was provided by the Stevenson Rubber Scheme of 1922. That was followed by the Coal Mines Act of 1930 and the Agricultural Marketing Act of 1933. The motive for the creation of monopoly was in these cases neither the receipt of some valuable consideration, nor the limitation of the grant of eminent domain to the least number of private or public bodies, but a belief that monopoly would contribute in some sense to the securing of business stability.

§ 2. *Price Control of Parliamentary Monopolies.* In almost all the earlier instances in which Parliament created a monopoly, it made some provision for the control of prices to be charged. In the case of the railways, under the Act of 1844 the companies were obliged to provide at least one daily " parliamentary " train at the fare of a penny a mile, and under the Act of 1921 each railway was further given a limited " standard revenue." If with a given scale of charges a railway earns more than its "standard revenue," the charges must be so reduced as to absorb 80 per cent of the surplus.

In the case of gas companies the Act governing a particular undertaking fixes, in many instances, a standard price per thousand cubic feet and permits a certain increase of dividend to correspond to a given reduction of price below the standard price. Similar sliding scales relating prices to profits were created also for electricity supply companies. But these in almost all cases are now a dead letter, since technical improvements have so far reduced costs below the standard price as to make it wholly inoperative. The McGowan Committee of 1936 has recommended the revision of the scales so as to adapt them to present conditions.

The exceptions to the general rule that where the Government establishes a monopoly, it regulates it also, are to be discovered almost entirely in the group of new monopolies created during the last decade. Under the Coal Mines Act every producer of coal must submit to the limitation of his output and the fixing of the price by a body responsible to the owners of coal mines, but to no wider authority. Under the Agricultural Marketing Act the prices of hops, milk, potatoes and various other products are regulated by marketing boards representative of the industries concerned. The Minister of Agriculture must, it is true, confirm their prices, and he must give consideration to the views of committees representing consumers. But it may be broadly said that unless the proposals of the marketing boards show a considerable advance on previous prices they are likely to be confirmed.

§ 3. *The Regulation of Private Monopolies.* Let us turn now to consider the regulation of monopolies which do not derive from grants by Parliament but from other artificial or natural limitations. If we cast our eyes back for a moment to much earlier periods, the control over monopolies was far more complete than it is to-day. Consumers were safeguarded against monopoly both by the common law and by a series of statutes. Already before the Conquest there were laws against engrossing, forestalling, regrating. These three closely interwoven offences consisted in attempts to " corner " some product, in the buying up of produce before it reached the market, and in buying in order to resell within a short time at an enhanced price. The series of laws defining these offences begins as early as the time of Edward the Elder in the tenth century. They were extended and amended under Henry III and Edward VI. In effect it was sought not only to repress serious attempts to establish monopolies, but also to secure that transactions were concentrated in the market. The motive was probably in part at least the obtaining of the market dues, but it had the effect, as we should now put it, of making the market more perfect by limiting it in space and time. It is interesting to find similar legislation being enacted for similar reasons in Kenya and Uganda to-day.

These laws were continued and further amended through Tudor and Stuart times down to the middle of the eighteenth century. By then the rapidly changing economic system, with improved facilities for transport, rendered them in their original form not merely obsolete but positively harmful. A committee appointed to consider them in 1767 reported that they " by preventing the circulation of and free trade in corn and other provisions had been the means of raising the price thereof in many parts of the Kingdom." Adam Smith, nine years later in *The Wealth of Nations*, added his famous tirade of condemnation : " The popular fear of engrossing and forestalling may be compared to the popular terrors and suspicions of witchcraft. The unfortunate wretches accused of this latter crime were not more innocent of the misfortunes imputed to them, than those who have been accused of the former." But to-day we should say, I think, that in part at least the popular fears were justified and the wholesale condemnation of these laws exaggerated.

The laws as they stood unquestionably created an undesirable obstacle to the performance of certain necessary economic functions. It is desirable that if a crop is short speculators should buy now, raise the price for immediate consumption, spread the stocks that will be available over the whole period until the shortage can be remedied, and at the same time provide an immediate incentive to redress the shortage. It is desirable that, where shortages or gluts are local, speculators shall buy in the overstocked and sell in the understocked market. Examples of such desirable functions can be further multiplied and should, of course, be permitted. But monopoly is not an illusory evil, and the repeal of the statutes in 1772 almost certainly went too far. The rapid improvement of means of transport was, it is true, helping to break down local monopolies. But the scale and form of monopolies were quickly adapted to the new circumstances, and the general widening of the possible field of competition proved an insufficient safeguard.

s

The repeal of these laws in 1772 breached the
defences, but did not immediately destroy them.
Distinguished lawyers, including the Lord Chief
Justice, held that prosecution was still possible under
the common law, and in one or two cases convictions
were upheld. But the doubt was so great that penalties
were nominal, prosecutions virtually ceased, and even
as a deterrent the law became ineffective. Finally, in
1844, by that perversity of fate which permits the
counsels of economists to prevail half a century after
the circumstances in which they were offered have
passed away, the doctrines of Adam Smith triumphed
and an Act was passed abolishing entirely the offences
of engrossing, forestalling and regrating.

§ 4. *Restraint of Trade.* The repeal of these statutes
threw the chief onus of defence on to a branch of the
law which had hitherto been wholly subsidiary. Contracts in restraint of trade had in general been held to
be void as contributing to the creation of monopoly, and
as being thus contrary to public policy. But from
Elizabethan times, at least, certain exceptions had been
recognized. If a man sold a business or a partnership
to another, its value would clearly depend upon the
amount of the goodwill that was being transferred. If
the vendor agreed not to compete, and thus attract to
himself again that part of the goodwill which was
purely personal, the value of the property sold would
be enhanced. Thus if an owner was to be in a position
to realize the full value of his own property, he had to
be in a position to restrain himself voluntarily from
competition. But if, having restrained himself in this
way, he were to break his undertaking, the purchaser

would have good grounds of objection. Thus the courts came to regard some such restraints as good and enforceable. But it was always held that the restraint must not be greater than was necessary to protect the property transferred, and that the public interest demanded that a man should not be wholly precluded from employing his particular skill to maintain himself. Thus for a restraint to be good there had to be some consideration for which it was imposed, and it had to be limited in space and also in time. For no purchaser could claim the right to be perpetually exempted from competition.

So long as production remained on a small scale, no serious difficulties were involved. A restraint from practising a trade within ten or twenty miles of the relevant town sufficed to protect the purchaser. But as the scale of industry grew, the necessary restraint grew also, until the public interest that a restraint must be limited came into conflict with the public interest that a man who has sold the intangible property involved in goodwill must not be allowed to detract from it by competition. The decisions of the courts soon made it clear that the latter interest was to prevail over the former, and where a general restraint was necessary, it would now ordinarily be held to be enforceable. The modern rule was approved by the House of Lords in the famous case of *Nordenfelt* v. *Maxim Nordenfelt*.

Another group of contracts in restraint of trade is that concerned with agreements to fix minimum prices, to divide the market, to pool profits, to assign contracts and refrain from undercutting, and so on. In general such contracts are not illegal, but they are unenforceable. It is not illegal for you and me to make a contract not to charge less than a certain price for some service. But if you decide that you do not wish to abide by your contract, the courts will not assist me in forcing you to do so. The consumers, who are obliged by our agreement to pay more for this service, cannot proceed against us for having made a contract in restraint of trade, unless they can show that we have done them some damage for which, even apart from the existence of the contract, they could have proceeded against us. But recent cases have shown that the limits of the grounds for such proceedings are most debatable. If, in the fulfilment of our agreement, we have injured others by the use of means which are in themselves unlawful (and which would, therefore, give ground for action against either of us individually) we are clearly liable. We are legally liable if we injure others by threats of unlawful action. But are we liable if we combine to injure others, but neither use, nor threaten to use, unlawful means ? Does the element of combination ever make unlawful what otherwise would be lawful ?

On this question English law is still in a state of indecision. A distinguished exponent of the law of tort has recently refused to commit himself to more than the following two propositions : first, that a combination of two or more persons *solely* to injure another in his trade is an actionable conspiracy if it results in damage to him ; second, that it is doubtful whether a combination of two or more persons to injure another person by conduct, other than that included under the first heading, which would apart from combination be lawful, is an actionable conspiracy. If it is, it is so only on the conditions that it both causes damage to the plaintiff and is also a crime.[1]

The first proposition is very unlikely to fit any circumstances that will arise in practice. The motives of trade " conspirators " will almost always be mixed. The second proposition, even apart from the serious doubt that it embodies, involves the importation into the definition of the *tort* of conspiracy of the elements of the *crime* of conspiracy. That crime has been notoriously flexible and undefined, and the limits of its application to individual and commercial situations have been much affected by legislation.

This simple principle that contracts in restraint of trade will not be enforced has unfortunately become hedged about by a number of exceptions which to the lay mind are extremely perplexing. The courts have been prepared to enforce contracts if some restraint has been shown to be necessary in order to protect property and capital and to prevent loss of employment. But the contract must be shown to be reasonable and made for some genuine consideration. Thus, in a famous case decided in 1815, an agreement between two competing coach-owners on the London-Edinburgh road not to run in competition with each other was held to be enforceable, as a " convenient mode of arranging two concerns which might otherwise ruin each other." Pooling agreements between railways, and a scheme for the division of work and the maintenance of prices by a group of stevedoring firms have similarly been held to be enforceable. In one of the railway cases the

[1] See Professor Winfield, *Law of Tort* (1937), Chap. XVII ; the leading cases are, *Mogul Steamship Co.* v. *McGregor, Gow & Co.* [1892] A.C. 25 ; *Allen* v. *Flood* [1898] A.C. 1 ; *Quinn* v. *Leathem* [1901] A.C. 495 ; *Sorrell* v. *Smith* [1925] A.C. 700

decision was justified on the grounds that " it is a mistaken notion that the public is benefited by pitting two railways against each other until one is ruined, the result being at last to raise the fares to the highest possible standard."

There is a third type of contract in restraint of trade that is relevant to our problem, the contract made between seller and buyer restricting the freedom of the latter with regard to terms of re-sale or to conditions of use. An example of such restriction is provided by the very common agreement between manufacturers and merchants requiring the merchant to charge a minimum wholesale price and to insist on a minimum retail price. Such contracts have been justified on the ground that they are necessary to prevent goods being used temporarily as unprofitable " loss-leaders " to attract customers into a shop where they may be induced to make other purchases. Such use drives other retailers to abandon the effort to sell the goods, or to cut price in turn. As a leading line the goods are no longer efficacious. As an ordinary line they are not sufficiently profitable to be pushed. Contracts of this type have been held by the courts to be enforceable.

" A manufacturer or merchant may refuse to sell his goods to anyone who wishes to buy them, or he may sell them on such conditions as he thinks fit to impose. If the buyer of goods who has acquired goods subject to terms or conditions subsequently deals with them in a manner contrary to the terms of his agreement he commits a breach of his contract with the seller, and the seller has a right of action against him."[1]

Such contracts may in particular circumstances be

[1] Report of Committee on Restraint of Trade, p. 6.

justified. But the power to impose contracts requiring conditions of re-sale has on occasion been misused, or has undesirably facilitated the establishment of monopoly. It has been vigorously opposed by the Co-operative Societies, since some (but by no means all) manufacturers of branded goods, sold ordinarily under price-maintenance agreements, have refused to supply the Societies on the ground that the subsequent dividend implies sale below the maintained price. The Committee on Restraint of Trade was unwilling to accept the Co-operative Societies' recommendation that traders should be prohibited by law from refusing to sell goods except where the solvency of the buyer is doubtful or the manufacturer owns or is owned by the selling units. The Committee hesitated to redress a real grievance by imposing on the freedom of individuals to select their customers a restriction which they thought generally undesirable. Such restrictions are, however, already imposed on certain, usually mono-polistic, undertakings, such as common carriers, public utilities and innkeepers, and differential treatment of undertakings so large as to approach monopoly is not evidently impolitic. It must, however, be remembered that the Co-operative Societies have a means of escape within their own control. If they agree not to reckon the expenditure on certain lines for purposes of individual dividends the grounds for refusal of supply are removed. And the profits made will nevertheless contribute to the raising of the general level of dividend that can be paid as the result of their whole trading.

Similar contracts restraining the freedom of buyers have been made a means of " whole line forcing." Of these the best-known instance is that of the contracts between the United Shoe Machinery Company and lessees of its machinery, which required the lessees not to use any machinery that they had not leased from the Company. This agreement was held in this country to be enforceable. There has, however, remained a sequence of cases in which restraints have been held unenforceable. The dividing line where public interest in enforcement has been separated from the public interest in unenforceability has become to the layman so blurred as to be indistinguishable and almost incomprehensible. But this much may be said in general terms. When considering the public interest the courts have come in recent years to measure it more by the interest that the sanctity of contracts should be upheld and property preserved, than by the interest that restraints which might conceivably lead to the raising of prices should be made difficult of enforcement. The reason for this is in part at least that the evidence on which the court might decide what is or is not the public interest is seldom available to it—by law or in fact. The courts have been brought, or have brought themselves into the anomalous situation that they cannot adequately consider, as they were enjoined to by the Maxim-Nordenfelt decision, the public interest, as well as the interests of the parties, in their adjudications upon contracts in restraint of trade. Nor indeed is the mechanism of the law-court well adapted to the balancing of opposing imponderables. Argument from precedent or principles is here inconclusive. Policy and judgment must play a part. This is indeed the justification for the creation of such special courts as we have seen to exist both in Germany (the Cartel Court), and in the United States (The Federal Trade

Commission), in which other outlooks and judgments are added to those of the lawyer. One of the principal recommendations of the Committee on Trusts which reported in 1919 was that a similar body should be created here with powers analogous to those of the Federal Trade Commission.

From this examination of the law with regard to restraint of trade we are driven, I think, to one inescapable conclusion. The desuetude of the law relating to monopoly and the repeal of the criminal laws against allied practices have imposed upon the law of contract and tort tasks which it is in no way fitted to bear. Protection against monopoly by the creation of disabilities at law for those who may be attempting to achieve it can at best be but occasionally effective. For in that majority of instances where the parties do not fall out, no control is exercised. It is, moreover, almost insuperably difficult to make the disabilities sufficient without allowing undesirable channels of escape from less harmful contracts. "If the monopoly established by the appellants and their mode of carrying on their business be as oppressive as is alleged . . ." said the Judicial Committee of the Privy Council,[1] "then the evil, if it exists, may be capable of cure by legislation or by competition, but not . . . by litigation."

§ 5. *The Extent and Gravity of the Problem in Great Britain.* Our attitude to the question whether we desire to see new legislation to strengthen the powers of the courts in dealing with monopolistic attempts to raise prices must depend, first, upon how serious we judge the problem of monopoly to be, and second, upon how

[1] *United Shoe Machinery Company of Canada* v. *Brunet.*

efficacious, or how desirable, we think alternative methods of meeting the situation.

The second of the questions will be postponed to the next chapter. The answer to the first we must attempt here. But to assess how serious is the problem of monopoly is most difficult. On the one hand we must admit that, as compared with the problems created by monopolies in the United States during the last four decades before 1914, ours have been less virulent and less formidable. Our comparative immunity from the worst extravagances has been attributed to various causes, amongst which the maintenance until recently of free trade, the possession of a rigorous and uniform company law administered under a unitary government, the absence of natural monopolies of materials, are probably the most significant. On the other hand, the Report of the Committee on Trusts of 1919 and the many valuable investigations into the extent and effects of monopolies in this country by such writers as Levy, Macrosty, Carter, Rees, Lucas and Fitzgerald can leave no reader under the illusion that monopolies are but occasional exceptions to a general rule of competition. Any broad judgment of the influence of monopolies must in any case be derived largely from personal impressions obtained from a wide study of the facts. We can probably do no better than to call to our aid the impression formed by Professor Hilton, who as secretary to the Committee on Trusts enjoyed an almost unparalleled opportunity of examining the evidence, and contributed an invaluable memorandum to the report.

" As to the extent to which concerted control has ousted competition as a ruling factor in the determination of price and output, and in the evolution of trade and industry, it is impossible to speak with any exactitude. Associations concerned with the regulation of price or output, or both, are to be found in almost every branch of British industry. Their number cannot be computed, for many are not registered either as companies or trade unions, and some are purposely carried on as secretly as possible. It may be taken, however, that there are considerably more than five hundred associations, all exerting a substantial influence on the course of industry and price, in being at the present time in the United Kingdom. The most painstaking inquiry yet undertaken into combination in any section of British industry is that made in respect of building materials, and the conclusion there reached was that 25 per cent of the materials that go to the building of an average house are subject to full control and 33 per cent are partially controlled. If particular industries in which combination has made most headway be taken it transpires that in innumerable lines of manufacture anything from 80 to 100 per cent of the whole national output of the articles concerned is either in the hands of one dominant consolidation or of manufacturers grouped together for purposes of price and other control in a trade association. It would, however, be fallacious to take these latter as typical of the whole range of industry. There are many industries, trades and services, great as well as small, in which combination has made hardly any headway, and competition is still the determining factor in the fixing of price."

He then quotes shipbuilding as an example of an industry in which competition was then always keen, and continues :

" Other industries and trades are to be found in which the rival manufacturers or traders are hardly on speaking terms, much less at that stage of mutual confidence which permits concerted regulation of the trade. These extremes of competition are to be set against the extremes of combi-

nation in forming any estimate of the relative value of the
two factors over the trade and industry of the country
as a whole. That relation cannot be expressed in figures ;
it must suffice to say that competition is no longer a
reliable regulator of prices over a very considerable field."

That estimate, we must remember, applied to 1919.
Since then there have been considerable changes.
Those three strongholds of Victorian small-scale competitive industry, coal, cotton and agriculture, have
all been brought into the field of semi-monopolistic
regulation. The shipbuilding industry, which Professor
Hilton quoted, has been the scene of a unique experiment in the co-operative scrapping of redundant building berths to scale capacity down to peace-time demand.
The regulation of road transport has limited the freedom of competition in passenger and goods transport.
In the wider sphere of general industry combination has
advanced rather than receded. The great organization
which dominates the chemical industries came into
existence only in 1926. In the heavy industries concentration and co-operation have gone at least a stage
farther.

It has been shown, moreover, in Chapter II, that
where competition is limited to a small number of
units, in the absence of destructive competition aimed
at achieving monopoly, a price not widely different
from that of monopoly may rule. The growth of the
scale of productive units has in recent years been such
as to bring almost the majority of industries into a
condition in which they are dominated by a few large
firms. Morris, Austin and Ford : Cadbury and
Rowntree : the Imperial Tobacco Company and
Carreras : the Dunlop Rubber Company dominate

their several industries, not perhaps to the extent of monopoly, certainly in most cases not to the extent of conscious monopoly, but so as to render the fixing of price a matter of policy rather than of acceptance of the inevitable. The same process of concentration has reduced the number of competitors and increased the dangers of monopoly in many more local trades and services.

But it would not be reasonable to suggest that the whole trend of the last twenty years has been toward the strengthening of monopolies. Scientific invention, geological survey, industrial and agricultural experiment have broken down many of the earlier monopolies based upon natural scarcities or patented processes. The nitrates of Chile, for example, the copper of North America, the transport of passengers by rail have lost their hold on their respective markets with the invention of synthetic fertilizers, with the exploitation of copper in Chile, Peru, Katanga and Northern Rhodesia, and with the development of the cheap motor car. Moreover, the possible field of expenditure has been so widened that apparent monopolies may, because of indirect competition, possess but little power to raise prices, and the existence of a trade association may for that reason be no indication of a really effective monopoly.

It is in the field within which substitution is virtually impossible that monopoly becomes a really serious problem. This is the field of necessary food-stuffs, fuel, clothing and housing. The most disquieting feature of the last two decades has been the increasing invasion of this field by monopolistic organizations. In part as the result of a sincere desire to help an impoverished agriculture and to raise standards of agricultural wages, the prices of milk, bacon and meat have been brought under the control of marketing boards, to the gain of the producer, but to the loss of the consumer. In addition to these organizations of primary producers, powerful monopolies or combines have emerged in the trades handling and distributing food-stuffs, in particular in those concerned with the importation of meat, with the milling of flour and the distribution of dairy produce. Coal prices have almost certainly been prevented from falling to levels which competition would have achieved. Housing costs have from time to time been affected by monopolistic prices for materials and components.

The problem of food prices was closely examined by the Royal Commission on Food Prices appointed in 1924. Its members showed some difference of opinion with regard to the urgency of the question. They were not prepared to level any general charge against large undertakings of abusing their powers. They saw economies as well as dangers in amalgamations. Yet in the more conservative majority report they say :

" it seems to us that the time has come to equip some body with power to deal with monopolies, trusts and combines which charge unduly high prices for the services they render to the public or suppress competition merely in order to maintain or expand their profits. We doubt whether public apprehension will be set at rest until the State has armed itself with the necessary powers to deal with anti-social actions by monopolies, trusts and combines."

But the dangers were not, they thought, confined to food prices, and discriminatory legislation against persons in these trades was in their opinion undesirable.

On their recommendation there was created in 1925 a Food Council charged with the duty of watching food prices. It was given no powers of enforcing the disclosure of information, and no sanctions to compel a firm to comply with its directions. It could merely lay before the President of the Board of Trade information where a firm or industry refused to obey its behests. It has from time to time made vigorous protests, more particularly regarding the prices charged for milk and bacon and other products regulated by marketing boards. Amongst other things, it established and sought to enforce a scale relating the price of flour to the price of bread, which despite an attempt by the master bakers to flout it in 1930, has generally been followed. That it has not been able in the absence of statutory powers to achieve much may reasonably be inferred from the words of Mr. W. Graham, then President of the Board of Trade, when introducing the abortive Consumers' Council Bill, which perished in the collapse of the Labour Government in 1931.

" The Food Council have made many important inquiries and to some extent they have made their wishes prevail, but there have been important fields in which they have not succeeded, and I trust that I shall be able to show that non-success has been clearly traceable to the absence in part of the statutory basis and the statutory powers for getting information, and I propose to go beyond that and show that it has been partly due to the absence of sanctions in trying to make fair prices prevail."

During the earlier years that have followed the war of 1914–18, we were protected against the more serious exactions of monopoly, not only by such legal bars as exist, but also by a far more effective barrier. The war itself and the luxuriant growth of the immediate post-war years led many trades into excessive expansion of productive capacity. The decline of the staple industries of the North of England curtailed consumption both of raw materials and of consumable goods. The consequent surplus capacity in a number of trades made prices low, and monopoly price often no more than a long-period normal price. In this situation monopoly often came to be regarded as desirable rather than undesirable. But it was not a situation that would persist indefinitely. Already before 1939 long-period developments had progressively reabsorbed many of the unemployed workers, and simultaneously had eliminated much of the redundant capacity. The weak monopolies of the depression had begun to show themselves to be stronger and more dangerous than we had reckoned. We might be protected in a period of expansion by the breakdown of some of the looser terminable associations. But many of them had now operated for long enough to have established some intangible community of interest and *modus vivendi* so that their collapse could not be a matter of calculation. It was not the wisdom of experience that led us from the Profiteering Act of 1920 to the Agricultural Marketing Act of 1933. It was a change of environment, a change almost certainly less permanent than many at the time supposed, and one which even before the present war was itself being progressively modified.

CHAPTER XII

FUTURE POLICY

§ 1. *Policy cannot be Derived wholly from Economic Arguments.* When we turn from the present to the future, and from what is to what ought to be, we move inevitably from the field of objective fact into the field of subjective judgments. We cannot prove by logic how we ought to act. Logic must build upon assumptions regarding right conduct which we must derive from our ethical or political or religious tenets. And with regard to the question of the maintenance or destruction of monopoly privilege of one kind or another political passions run hottest. We cannot prove by logic, or by economics as a branch of logic, that human welfare will be maximized if the distribution of wealth is made as equal as is possible, however clearly our intuitions may recommend this to us. We cannot prove that there are things of fundamental value to be conserved by maintaining the traditions and structures of our social organization, however passionately we may ourselves believe it. And so we must not expect complete unanimity of opinion as to how the problems of monopoly privilege should be handled.

In these circumstances we can profit more by attempting to understand the alternative motives and

T

policies that are possible, than by establishing one line of action and seeking to prove that it alone can be justified. Let us try then, as objectively and dispassionately as may be, to examine the various alternatives open to us.

§ 2. *A Policy of Inaction.* The first, and by far the simplest, course is to do nothing. We may justify inaction by saying that, though in theory monopoly may appear a most serious evil, in practice the damage that it does is not very great, and is outweighed by those improvements in efficiency which we have seen that it often brings. The evil is not great, it is argued, because the establishment of long-period monopolies is seldom possible, and where possible their strength is inconsiderable. Competition arises not only from identical articles or services, but in most cases also from alternative means of satisfying a not very specific want. Monopoly of one outlet merely diverts demand into alternative outlets, and the monopoly power is rendered negligible. Moreover, it is said, the very existence of monopolies serves to stimulate the development of new sources of supply or of new substitutes or improved methods. Should we have had £40 copper without the earlier extortions of Copper Exporters Incorporated ? Should we have had 6d. rubber without the Stevenson restriction scheme ? Should we have had the present range of artificial manures without the monopoly of Chilean nitrates ?

This argument from technical progress must not, however, be pressed too far. We must remember that a stimulus to invention almost, if not quite, as great is provided by the ordinary processes of competition ;

that losses may be an even greater encouragement to economic invention, in the sense of the development of cheaper ways of doing things, than are exceptional profits ; that it has been the collapse of monopolies, rather than their existence, which has brought technical improvements.

The view that it is best to do nothing drastic to outlaw monopoly, but rather to leave the door open for its encouragement, derives support also from those who would hold that control of the rate of economic change is often necessary. New inventions may bring changes of demand which, while benefiting society as a whole, do great and lasting damage to existing industries and to those supported by them. Both the coal industry and agriculture, in this country, have provided examples of the few being asked to suffer for the benefit of the many. Similar, and far more severe, problems of economic adjustment are facing those African or eastern countries where the exploitation of minerals, or the growth of agricultural products such as rubber or sugar for world markets, has brought them suddenly into contact with western European economic methods. The social and political framework of society is so closely intertwined with the economic structure that there may be, almost certainly are, instances in which it is undesirable that economic changes should be allowed to exert their full disruptive power upon society. In such instances a monopoly may help, as it probably does in the case of the British coal industry to-day, to mitigate the extreme violence of the transition. But it must be remembered that it is a dangerous device. We are screwing down the safety valve to get us out of our difficulties. If we use the opportunity merely to stand still and do nothing, rather than to make the most rapid possible change, the ultimate explosion may be far more violent than the earlier would have been. Monopoly, moreover, while it might assist in easing the transition if suitably administered for that purpose, is directed ordinarily to the immediate private profit of investors, and profit is almost as likely to be secured by more drastic transition as by less. In the case of concentration of output in the process of " rationalization," monopoly has in many instances aggravated the social damage by intense concentration of it in certain districts.

But by far the strongest resistance to drastic action comes from those who would say, if they sought at all to express their motives, that inequality of incomes is inevitable and even desirable in a world in which individuals are born with unequal talents. You must leave the efficient man as well as the inefficient the motive to exert himself to the utmost. The great merit of the capitalist system, it has been said, is that it succeeds in using the nastiest motives of nasty people for the ultimate benefit of society. They would point to the emergence of the problem of incentive in Russia, and the apparently growing inequalities consequent upon the introduction of methods of payment required in the interests of output. But the efficacy of a given incentive depends upon what you possess already. The carrot that would tempt the hungry donkey would stir the replete millionaire to violence of language rather than of action.

Allied to those who seek to restrain action against monopolies from the narrowest and most selfish of reasons we find many whose disinterested concern

with human welfare it is impossible to doubt. There
are many responsible economists who believe that it is
as true now as when Adam Smith, Bentham, Malthus
and Ricardo shaped the framework of economic
analysis, that there is more danger in an excess than
in a deficiency of regulation ; that the reaction against
an over-simplified belief in the economic harmonies
has gone too far, until it is popularly supposed that any
form of organization, however top-heavy or unnecessary, is superior to the absence of visible control ;
that a little less anxiety to introduce the plasticine of
regulation into the clockwork of State would result in
its more regular working ; that a properly and freely
working price system is a necessary condition of the
perfectly operating economic system, with all its
resources employed, and with all resources devoted to
their best possible uses.

For those who hold this view the problem of their
right attitude to monopoly has always been a difficult
one. In the competitive struggle the State has certain
functions to perform. It must keep the ring, and see
that certain rules are observed—the rules, for instance,
requiring contracts to be performed, or the rights of
property to be observed. Is the freedom of the individual to form combinations one of the rights that
the State should maintain, or is combination an
infringement of the rules ? That problem was fought
out, of course, at the beginning of the last century in
connection with the right of workmen to combine in
Unions. When the earlier attitude of restraint of such
combinations gave way later to their permission, it was
difficult not to extend the same freedom of combination
to manufacturers as to workers. But if we look at the

effects of combination, they are disastrous to that economic harmony that competition might be expected to create. The amount of output is no longer that, or even approximately that, at which marginal utility equals marginal disutility. Resources are no longer so distributed that everywhere the marginal product of labour is, within reasonable limits, identical.

And so the *laisser-faire* economist finds himself in a quandary. Is a given rise of prices to be suppressed as an indication of monopoly, or to be permitted as a necessary, but not yet sufficient, inducement to new competition ? If monopolies were all permanent, stable, powerful, the answer might not be difficult. But many short-period monopolies are essentially unstable and impermanent. Allow a sufficient price rise and the motive to combine will often disappear, the bait of easy profits will lead low-cost producers to break away and to expand, new producers will come in, and the monopoly is at a much more satisfactory end than the legal big stick could have achieved. But the gradual changes of the last century have indisputably strengthened monopoly. It can no longer be treated ordinarily as an unfortunate and occasional exception which had best be disregarded in the framing of general policy. Policy must now take full account of its existence.

§ 3. *A Policy of Mitigation.* The line between those who think that no fundamental change should be made, and those who think that something should be done, is naturally ill-defined. A belief in the need for the strengthening and rigorous enforcement of the Company Laws, or the requirement of adequate publicity is compatible with that general attitude to the problem that has already been described. Nor is there unanimity among those who believe that, within the general framework of the capitalist system, effective control of monopoly is desirable and possible. But we may take the recommendations of the Liberal Industrial Inquiry[1] of 1928 as representative of this general attitude, and briefly consider them.

The authors started by drawing attention to the very wide field already covered, exclusively or in part, by the activities of concerns not operated for private profit, or subject to a large measure of public control. Productive undertakings of this nature (including those concerns run by the national and local governments, both directly and through appointed *ad hoc* bodies), parliamentary companies, co-operative societies and charitable societies, such as universities and schools, were employing a capital amounting at that date to about £3,000,000,000, or if we add the roads of the country, about £4,250,000,000. These figures include, however, the parliamentary companies operating railways, tramways, gas, water and electricity under a large measure of parliamentary control. While publicly controlled, it is scarcely accurate to include them in the total of companies not operating for private profit, which is here our immediate concern. The parliamentary companies employed about £1,376,000,000 of the total, leaving a little under £3,000,000,000 as the total we are seeking. This figure has been substantially increased since 1928 by extensions of municipal gas and electricity, of local transport services, and of

---

[1] *Britain's Industrial Future*, 1928, pp. 59–100. See also *The Next Five Years*, 1935, pp. 78–96.

municipal housing. The value of the fixed capital of
Great Britain in 1928, apart from land values, may be
put approximately at £14,000,000,000, so that already
some 20 per cent of the whole was controlled otherwise
than for private profit.

The Liberal Report did not recommend any general
extension of the field of public concerns. But it is
already so wide that mere growth of existing services
might greatly increase the proportion of all economic
activity so administered. The Report did, however,
recommend that greater efficiency should be sought
along the lines of the transfer of the economic functions
of central and local governments from the political
bodies themselves (or from committees of the political
bodies) to special, *ad hoc*, bodies of a more permanent
character, not recruited from the membership of
parliament, or of the councils concerned, though
responsible, of course, to them. Instances of such *ad
hoc* bodies are afforded by the B.B.C., the Central
Electricity Board, the London Port Authority, or the
Mersey Docks and Harbour Board, the Metropolitan
Water Board. Several new examples, such as the
London Passenger Transport Board, have come into
existence since 1928.

To deal with the problem of private monopoly they
recommend two main lines of action. The first, a
strengthening of the existing Company Law, the
second, the creation of a new category of public
companies. They wished to strengthen the Company
Law mainly as regards the publication of the information necessary to make the control of directors by
shareholders a little more of a reality than it ordinarily
is, and to make it more certain that directors are

controlling the firm in the interests of the whole body of
shareholders and not of their own private pockets. For
this purpose they recommend far fuller publication
than was then required of the nature of a company's
assets and liabilities : of the main sources of revenue
(trading profits, dividends and interest, profits on sales
of capital assets, etc.) : of payments to directors :
and of the share holdings of directors, which were to
be changed only with the consent of the whole Board.
They recommend also that an increased responsibility
be imposed on auditors, who were to be required to
satisfy themselves that assets were rightly (and not
merely not excessively) valued, and to draw attention
to any item in the balance sheet that might mislead.
Their status and tenure were to be improved so that a
public-spirited auditor should not be victimized by an
angry board of directors, and they were to have the
right to attend and to speak at all general meetings of
the company.

These were minor, but nevertheless important,
matters, some of which have in part been remedied by
subsequent Company Acts. Two more important
recommendations remain. First it was suggested that
some better measure of control over Boards of Directors
was desirable than can be exercised by a general
meeting of shareholders. Methods of appointment and
reappointment of directors needed overhaul. " Direc-
torships are," they said, " the pocket boroughs of the
present day." For this purpose they advised the
establishment of Supervisory Councils, analogous to
those that exist for certain types of companies in
Germany, whose functions would be to hear detailed
reports, to cross-examine and criticize the Board of

Directors and to exercise authority over higher appoint-
ments, including those of directors. Though not
suggested in the Report, one might expect the nomina-
tion of auditors to be added to their duties.

Finally, to give increased control over certain types of
large-scale concerns other than public utilities, they
recommended the establishment of a new category of
Public Corporations. The distinction between the
public company and the public corporation would
depend partly on absolute size, partly on relative
preponderance in its industry. It was suggested that
the Board of Trade should have power to require a
company to be registered as a Public Corporation if
its assets exceeded one million pounds or its share of
the output of the industry was greater than a half.
Such a corporation would be subject to inspection at
intervals by the Board of Trade, which would report
its rate of profit on capital and turnover, its reserves
and provision for depreciation, its scale of salaries, the
extent of its monopoly, and its various price or output
agreements. If such examination brought abuses to
light, they recommended the adoption of the methods
of investigation and control recommended by the
Committee on Trusts of 1919.

It will be seen that the Liberal proposals relied
chiefly upon the weapon of publicity. Though they
could scarcely hope that publicity would " protect the
born gull from the born crook," yet they did hold that

" the necessary condition for the right use by the consumer of his ultimate weapon against this type of combine,
namely his power in the last resort to carry his custom
elsewhere, calling into being, if necessary, an elsewhere to
carry it to, is Publicity. Publicity will protect the combine

from unfair criticism on the part of the public and from blackmail by other powerful interests (by the Press for example), and it will protect the public by keeping them informed of any case where there is occasion for them to put forth their ultimate weapons of reprisal."

Few disinterested observers would deny the need for added light upon the affairs of such powerful corporations as do not themselves willingly provide it. Many shady transactions are possible only because of the obscurity that surrounds the facts that ought to be known to shareholders. American traditions of wider publicity of many of the vital facts of costs, output, sales and revenues have not been found to impair competitive powers. But whether we can trust to little else than publicity to control our monopolies is a question far more difficult to answer. In the United States in the period before the passing of the Sherman Act the activities of the " muck-rakers " provided wide publicity of facts, but did little or nothing immediately to curb the offenders. It may be that our monopolists are less pachydermatous, that social pressure is more powerful here. It is a problem that cannot be profitably discussed apart from a discussion of the power and the politics of the Press, and of the intentions of those that control it. It would be rash to say that anything is impossible to a determined autocrat in Fleet Street. It would be rasher to say that we can always rely on that power being exercised as a jury of philosophers might have recommended.

The type of policy recommended by the Liberal Inquiry merges by imperceptible gradations into the policies advanced from time to time by the official Labour Party, with their greater emphasis on the exten-

sion of State socialism and upon the extension of
consumers' co-operation, and their smaller trust in the
efficacy of mere publicity as a weapon of defence.
They are already sufficiently well known to readers
and since in character they lie between the Liberal
approach that we have just examined and the more
extreme views that we shall now have to consider, we
may, despite their greater political importance, for the
moment pass them by.

§ 4.   *A Policy of Abolition.*   Let us turn now to a rather
more dramatic analysis of the situation.   To this way
of thinking, monopoly and privilege are among the
greatest obstacles to human progress.   The central
economic problem is the cure of poverty and the
creation, so far as our limited resources permit, of
plenty.   But the motive of action is profit.   In a
perfectly competitive world the motive of profit is
compatible with maximum output.   But in any world
in which competition is not perfect, there is a motive
to restrict.   Moreover in such a world there may in the
complete sense be no equilibrium short of monopoly,
since by progressive combination profits are progressively increased.   The restriction which would in
any case be dictated by self-interest, is furthered by
errors of judgment and the tendency to excesses of
investment in certain types of capital, errors which
can only be retrieved by agreements of producers to
limit output.   This growing conflict between the general
interest in plenty and the capital-owner's interest in
scarcity can only be resolved, it is said, by the complete
destruction of monopoly and economic privilege.

There   is   a   further   problem   which   monopoly

gravely complicates. The level of real wages that is
consistent with a given level of employment will be
lower, the greater is the degree of monopoly. The
consequent effects on the distribution of wealth are
themselves sufficiently injurious, but there is an added
difficulty. With a high degree of monopoly the proportion of the national dividend likely to accrue to wealthy
persons and be saved, may, as was seen in Chapter VII,
be in excess of the amount that, with that distribution
of wealth, can find profitable investment at any practic-
able rate of interest. The inability to find a use for
all the savings that would be made in conditions of
full employment, may condemn us to the paradoxical
fate of unemployment in the midst of poverty and
want. From this impasse, it is said, we can escape only
by securing a transfer of wealth from rich to poor.
But merely to increase money wages would result
either in unemployment or in a general rise of prices,
leaving profits in real terms as high as before. We can
secure a redistribution of wealth with a constant level
of employment only by reducing the degree of monopoly, or by heavy redistributional taxation. Thus
the problem of monopoly, it is argued, is fundamental
to the whole problem of economic stability and
progress.

It is fundamental also, it is argued, to the whole
system of world politics and world peace. For through
monopoly and the growing preponderance of the
financier over the industrialist, comes, it is said, the
highest stage of capitalism, that of imperialism. In
this stage the monopolists of different countries, having
outgrown the limits of their own territories and having
exhausted the possibilities for peaceful expropriation,

U

begin a struggle for markets and spheres of influence which involves the rival nations in war.

But it is one thing, those who hold this view would argue, to say that monopoly must be abolished, another to achieve its abolition. For the whole class of those who depend on profits for their incomes will rally to the defence of the system of economic organization which makes possible their well-being. They will, by their own criteria, be acting in the best interests of the nation. They will not consciously be preferring a sectional to the general welfare. But they will none the less use all the powers at their command to preserve the existing situation. And since it is impossible to separate economic power from political power they will not improbably succeed, even though politically outnumbered, in frustrating the desired change.

There must, therefore, inevitably come a painful struggle between the class that represents monopoly and privilege, and the class that represents the ordinary wage or salary earner, and consumer. There must always, it has been said, be a revolution, when the forms of power do not correspond with the realities of power. The forms of power to-day are, in Great Britain, those of democracy ; the realities of power are those of a commercial oligarchy. You may have a democratic form of government, you may elect a socialist majority, but big business controls the switchboard in the power-station of economic activity, and can bring the whole system to a standstill when it wishes. No body of moderate evolutionists, unprepared to rebuild if necessary from the very foundations, can exert sufficient control to make the radical changes that are demanded. Progress by slow evolution is impossible : it would be frustrated by those whose powerful interests are at stake. Socialization by compensation is impossible ; economic and political power would still rest in the hands of those who from being owners have become creditors. There is no way from the old to the new, save through the painful process of expropriation and, in the extremity, destruction. During the last century the forms of power have been changed in this country from those of oligarchy to those of democracy. For our century remains the vastly greater task of completing this process, by making the realities of power also those of democracy.

Many of us who have been brought up to believe that the British genius can best be defined as an infinite capacity for muddling through, will feel an instinctive repugnance to this melodramatic, un-English, analysis of the situation—a repugnance which, our more revolutionary friends will tell us, discloses at once a refusal to face facts and indisputable evidence of class prejudice. Is this an occasion on which once again the tortuous road of compromise and adjustment will deliver us at our goal more rapidly than direct onslaught ? Can we deal with monopoly not by a massed attack along the whole front, but by enveloping first one and then another salient ? Cannot death duties and supertax be left to deal slowly but effectively with the undesired survivals of excessive economic power, if such there be ? Have ordinary investors in Central Electricity Board stock or in Local Loans any more real monopolist stranglehold over consumers of electricity or occupiers of council houses, than have the subscribers of the various Russian State Loans over Russian consumers ?

In Central Africa there are to be found two methods of road building. In the Belgian Congo the roads march with undeviating straightness from horizon to horizon. When the Belgian road encounters an ant-hill (and the industrious African ant makes hills fully as high as a house) it turns neither to right nor to left. The ant-hill must go. When you cross to Rhodesia, the road resembles the familiar English lane. When it encounters an ant-hill it passes it by with a sweep. Which of the two has the right sense of fitness and economy ?

§ 5. *The Problem of Choice.* Between the limits set by these alternative policies of inaction, of mitigation, of abolition, choice must lie. The problems are far wider than can be settled on economic grounds alone. For decisions made in the economic field will affect the whole social framework of our country. They involve our most deep-rooted political, social, economic, even religious principles. But we cannot be blind to these broader issues which impinge upon our studies, and pretend that they lie beyond the horizon of a strictly defined economics. If we seek to exclude them wholly from our scope, and more especially from the scope of an examination of monopoly, we shall confine ourselves to a profitless academic discussion of an unreal world.

But though we cannot hope to reach any unassailable conclusion, free from the ambiguities that are inherent in honest differences of judgment with regard to the proper ends of society, it is nevertheless incumbent upon us to learn what we can from experience. From those who would plead for inaction we must inquire : Has comparative inaction during the last century left us with no serious present problem of monopoly ? Were the United States and Germany wrong in thinking that special legislation was necessary ? Has the growing scale of business and the growing concentration of economic power caused us no problems that call for control ? From those who believe in a policy of mitigation we must ask : Has control in fact proved effective ? Did the experience of the United States suggest that " trust-busting " was effective ? Were monopolies under sufficient control in Weimar Germany, or in the United States to-day ? Can such bodies as the Cartel Court, or the Federal Trade Commission, be given powers, and expected to exercise them in such a way as to protect the consumer and not merely the weaker producer ? Has publicity proved itself an adequate weapon ? From those who believe in root and branch extirpation we must demand : Can the end that you, and perhaps we also, have in view, be achieved by no less painful process ? Cannot piecemeal elimination effect the same result without so much damage ? Does the advantage of a speedier transition outweigh the loss of continuity, the destruction of so much that is valuable in tradition and experience, the probable wastage of organizing and technical ability, the chances of bloodshed and warfare ? Are you not guilty of that greatest of all sins against society, the desire to compress the slow evolution of future history into the compass of your own lifetime ?

APPENDIX

PRINCIPAL SOURCES
AND
SUGGESTIONS FOR FURTHER READING

(The books most suitable for immediate supplementary reading are marked with an asterisk *.)

Chapter I. MONOPOLY PRICE

JOAN ROBINSON. *The Economics of Imperfect Competition.* Chaps. 1–3 and 6–7.

J. E. MEADE. *Economic Analysis and Policy.* Part II. Chaps. 1–2 and 4.

Chapter II. QUASI-MONOPOLY

A. R. BURNS. *The Decline of Competition.*

Chapter III. TYPES OF MONOPOLY

A. MARSHALL. *Industry and Trade.* Book III. Chaps. 1–2.

D. H. MACGREGOR. *Industrial Combination.*

A. C. PIGOU. *Economics of Welfare.* Chap. 14.

F. GARDNER WILLIAMS. *The Diamond Mines of South Africa.*

A. PLANT. *The Cambridge History of the British Empire.* Vol. VIII. Chap. 29.

*P. FITZGERALD. *Industrial Combination in Great Britain.*

**Report of Committee on Trusts*, 1919.*

Chapter IV. DEVICES FOR STRENGTHENING MONOPOLY

*W. H. S. STEVENS. Unfair Competition.

J. E. DAVIES. *Trust Laws and Unfair Competition.*

Chapter V. FORMS OF MONOPOLY ORGANIZATION

*Report of the (Balfour) Committee on Industry and Trade. Factors in Industrial and Commercial Efficiency. Chap. 1.

H. LEVY. *Monopoly and Competition.*

H. W. MACROSTY. *The Trust Movement in British Industry.*

G. R. CARTER. *The Tendency towards Industrial Combination.*

J. MORGAN REES. *Trusts in British Industry.*

*J. W. F. ROWE. *Markets and Men.*

*A. F. LUCAS. *Industrial Reconstruction and the Control of Competition.*

Chapter VI. MONOPOLY AND INDUSTRIAL EFFICIENCY

National Industrial Conference Board. Mergers in Industry.

*E. A. G. ROBINSON. *The Structure of Competitive Industry.*

Chapter VII. MONOPOLY AND INDUSTRIAL STABILITY

A. C. PIGOU. *Economic Essays and Addresses.* Chap. 3.

*J. W. F. ROWE. *Markets and Men.*

Chapter VIII. THE PROBLEM OF THE CONTROL OF MONOPOLY

A. C. PIGOU. *Economics of Welfare.* Chaps. 19–22.

J. E. MEADE. *Economic Analysis and Policy.* Part II. Chaps. 7–8.

A. A. BERLE AND G. C. MEANS. *The Modern Corporation and Private Property.*

Chapter IX. THE LAW AND MONOPOLY IN THE U.S.A.

*F. L. ALLEN. *The Lords of Creation.*

*H. R. SEAGER AND C. A. GULICK. *Trust and Corporation Problems.*

ELIOT JONES. *The Trust Problem in the United States.*

J. W. JENKS AND W. E. CLARK. *The Trust Problem.*

I. M. TARBELL. *History of the Standard Oil Company.*

J. T. FLYNN. *God's Gold.*

(The literature of the American Trust Problem is far too extensive to be summarized here. A useful bibliography will be found in Seager and Gulick.)

Chapter X. THE LAW AND MONOPOLY IN GERMANY

H. LEVY. *Industrial Germany.*

R. LIEFMAN. *Cartels, Concerns and Trusts.*

*A. P. L. GORDON. *The Problem of Trust and Monopoly Control.*

A. K. MICHELS. *Cartels, Combines and Trusts in Post-War Germany.*

D. WARRINER. *Combines and Nationalization in Germany.*

*H. R. SEAGER AND C. A. GULICK. *Trust and Corporation Problems.* Chaps. 24-5.

(Those who read German will find a useful summary of the German literature in an Appendix to Levy.)

Chapter XI. THE LAW AND MONOPOLY IN GREAT BRITAIN

W. A. SANDERSON. *Restraint of Trade in English Law.*

F. D. SIMPSON AND F. POLLOCK. Principles of Contract. (*Law Quarterly Review ;* Oct., 1925.)

C. A. COOKE. Legal Rule and Restraint of Trade (*Economic Journal ;* March, 1936.)

Chapter XII.   FUTURE POLICY

Britain's Industrial Future, being the Report of the Liberal Industrial Inquiry, 1928.

The Next Five Years, 1935.

Britain without Capitalists.

V. I. LENIN.   *Imperialism—The Highest Stage of Capitalism.*

INDEX

Printed in Great Britain by Butler & Tanner Ltd.. Frome and London

Date Due

Nov 29			
May 23 58			
Oct 16 63			
Dec 20 6:			
Jan 6'64			
1 6 MAY 1970			
1 4 MAY 1975			
2 9 OCT 1979			
SEP 0 3 1993			
MAY 0 6 1993			